DATE		

Political
Stability
in
Federal
Governments

POLITICAL STABILITY IN FEDERAL GOVERNMENTS

JONATHAN LEMCO

PRAEGER

New York
Westport, Connecticut
London

Library of Congress Cataloging-in-Publication Data

Lemco, Jonathan.
    Political stability in federal governments / Jonathan Lemco.
        p.   cm.
    Includes bibliographical references (p.   ) and index.
    ISBN 0–275–93854–9 (alk. paper)
    1. Federal government.   2. Political stability.   I. Title.
JC355.L46   1991
321.02—dc20   91–6777

British Library Cataloguing in Publication Data is available.

Library of Congress Catalog Card Number: 91–6777
ISBN: 0–275–93854–9

First published in 1991

Praeger Publishers, One Madison Avenue, New York, NY 10010
An imprint of Greenwood Publishing Group, Inc.

Printed in the United States of America

The paper used in this book complies with the
Permanent Paper Standard issued by the National
Information Standards Organization (Z39.48–1984).

10 9 8 7 6 5 4 3 2 1

CONTENTS

PREFACE

In this study, the conditions affecting the emergence of political stability in the forty-four federations known to have existed in the past two hundred years are identified and tested. Federal systems have been chosen as avenues of study for a number of reasons. First, they possess a specific form of constitutional structure that lends itself to statistical analysis. In addition, they enjoy an unsubstantiated reputation for protecting regionally grouped diversities, thereby enabling human diversity to flourish. Finally, and most important, federal nation-states can concentrate power and authority in large central governments while diffusing the exercise of powers so as to give most, if not all, segments of society a constitutionally guaranteed share in the governing process.

After the theoretical literature concerning federalism and political stability is reviewed, data pertaining to political, social, and economic conditions that have been said to be related to federal political stability are collected and tested. These conditions include the structure of polities, the impact of political freedom, the importance of the party system, and the relevance of ethnically and territorially based cleavages. The association among economic modernization, social mobilization, relative deprivation, and federal political stability is also investigated.

The dependent variable "stability" is classified into five categories of long-term and short-term stability, each encompassing various related conditions including riots, protests, revolutions, and so on. The variables are then tested using a series of multivariate tests, including Discriminant analysis, Multiple Regression analysis, and most important, N-Chotomous Probit analysis.

Given only forty-four cases, causality cannot be presumed. Neverthe-less, several conditions emerge as significantly associated with federal stability. Indeed, if one were to construct a stable federation based on the histories of previous federations, one might seek the following attributes:

Such a federation would comprise many small constituent units owing their first allegiance to a strong central government. It would have an effective two- or multiparty system that would allow for a great deal of political freedom. Furthermore, the federation would be created in the face of a strong military or economic threat, and this threat would not dissipate until a strong sense of national legitimacy had developed. This sense of legitimacy would be threatened, however, if there were many frequent major constitutional changes.

To further minimize the potential for federal instability, the political elites of such an ideal federation would avoid concentrating national minorities in a small number of constituent units, where they would be in the majority. In addition, the evidence suggests that if one religious grouping was especially dominant in the federation, there would be a struggle between religious and secular interests for the primary allegiance of the population. Historically, this competition has been often associated with federal instability.

Finally, the political elites of such a model federation would be well advised to discourage rapid economic modernization. The evidence sug-gests that where rapid economic change exceeds the adaptive capacity of the nation's political institutions, as has often historically been the case, there has been a great deal of internal divisiveness.

ACKNOWLEDGMENTS

I would like to thank all of those who contributed to the creation of this book. Art Frank and John Guthrie provided excellent methodological advice at various stages of this work. Peter Regenstreif and Tony Birch contributed wise counsel and moral support. William Riker first inspired me to investigate federal stability. I owe him an enormous intellectual debt. Finally, I would like to thank my family for their love, guidance, and support.

Political
Stability
in
Federal
Governments

INTRODUCTION

This study is an investigation of certain of those political, economic, and social conditions that theorists of federalism have associated with the stability and instability of federations. For many years, there have been persuasive arguments that federalism provides the best government possible for a nation of considerable ethnic and regional disparity. These students of federations have suggested that a centralized federal government that protects the national interest, and the governments of the constituent units that protect local and regional interests, are the most responsive administrative forms for a society of great diversity.

Although a cogent case can be made that a federal administrative and political structure is often appropriate to a nation of great heterogeneity, it would be a mistake to regard federalism as a panacea for all the ills of a diverse society. The point is best exemplified by the glaring fact that twenty-seven of the forty-four federations formed in the past two hundred or so years have failed either by breaking apart or by becoming fully centralized, unitary states. The imposition of a federal structure will not, of itself, solve all of the problems of a heterogeneous society. If the most advantageous political, economic, and social features are present in the federation, however, I suggest that the country stands an excellent chance of survival.

The task of the creators of federal systems is first to examine and identify those features that seem to benefit or damage federations as a whole and then to try and create an appropriate constitutional and administrative structure that will embody the benefits rather than the defects.[1] If the near-universal conditions peculiar to federations can be identified, and then preliminary recommendations for the application of those conditions that seem to be associated with federal stability provided, then this study will have made a contribution.

Why study federations? Federations, and the conditions associated with their stability, are important fields of study because they are devices whereby nation-states can concentrate power and authority in large, central governments while, at the same time, diffusing the exercise of powers so as to give most, if not all, segments of society a constitutionally guaranteed share in the governing process.[2] It is in this regard that federations are unique.

On the other hand, federations are artificial constructs that have often proven all too fragile. Furthermore, William Riker and others have shown that federations may not protect diversity better than other governmental services.[3] So the practical reason for studying federalism is to try to discover ways to make this attractive but fragile constitutional form work better.

Federations are also an interesting subject of study because the federal constitutional structure has become especially popular in this century. More than a billion people, or approximately 40 percent of the world, live in federal countries. Federal constitutions have been adopted in many of the world's most powerful nations in terms of economic, technological, and military strength. Furthermore, federalism has been especially attractive in many of the geographically largest countries of the world: the Soviet Union, Canada, India, the United States, Brazil, and Australia.

It must also be noted, however, that federalism is not necessarily appropriate everywhere. For example, many have argued that federalism is usually unsuitable for countries of comparatively small area (although Switzerland is a notable exception) and with a relatively homogeneous population (Mexico is one exception to this). In addition, Gilles Lalande has stressed that the federal structure is not well suited to countries where majority rights are fundamental or where sovereignty is seen as one and indivisible,[4] that is, where a concern for unity overrides considerations of diversity (as in Italy in the nineteenth century or in Algeria or Chile today).

In review, the primary purpose of this study is to investigate those conditions that seem to raise or lower the level of political stability in a federation. The chapters focus on the following general themes:

Chapter 1 contains a brief review of the history of federal thought and the conditions associated with federal stability.

In chapter 2, the theoretical literature concerned with political stability, and how it relates to federations, is discussed. A variety of authors, notably Ted Robert Gurr, Douglas Hibbs, and Uriel Rosenthal, have examined both empirical and nonempirical studies of political stability. The concept of stability is defined, and its operationalization as the dependent variable is then outlined.

In chapter 3, certain independent variables believed to be especially important to federal stability are examined. These variables are related to the wealth, the language fractionalization, the degree of political freedom, and the political structure of the federation. Following William Riker and Jonathan Lemco, it is suggested that the presence of a highly centralized federation of many constituent units of small size is highly conducive to federal harmony. All together, the variables discussed in this chapter act as an overview to the rest of this study and are tested in greater depth throughout the course of this study.

Chapter 4 is a brief examination of the role of freedom in federal political stability. An attempt is made to ascertain whether freedom is a concept related to political stability and whether democratic or non-democratic federations, as classified by Raymond Gastil in his *Freedom in the World* study, are likely to be the more politically stable.

Chapter 5 includes a more comprehensive exploration of the impact of political centralization on federal stability. The independent variables pertaining to centralization include those that refer to federal political parties, the federal constitution, and crosscutting cleavages.

In chapter 6, the role of political cleavage is analyzed. After the literature is reviewed, the relationship between ethnic, language, racial, and religious cleavage and federal political stability is tested.

Chapter 7 includes a review of the literature concerning modernization, social mobilization, and relative deprivation. Certain variables pertaining to these general concepts are then identified and tested against the dependent variables. Following the work of Ted Robert Gurr, this study investigates a series of economic variables, and it is hypothesized that the greater the level of economic development, but the slower its rate of growth, the more likely there is to be political stability.

Chapter 8 is a review of many of the conditions deemed necessary for the inception and continued existence of federations as postulated by the theorists discussed in chapter 1. It concludes with a discussion of the most significant independent variables, the prospects for future research, and a focus on the extent to which federal and unitary structures can protect minority rights effectively.

NOTES

1. William H. Riker and Jonathan Lemco, "The Relations between Structure and Stability in Federal Governments," in William Riker, ed., *The Development of American Federalism* (Norwell, Mass.: Kluwer, 1987).

2. This point is expressed by Daniel J. Elazer in *Federalism and Political Integration* (Jerusalem: Turtledove Publishing Co., 1979), p. 49.

3. William H. Riker, "Six Books in Search of a Subject, or Does Federalism Exist and Does It Matter?" in *Comparative Politics* (October 1969), pp. 135–46.

4. Gilles Lalande, *In Defence of Federalism: The View from Quebec* (Toronto: McClelland and Stewart, 1978), p. 12.

1

THE FEDERAL "PRINCIPLE"

Several definitions of *federalism*, and some of the conditions usually associated with the term, are discussed in this chapter. The role of the constitution in designating two levels of authority is also noted. A brief history of federal thought, and the conditions associated with the origins of federations, as suggested by the most celebrated federal theorists, are then presented. This discussion is followed by an investigation of the social and political conditions conducive to the continued survival of federations. The chapter concludes with a summary of the specific hypotheses to be tested in the course of this study.

HOW SHOULD THE TERM *FEDERATION* BE DEFINED AND THE CONCEPT OPERATIONALIZED? A REVIEW OF THE FEDERAL LITERATURE

Despite its constant use, the term *federation* is still ambiguous. Not only does it connote different things, but policymakers and those who study the field professionally have historically ascribed a wide variety of meanings to the term. There is no universally accepted definition.

Most writers would agree that a federation is always a form of rule by constitution, at least in the formal sense. A federation is something like an alliance; it is something consciously created and must have a set of structural rules. All federal commentators would also probably agree that a federal form of government must operate on two levels: (1) as a polity and (2) as a series of constituent units (provinces, states, länder, etc.).

A federation, which can be interpreted as the next stage of amalgamation after an alliance, aims at creating and maintaining a nation while preserving the identity and traditions of the constituent units. It is, therefore, implied that there should be a common financial policy across the states and free movement of labor and capital from one state to another. However, neither federal nor constituent governments can exercise absolute sovereignty in the true federation, for this would violate the constitutional rights of the federation and, in fact, remove the whole raison d'être of federalism. Furthermore, although residual powers for the constituent units should and do exist in many federations, the national government should act in the national interest at all times, showing no prejudice toward any single unit.[1]

What we have, then, is a guaranteed division of power between central and regional governments. William Riker has provided what is one of the best overall definitions of a federal government:

> a political organization in which the activities of government are divided between regional governments and a central government in such a way that each kind of government has some activities on which it makes final decisions.[2]

HOW CAN FEDERAL CONSTITUTIONS BE CLASSIFIED?

The federal constitution is a contractual arrangement that provides for the division of power or the distribution of legislative authority between two levels of government: the central government and the constituent units. The division of powers is quite specific as written but differs radically across different federal regimes. Certain fields, such as foreign affairs, always come under the jurisdiction of the federal authority. Other fields, such as education, social affairs, and fiscal administration, are often delegated to both levels of government. Furthermore, Ronald Watts shows that in the newer federations, the allocation of the powers to levy and to collect taxes and other revenues has tended to conform to the principles of economic efficiency and national welfare. Those federations that have failed (the West Indian Federation is notable in this regard) have not had the same degree of economic efficiency.[3]

Daniel Elazer, Ronald Watts, and others agree that one of a federation's greatest strengths is its flexible constitution. The flexible constitution is but one means, however, whereby the rights of constituent groups can be protected and conflict mediated. Watts asserts that federal harmony is also dependent on "the size, number, and internal homogeneity of the provincial [constituent] units, the distribution of legislative and executive responsibilities and financial resources, the machinery of intergovernmental consultation and cooperation, the way regional groups are represented in the institutions of the central government . . . and the flexibility of the political institutions in adapting to changing needs."[4] Subsequent sections of this chapter address these issues more specifically.

THE ROLE OF THE FEDERAL CONSTITUTION IN ASCRIBING DEGREES OF CENTRALIZATION

Whether a federal union is highly centralized or highly peripheralized is usually determined by the division of powers between the central government and the constituent units. If the central government reserves most of the powers, then the system is highly centralized. However, if most powers are delegated to the constituent units, the system is not necessarily decentralized. The constituent units might, for example, have a great deal in common with one another and could create a uniform policy, or more likely, the central government might centralize the union through the legislative and administrative processes. Thus, over a period of time, a decentralized union could become highly centralized.[5]

Since federalism is a process, the degree of centralization or decentralization is constantly changing. As consensus within each ethnic or communal group and across the various communal groups changes, movements toward or away from centralization develop. Additionally, depending on the powers that are reserved, delegated, or assumed by the central government, many different variants of federalism can and do emerge.[6] These variants of federation often take the form of nondemocratic federations.[7]

THE FIRST FEDERATIONS

The term *federal* comes from the Latin *feodus*, referring to a contract, treaty, or alliance. Elazer argues that the first political system to embody the essential aspects of federalism as we recognize it today was the ancient Hebrew state, whose principles are even mentioned in the Bible.[8] Later on, there was a series of other early federal experiments, including the Greek Leagues which united to fight Persia and Rome. By 1291, the original Swiss Confederation was created, a structure that exists to this day. It was one of a number of central European and Italian federations created in the thirteenth, fourteenth, and fifteenth centuries, the culmination of which was the successful United Provinces of the Netherlands. This federation lasted more than two hundred years and is the first case to be included in this study (the Swiss federation having been reactivated in modern form only after the defeat of Napoleon and the dissolution of his puppet Helvetian Republic in 1814).

The emergence of the concept of the nation-state in the sixteenth and seventeenth centuries necessarily led to a reexamination of the application of the federal structure. "From an overemphasis on the defence and military security of the contracting states, attention turned to the contribution federalism could make to the formation of states and to the unification of nations."[9]

This is best demonstrated by the freeing of some of the British colonies of North America in 1776, which formed the United States of America, a "classic" federation. Many other federal experiments soon followed this American model. Unfortunately, most of them, particularly in nineteenth-century Latin America and twentieth-century Africa and the Caribbean, have proven to be dismal failures. One of the reasons for these failures may be that a federal constitutional form of government cannot be imposed on a populace without the political sophistication to live by its rules. There is probably a great deal of merit to this assertion. However, it is also the case that the shattering of several colonial empires paved the way for several successful present-day federations. The United States, Australia, and possibly Canada are but a few of the former colonies that still survive with what appears to be a fairly high degree of political stability.

THE NECESSARY CONDITIONS FOR POLITICAL STABILITY AT THE INCEPTION OF FEDERATIONS

Federalism has been a topic of scholarly discussion and writing ever since the era of the ancient Greeks, but little of this literature has thoroughly explained federalism or its development. (*The Federalist Papers* may be an exception.) Typically, none of the writers who supported federalism (Pierre-Joseph Proudhon)[10] or failed to support it (Harold Laski)[11] attempted to examine the system analytically.

Since 1940, however, a number of writers, beginning with K. C. Wheare, have tried to describe the origins of federalism. Anthony Birch has integrated this literature on federal stability into four avenues of exploration:

1. *The institutional or constitutional approach*, encompassing the work of K. C. Wheare and William Maddox
2. *The sociological approach*, highlighting the work of W. S. Livingston

3. *The process or developmental approach*, reflecting the views of Carl Friedrich and Karl Deutsch

4. *The political approach*, in which federalism is regarded as an exercise in the making of bargains and which is best represented by the work of William Riker[12]

Each of these approaches has a great deal of merit if we are to fully comprehend those features associated with federal stability.

The Institutional or Constitutional Approach

Wheare conceived of federation as a bargain among territorial political units. Using the United States as a model, Wheare described federalism as a system of government in which the federal and regional governments are both coordinate and independent. He stressed the sharp division in the powers and functions of two coequal sovereign governments as a basis for classifying systems of government as federal.[13] And he maintained that two sets of incentives made a federal structure desirable. One was the advantage perceived by each authority in establishing a single central government charged with certain functions involving all the parties. The second incentive for a federal structure stemmed from the expected benefits from the retention by regional governments of authority over issues peculiar to each region.

> Federal government exists when the powers of government for a community are divided substantially according to the principle that there is a single independent authority for the whole area in respect of some matters and that there are independent regional authorities for other matters, each set of authorities being co-ordinate with and not subordinate to the others within its own prescribed sphere.[14]

Wheare concluded his federalism treatise by stating: "Or, to put it shortly, they must desire to be united, but not to be unitary."[15]

The conditions that Wheare believed contribute to federal stability include:

1. A sense of military insecurity and the consequent need for common defense

2. A desire to be independent of foreign powers, which makes union a necessity

3. A hope of economic advantage
4. The experience of some previous political association
5. Geographical proximity among states
6. A similarity of political institutions[16]

A close investigation of Wheare's thesis reveals that he perceived federalism to be a form of governmental arrangement that is the product of only a minimal level of consensus. Wheare implicitly argued that federalism is itself a valid indicator of the very lack of a community of interest encouraged by similarity of language, race, religion, or culture that is hypothesized to be productive of consensus.

Wheare tended to ignore the role that certain underlying societal conditions played in the development of federalism. Instead, he placed more emphasis on considerations of defense, expansion, and economic security as the primary underlying forces encouraging a federal system of government. Wheare considered the act of federation to be the product of a decision-making mechanism involving real leaders and real objectives, and he rejected the idea of federalism as the inevitable product of some conflux of social forces.

Birch states that the approach used by Wheare "cannot usefully be applied to many of the federations that have been established, successfully or otherwise, since the [Second World] war."[17] This is partly because his conditions have been considered too legalistic by certain commentators but mostly because the conditions he sets forth are simply not evident in many of the postwar federations. It is difficult to find many of his conditions present in the Mali Federation, Uganda, the Cameroons, Pakistan, or Indonesia, to name a few examples. Nevertheless, Michael Stein and others have stressed that Wheare's ideal-type federation became the most widely accepted basis for a classificatory scheme and for comparing federal systems of government in such problem areas as financial and administrative relations between the two levels of government, relationships between the court systems of both levels, and the composition of legislatures at the two levels of government.[18]

Finally, William Maddox also suggested six conditions conducive to stability during the federations' inception:

1. The presence of military insecurity
2. The presence of economic insecurity
3. The existence of uniformity among states of size, culture, and political and social development

4. The existence of unifying spiritual, emotional, or ideological forces
5. Geographic contiguity among states
6. The presence of independent sources of political, financial, and military power for the central government[19]

It is clear that Maddox's conditions are very similar to Wheare's.

The Sociological Approach

Birch contends that one of the major shortcomings of Wheare's approach to a definition of federalism is that it is not particularly applicable to many of the post–World War II federations.[20] W. S. Livingston has provided an alternative to the purely institutional approach, an alternative that Birch and others refer to as the "sociological approach." This view attempts to explain federalism as congruence between a set of federal institutions and a pattern of societal diversity.[21] Livingston contends that the essential characteristic of federalism lies within society itself, not in the polities' division of powers or in the resulting institutional framework. Indeed, he believes that certain societies are intrinsically federal because they are pluralist and that, under these circumstances, federalism is simply their particular translation of the relations among the economic, social, political, and cultural forces that exist in these societies. Livingston makes two important assumptions:

1. Since federations are more than mere bargains, the study of federalism should include more than the bargaining process.
2. The nominal category of federation contains a great variety of structures that correlate with the diversity found in society.

Therefore, although the act of federation itself may be less attributable to the influence of social forces than to conditions of security and economic necessity, the ultimate success of federalism depends on how the congruence of governmental structure and underlying consensus is achieved. So, according to Livingston, social cleavages of an ethnic, linguistic, cultural, and religious nature are crucial factors for the longevity of federations. Livingston maintains that these cleavages become important when communal groups attain sufficient power to permit their political representatives to insist on retaining important functions in the geographic areas where they constitute an overall majority.[22] Birch presents a convincing argument, however, to show that given Livingston's approach to federal countries, it is still very difficult to make any firm generalizations about the members of a category (or ethnic group) of which the membership is undefined.[23] We have no way of predicting what particular form of diversity in what specific kind of federation will produce cleavage and what particular form will not. Thus, Livingston's theory appears to have limited predictive power.

The Process or Developmental Approach

Carl Friedrich and Karl Deutsch are both convinced of the importance of communications systems in politics. Friedrich, reacting to Wheare's institutional approach, maintains that federalism should not be seen as a static system, characterized by a precise and definitive division of power between two levels of government. Specifically, he says that federalism is also, and possibly most tellingly, "a developmental federalization of a political society," that is, the mechanism whereby separate political communities agree to negotiate solutions or decisions on common problems. Friedrich also believes that all federal systems have in common a balancing of their goals.[24]

Deutsch speaks of the "amalgamated security-community," which includes federal states and which, according to him, also includes uninterrupted internal connections at the social level as well as a vast range of means of communications and transactions.[25] This approach seeks to combine Wheare's institutionalist insights and the sociological approach of Livingston in interpreting federalism as a political society in which the internal communications system plays a key role. The necessary conditions that Deutsch cites for the "amalgamated security-community," based on the thirty-three cases he uses, include "a distinctive way of life," "expectation of economic gains," and "unbroken links of social communication." More specifically, his conditions for federal stability include:

1. A mutual compatibility of primary values shared by the federal partners
2. A distinctive way of life within each constituent unit
3. The presence of popular expectations of stronger economic ties or gains to be made from a federal union
4. A marked increase in political and administrative capabilities of at least some participating units
5. The presence of superior economic growth on the part of at least some participating constituent units directly attributable to federation

6. The presence of unbroken links of social communications, both geographically between territories and sociologically between different strata
7. A broadening of the political elite throughout the federation
8. The mobility of persons, at least among the politically relevant strata
9. A multiplicity of ranges of communications and transactions within the federation[26]

Deutsch makes little mention of the political circumstances that would bring about these conditions, and Riker has presented a cogent argument to show that the conditions Deutsch presents are neither necessary nor sufficient for the amalgamation of political units.[27] Riker emphasizes that Deutsch makes little mention of military, diplomatic, or political factors as important concerns in the development of federations.

In the course of this analysis, Deutsch's conditions are tested empirically for their presence, or absence, during the origins and maintenance of the forty-four federations known to have existed in the past two hundred-odd years.

The Political Approach

As noted, William Riker demonstrates that the aforementioned conditions are neither necessary nor sufficient at the inception of federations. Instead, he discusses the dynamics of the division of power between two levels of government. Riker believes that the guarantee that the constitutional act grants the two levels of government in terms of their respective areas of autonomy remains subject to the pull of political forces.[28] He suggests that the bargain depends on each side receiving more benefits as a member of the federation then it would have outside the federal structure. The groups offering and receiving federal benefits expect to gain increased economic and military resources, whereas the cost to both parties is a diminished degree of autonomy. In focusing on the political aspects of the federation, Riker identifies two necessary conditions:

1. A desire on the part of politicians who offer the bargain to expand their area of influence by peaceful means, usually either to meet an external military or diplomatic threat or to prepare for military or diplomatic aggression
2. A willingness on the part of politicians who accept the bargain to give up independence for the sake of union, either because

they wish protection from a military or diplomatic threat or because they desire to participate in the potential aggression of the federation[29]

It is important to note that Riker is no longer convinced that an external threat is present during the inception of every federation. Rather, following Birch, Riker now recognizes the importance of internal divisiveness at a federation's inception.[30]

Watts attempts to integrate the aforementioned conditions as they apply to the post–World War II federations. He looks for the following:

1. The desire for political independence
2. The hope of economic advantage
3. The need for administrative efficiency
4. The enhancement of the conduct of external relations, both diplomatic and military
5. A community of outlook based on race, religion, language, or culture
6. The presence of specific geographical factors
7. The influence of history
8. The presence of particular similarities and differences in colonial and indigenous political and social institutions
9. The character of political leadership
10. The existence of successful older models of federal union
11. The influence of the British government in constitution making

Watts concludes that certain of these conditions have been present in the six new federations he examines but that two underlying factors are always present: the existence of diversity within a federation and the desire of constituent units to form a union for whatever reason.[31]

Ramesh Dikshit argues as well that external military threat and internal divisiveness are not always present during the formation of successful federations. Bruce Berkowitz concurs and points out that at least in the case of Australia, an external military threat was not a necessary condition for unification.[32] Dikshit concludes that federalism is influenced by a myriad of economic, political, and cultural factors. He places less stress than does Riker on the influence of political parties in maintaining the federal bargain and argues that parties must reflect the political, social, and economic interactions in their environment.[33] Thus it is clear that no single factor is universal to the creation of federal states; as Dikshit shows, a variety of factors contribute to the formation of a federal structure.

In this brief review of the theoretical literature, several of the conditions that may be conducive to federal stability have been discussed. It is our task to test many of the aforementioned conditions and others, both for their universality and for their relation to the political stability of federations at inception. The reader will note that not all of the conditions will be tested because there do not exist enough data to conduct an unbiased test. Causality cannot be proven here either, of course, but if it can be shown that certain conditions seem to be both near-universal and concurrent with the stability or instability of most of the modern federations, then perhaps concrete recommendations for more effective, long-term federal unions can be provided.

The independent conditions that have been adapted from the work of the mentioned commentators and that will be tested against dependent variables measuring degrees of stability (in chapter 8) include:

1. The presence of territorial or spatial divisions of power
2. A written, flexible constitution specifying center-constituent unit powers
3. A bicameral form of government
4. The desire for an improved economic condition
5. A prior political association among constituent units
6. The similarity of political and social institutions
7. Geographical neighborhood among states
8. The presence of flexible elites
9. The need for administrative efficiency
10. A general community of outlook
11. The existence of role models (i.e., constitutional advice and recommendations from Great Britain, France, the United States, etc.)

To reiterate, these independent variables represent factors that, hypothetically, have some impact during the formation of federal states. It must be stressed, however, that this list is by no means all-inclusive. In succeeding chapters, a variety of other independent variables that are relevant to specific aspects of stability at the federations' inception will be tested.

WHAT CONDITIONS CONTRIBUTE TO THE
MAINTENANCE OR DISSOLUTION OF FEDERATIONS?

In addition to describing the conditions that must exist to create federations, many writers have also suggested conditions that contribute to the maintenance or demise of federations. These hypothesized conditions are quite diverse, but it appears that all successful federations have retained a strong central government influence while retaining weaker levels of constituent autonomy. As well, it seems that most successful federations experience some association before union but that with federalization the constituent units wish to maintain some degree of autonomy.

For most successful federations, leaders of constituent units have been convinced that their best interests will be served if they give up some independence for the sake of the federation as a whole. Most successful federations have also found that in unity there is strength against a common military or economic threat and cohesion against internal threat caused by dissatisfaction. The unsuccessful federations have not been able to realize many of these qualities.

It is important to note the work of S. M. Lipset, Watts, and others who have argued that one of the important reasons for the fragmentation of some federations was that cultural, economic, and social cleavages, instead of overlapping or cutting across one another and thereby canceling one another out, reinforced one another and so created polarization and conflict among regional groups.[34] In these cases, the federal institutions were unable to perform the dual functions of accommodating minority fears through the promise of adequate provincial autonomy and of encouraging federal cohesion through representative and effective central policy-making. Thomas Franck and later Watts argued that a decline in support for political compromise or for the federal solution will result in the federation's fragmentation.[35] Watts shows that intransigence then becomes the order of the day and that only a small incident is necessary to spark secession or civil war.[36] Thus reinforcing cleavages, rather than crosscutting cleavages, are crucial elements of instability.

Watts also maintains that established federations experience severe tensions when there is regional divergence of political demands, a weakness of interregional communication, the evaporation of traditional inducements to unity, and external influences.[37] Deutsch presents an argument that is somewhat less convincing. He believes that factors such as social mobility and communication pattern, not political factors, are most crucial to the continued existence of federations. He argues that an increased amount of interaction between constituent units positively encourages federal integration and that a diminished degree of interaction has a fragmentary effect.[38] Arend Lijphart contends in his "consociational democracy" thesis, on the other hand, that federations break up when there is a weakening of elite accommodation or an increase in communication between subcultures at the mass level.[39] This is a more reasonable analysis, but it does not explain the entire process.

Although the importance of sociological factors in both the integration and the disintegration of federal systems cannot be denied, political and economic variables are far too often underemphasized. Riker's focus on political parties in maintaining the federal bargain, Richard Simeon's discussion of intergovernmental bargaining relationships, and Watts's work stressing economic disparities, exploitation, competition, and military factors all deal with such factors.[40] However, an exclusive emphasis on institutional, sociological, political, or economic factors is probably insufficient to account for the actual performance and disintegrative cleavages within a federal system. Rather, there is a complex interplay among all the variables.

As a related point, Dikshit argues that regionally grouped diversity within unity is vital to the maintenance of federalism. Effective regional autonomy coupled with increased centralization of certain essential government powers and functions is, he notes, necessary for the survival of federalism. The former prevents the transformation of federalism into unitary government, whereas the latter enables the government to exploit the advantages of a larger base and better perform its functions.[41] By contrast, it is argued in the course of this study that, in fact, the more centralized federations are more likely to remain politically stable. Indeed, it is proposed that high levels of regional autonomy inhibit the survival of most federations and should be minimized if one wants to preserve the federal structure. Although several federations have become so centralized as to resemble unitary states, by and large the most successful federal states (with Switzerland the notable exception) retain the federal structure and process while stressing a high level of political centralization. A more detailed discussion of this point follows in chapters 3 and 5.

It has also been suggested in the theoretical literature that a condition important to the maintenance of a federation is that there be no one state, or two states, large enough to dominate the federation or threaten secession. There are many historical examples of federations that have overly large constituent units and that have had such problems. (See the discussion by John Stuart Mill in *Representative Government*, chapter 17.)

Charles Tarlton maintains that great disparity in the size and influence of the different constituent units fosters an "asymmetrical" federation. When provinces become too diverse, argues Tarlton, they are likely to form a federal government if they have sufficient political power and motivation to achieve unity. If the provinces become convinced that a harmonious relationship can no longer exist, however, then dissolution of the federation becomes a real possibility.[42]

For a federation to be maintained, it is also necessary to have a sufficient number of federating units. Too few small constituent units might have a great deal of trouble remaining economically viable and self-protecting. Further, a sufficient number minimizes the possibility of an overwhelmingly dominant state. Scholars are divided on this issue, but perhaps it may be that a minimum number of ten provinces is necessary. Such a number would reduce the possibilities of continuous face-to-face conflict between rival constituent units.

To conclude this review of the conditions that may be conducive to the maintenance of federations, let us ask, with William Riker, "Why should a majority (i.e., when such exists) that has been hurt by the federation choose to maintain it?" Riker concludes that the costs of maintaining the federation may be fairly low but that the costs of getting rid of it may be too expensive.[43] So, for those cases in which the majority should be or is dissatisfied with the federation as it is, the time, material, or other costs of changing may outweigh the benefits of a new political structure.

Throughout the course of this study, several conditions are tested for their importance to the maintenance of federations. Those that have been suggested by the theorists mentioned and that will be tested include:

1. The presence of a continued external threat
2. The desire to deter internal division or separation
3. The existence of "strong" party systems
4. The degree of political freedom
5. The presence of continued economic advantage with a federal structure
6. The presence of crosscutting cleavages
7. Easy communication across political spheres
8. Easy transportation across constituent units
9. The existence of flexible elites
10. The size and number of constituent units

THE ASSUMPTIONS AND HYPOTHESES OF THIS STUDY

The following dependent variables are assumed to be related to, and are measures and definitions of, political instability: riots, armed attacks, political assassinations, coups d'état, internal or civil wars, revolution, electoral violence, abuse of high office, small-scale terrorism, mutiny, plots against the regime, purges, general strikes, irregular executive transfers, unsuccessful irregular executive transfers, constitutional crises, and major cabinet changes.

The following dependent variables are associated with political stability: collective nonviolent protests, executive effectiveness, regular executive transfers, and the years of existence in the federation's present form.

The specific hypotheses to be tested in this study follow.

Chapter 3—Structure and Stability in Federal Governments

H2a: That centralization, many constituent units, and the absence of especially large units are positively correlated with federal stability and the absence of political secession in particular

H2b: That the degree of wealth, the degree of language cleavage, and the degree of political freedom are not strongly associated with federal stability

It is argued that these independent variables are the most important conditions associated with federal stability. These six conditions form a basis for the rest of this thesis.

Chapter 4—Political Freedom

H3a: That political freedom, political rights, civil liberties, and political terror (as defined by Raymond Gastil) are not strongly associated with federal stability

Chapter 5—Centralization

H4a: That a centralized constitution is positively correlated with federal stability

H5a: That the higher the level of political party centralization, the more likely is there to be federal stability, that is, in highly centralized states, the central government organizes lower levels of government primarily for reasons of efficiency

H6a: That crosscutting cleavages are positively correlated with federal stability

H6b: That language-region correspondence, race-region correspondence, and religion-region correspondence are negatively correlated with federal political stability

Chapter 6—Political Cleavage

H7a: That religious, language, and racial cleavages are not strongly associated with federal stability (no assumptions are made relating to the correspondence between region and cleavage in this chapter)

H7b: That balanced communal competition (as discussed by Alvin Rabushka and Kenneth Shepsle) is positively correlated with federal political stability

Chapter 7—Modernization and Social Mobilization

H8a: That the more modern the federation, the more likely it is to be politically stable

H8b: That a long-lasting national constitution, an effective legislature, and long-lasting political parties are positively associated with federal stability

H8c: That the number of newspaper readers per population of 1,000, the number of radios owned per population of 1,000, the literacy rate among those over the age of fifteen, the proportion of university students, and the percent of population in cities of more than 50,000 are positively associated with federal stability

Relative Deprivation

H9a: That the hope of economic gain at the inception of the federation is positively correlated with federal stability

H9b: That the presence of one or two constituent units prosperous enough to entice the others to join, the level of economic development, the percentage of wealth controlled by the wealthiest 5 percent of the population, and the form of economic system are not strongly associated with political stability

H9c: That the rate of economic growth is negatively correlated with federal stability

Chapter 8—The Origins and Maintenance of Federations

The conditions discussed in chapter 1 by the federal theorists are here tested for their relevance to political stability. No specific hypotheses are derived, however.

NOTES

1. The first cogent treatise on this subject was probably *The Federalist Papers* by Alexander Hamilton, James Madison, and John Jay. See also Edward McWhinney, *Federal Constitution-Making for a Multinational World* (Leyden: A. W. Sythoff, 1966).

2. William H. Riker, "Federalism," in Fred Greenstein and Nelson W. Polsby, eds., *Handbook of Political Science: Governmental Institutions and Processes* (Reading: Addison-Wesley, 1975): 101

3. Ronald L. Watts, *New Federations: Experiments in the Commonwealth* (Oxford: Oxford University Press, 1966): 50.

4. Ronald L. Watts, "Survival or Disintegration," in Richard Simeon, ed., *Must Canada Fail?* (Montreal and London: McGill-Queens University Press, 1977): 42–60.

5. James Peter Oberle, "Consociational Democracy and the Canadian Political System" (Ph.D. dissertation, University of Maryland, 1976).

6. See especially Ivo Duchacek, "Antagonistic Cooperation: Territorial and Political Communities," *Publius* 7, no. 4 (Fall 1977): 3–29.

7. Such authoritarian or totalitarian federal systems are still valid examples of federalism, at least according to the letter of their constitutions, and will be included as part of the sample of federations in this study.

8. Daniel J. Elazer, "Federalism," in David L. Sills, ed., *The International Encyclopedia of the Social Sciences* (New York: Macmillan Co. and Free Press, 1968), 5: 353–65.

9. Gilles Lalande, *In Defence of Federalism: The View from Quebec* (Toronto: McClelland and Stewart, 1978), p. 15.

10. Ibid., p. 13.

11. Harold J. Laski, "The Obsolescence of Federalism," *New Republic* (May 3, 1939).

12. Anthony Birch, "Approaches to the Study of Federalism," *Political Studies* 14, no. 1 (1966): 15–33.

13. K. C. Wheare, *Federal Government*, 4th ed. (London: Oxford University Press, 1963).

14. Ibid., p. 35.

15. Ibid., p. 36.

16. Ibid.

17. Birch, op. cit., pp. 15–33.

18. Michael B. Stein, "Federal Political Systems and Federal Societies," *World Politics* 20 (1968): 727.

19. William P. Maddox, "The Political Basis of Federation," *American Political Science Review* 35 (1941): 1120–27.

20. Birch, op. cit., p. 16.

21. W. S. Livingston, "A Note on the Nature of Federalism," in *Political Science Quarterly* 67 (March 1952): 81–95, and W. S. Livingston, *Federalism and Constitutional Change* (Oxford: Oxford University Press, 1956).

22. Livingston, "Nature of Federalism," pp. 81–95.

23. Birch, op. cit., p. 17.

24. Carl J. Friedrich, *Trends of Federalism in Theory and Practice* (New York: Frederick A. Praeger, 1968), p. 7.

25. Karl Deutsch, et al., *Political Community in the North Atlantic Area* (Princeton: Princeton University Press, 1957).

26. Ibid.

27. Riker, op. cit.

28. Ibid., and William H. Riker, *Federalism: Origin, Operation, Significance* (Boston: Little, Brown and Co., 1964).

29. Riker, "Federalism."

30. Ibid.

31. Watts, "Survival or Disintegration."

32. Bruce David Berkowitz, "Stability in Political Systems: The Decision to Be Governed" (Ph.D. dissertation, University of Rochester, 1981).

33. Ramesh Dutta Dikshit, *The Political Geography of Federalism* (New Delhi: Macmillan Co., 1975).

34. See, for example, Seymour Martin Lipset, *Political Man* (Garden City: Doubleday and Co., 1960), and Watts, "Survival or Disintegration," pp. 53–54.

35. Thomas M. Franck, *Why Federations Fail: An Inquiry into the Provisions for Successful Federation* (New York: New York University Press, 1968).

36. Watts, "Survival or Disintegration."

37. Ibid.

38. Deutsch, op. cit.

39. Arend Lijphart, *Democracy in Plural Societies: A Comparative Exploration* (New Haven: Yale University Press, 1977).

40. Riker, "Federalism," and Richard Simeon, *Federal Provincial Diplomacy: The Making of Recent Policy in Canada* (Toronto: University of Toronto Press, 1972), and Watts, "Survival or Disintegration."

41. Dikshit, op. cit.

42. Charles D. Tarlton, "Symmetry and Asymmetry As Elements of Federalism: A Theoretical Speculation," *Journal of Politics* 27 (1965): 861–74.

43. Riker, "Federalism."

2

WHAT IS POLITICAL STABILITY?

There are many interpretations of political stability in the literature, but in this study, and in this chapter in particular, of greatest interest are those conditions that are relevant to the endurance of federal political structures. First, a definition of the term *political stability* is presented, its operationalization is discussed by several theorists, and the prospects for instability are considered. A typical question asked is, what, in the most general sense, is the process of national disintegration?

Second, the method of analyzing stability is outlined. Federations are divided into five definitions or subdivisions of stability, each with various associated variables, or "classifying indicators." Different aspects of stability are tested under this framework because the concept is not a very clear one and its elements are not commensurate. These definitions of stability are discussed in some detail in the course of this chapter and are then tested as the dependent variables throughout the study against a variety of independent variables related to federations. In other words, in chapters 4–8, each of the five ways of defining the dependent variables is tested against the same set of independent variables. In chapter 3, the independent variables are tested against only the first measure of stability, "the absence of secession potential."

1. The absence of secession potential
   Federations in this section will be tested based on their potential for secession. They will be divided into current federations that display little evidence of internal divisiveness, current federations that are threatened with secession, and federations that have dissolved.

2. Long-term stability with destabilizing potential: the absence of
    structural change and the amount of political violence
    This dependent variable definition includes variables or condi-
    tions that are particularly violent and regime-threatening. It is
    suggested that the variables in this aspect of stability are strongly
    associated with the relatively quick demise of federal regimes.
    This subdivision and those to follow are adapted from similar
    ones devised by Uriel Rosenthal.[1]

3. Long-term stability: legitimacy or the degree of loyalty
    The variables associated with this category are related to the
    legitimacy of federal regimes. It is argued that their presence
    does not directly threaten the existence of the regime. In this
    sense, this definition of stability differs from the one just pre-
    vious in that there are less violent variables with associated
    destabilizing potential.

4. Long-term stability: the limitation of violence—collective
    protests
    In this definition, collective protests act to defuse the potential
    for more violent acts and, in this way and others, are positively
    associated with the limitation of violence and political stability.

5. Short-term stability: stability of the chief executive
    These classifying indicators are concerned with threats to the
    existing federal regime and not the federal structure as such.

A DEFINITION

Donald Morrison and Hugh Stevenson define political instability as "a
condition in national political systems in which the institutionalized patterns of authority break down, and the expected compliance to political
authorities is replaced by violence intended to change the personnel,
policies, or sovereignty of the political authorities by injury to persons or
property."[2]

In this study, two important conditions are added to this definition:

1. Following Phillips Cutright, interruptions in the regular flow of
    political succession must be included in any definition of politi-
    cal instability.[3]

2. Following Morrison and Stevenson and the Fierabends, a system
    should be considered relatively unstable depending on the fre-
    quency or magnitude of particular disruptive events.[4]

THE MEASUREMENT OF POLITICAL STABILITY: A BRIEF REVIEW

The first widely cited studies of political stability in the literature were those of Rudolph Rummel[5] and Raymond Tanter.[6] These and many subsequent investigations (Arthur Banks; Douglas Bwy; Leo Hazlewood; Donald Morrison and H. M. Stevenson[7]) were essentially atheoretical: they attempted to "discover" conditions related to political stability by a statistical method of classification known as "factor analysis." In this technique, categorizations of political instability, based on factor analysis of variables, measured the frequency of different kinds of events involving political violence in nations. Morrison and Stevenson, however, were quick to point out, "These factor categorizations suffer . . . from ambiguities in the definition and coding of variables included in the factor analysis, and in the labelling of the dimensions, or factors, and they have been justifiably criticized as being more dependent on statistical explanation than on analytic needs."[8]

Another important criticism of the factor analytic technique is that it remains a nontheoretical classification tool, which in the absence of a sound conceptual foundation does not allow one to infer a closely fitting causal explanation. Accordingly, the researcher must be very wary of employing this method.[9]

Morrison and Stevenson are also particularly notable for clearly distinguishing among

1. elite instability, in which members of the political elite, or some alternative elite, use violent action or the threat of violence to remove persons from their command positions in the national government;

2. communal instability, in which members of communal groups—that is, groups whose members share characteristics of ethnicity, language, religion, or territory—use violence to change the distribution of authority among communal groups within the national population; and

3. mass instability, in which a mass movement that is based on commitment to a specific political program seeks to alter the structure and policy of the national government.[10]

This typology of political instability is based on the theoretical assumption that instability is a consequence of conflict among different actors in a political system.

Ted Robert Gurr, on the other hand, asserts that political instability can be seen in terms of differing degrees of intensity of violence. His typology categorizes kinds of instability in terms of their degree of divisiveness.[11]

Samuel Huntington is an extremely important theorist of political instability, particularly as the concept relates to modernizing states. He discusses the relation between social groups and political institutions in changing societies and suggests that at the outset of political change, popular expectations usually exceed a society's social and economic potential. Thus, citizens become frustrated with the inability of government to meet their demands. For example, scarcity of resources in most modernizing societies increases the likelihood of social frustration. Frustrated expectations then are pushed into the political arena, where they become forces for violence.

According to Huntington, the input of these violent forces into the political sphere entails a high degree of political participation. Here a crucial step is taken. Political participation by itself threatens to disrupt the political fabric. It needs to be absorbed by political institutions in order to secure political stability. When political participation outgrows political institutionalization, political instability increases.

The structure of the historical process to political order, according to Huntington,[12] would be as follows: political order is dependent on the ratio of participation to institutionalization, and participation depends on a series of social and economic factors. Huntington has in mind the politicizing effect of social mobilization, which Deutsch calls "the process in which major clusters of old social, economic and psychological commitments are eroded or broken and people become available for new patterns of socialization and behavior."[13] To survive, a polity must have at its disposal political institutions capable of absorbing the pressures derived from the divisive conditions brought about by these social groups.[14] Huntington's thesis is probably the best overall explanation of the causes and consequences of political instability in nation-states.

THE STABILITY DEPENDENT VARIABLES

In the next section of this chapter, the five divisions of instability utilized in this study and the conditions associated with these categories are presented. The results of the five tests will then be analyzed in terms of the independent variables in this study.

The Absence of Secession Potential

The dependent variable "political stability" is categorized in several ways. The first category mirrors that presented by Riker and Lemco, where stability is discussed as political separation and is divided into

1. federations that no longer exist and are therefore "not stable" as of 1983 (twenty-seven such cases);
2. federations that are "partly stable"—that is, those that have experienced or are experiencing severe problems of secession or civil war but that continue to exist as of 1983 (four such cases); and
3. federations that are "stable" in the sense that they continue today with no serious expectation of secession or civil war as of 1983 (thirteen such cases).[15]

Up to now, the most important aspect of stability, which is political secession or separation, has not been discussed. As conceived by Gurr, political separatism identifies the degree of "widespread demands for greater political autonomy" by regional or ethnic groups that are "dissatisfied with the polity, of which they are formally members."[16] John Wood concurs, adding that the conditions necessary for secession must include a separable territory and cultural homogeneity among the secessionists. The secessionist group must feel both economically deprived and culturally threatened in a state that it regards as less legitimate than it once was.[17] There are problems with these assertions, however. Although it is clear that a secessionist state, by definition, must have separable territory and less legitimacy to its dissidents, it is easy to find examples of nonculturally based secessionist groups (Jamaica in the West Indies Federation) and noneconomically based movements (The United Netherlands or many of the early Latin American federations). The argument that groups secede from states that threaten their identities is easily refuted by the lack of such examples in several federations, including the first Austrian federation, the West Indies Federation, Chile, Libya, and the first Mexican federation.

I would instead postulate that the structure of a federation plays a very important role with respect to political secession. Data are derived for political secession from studies of individual countries as of 1983.

Long-Term Stability with Destabilizing Potential: The Absence of Structural Change and the Amount of Political Violence

One common approach to political stability relates the concept to the absence of structural change, that is, change brought about by violent acts against the political structure. According to this theoretical approach, the first series of breakdowns in the political structure occurs as pressures increase on existing political patterns. The prototypical examples of such structural change include riots, coups d'état, civil wars, and revolutions. There are some problems associated with this approach, however. For example, a number of countries have withstood political upheavals and institutional rearrangements throughout their history, yet their social and political systems have not disappeared. (A good example would be France.) Furthermore, minor upheavals in one country may be considered of major importance in another, so it is difficult to generalize about the relative importance of structural change from one polity to another. Indeed, to regard such events as assassinations or cabinet changes as equally important across different nations and political cultures may be a serious error. In this study, this problem is partially avoided by collecting several violence variables that many commentators have suggested are associated with political stability and by trying to judge the variables' relevance to federations.

Let us look more closely at the definitions of the dependent variables in this section. Michael Hudson, G. Bingham Powell, Jr., Douglas Hibbs, Jr., and others define *riots* as violent, but short-lived, demonstrations or disturbances involving a large number of people and characterized by material damage or bloodshed.[18] Riots are relatively disorganized protest gatherings resulting from what Powell calls "a shared sense of frustration" and often directed against vaguely specified targets.[19] *Armed attacks* are acts of violent political conflict, often carried out by small organized groups that are aimed at weakening or destroying the power exercised by other organized groups.[20] *Political assassinations* are defined as any politically motivated murder or attempted murder of a high government official or politician. In addition to national, state, and provincial leaders, included are mayors of large cities, members of the cabinet and national legislature, members of the inner core of the ruling party or group, leaders of the opposition, and newspaper editors. Arthur Banks defines *coups d'état* as "extraconstitutional or forced changes in the top government elite and/or its effective control of the nation's power structure."[21]

The dependent variables and their data sources in this section include:

1. Riots: Arthur Banks, *Cross-Polity Time-Series Data*, and Charles Lewis Taylor and Michael C. Hudson, *World Handbook of Political and Social Indicators*
2. Armed attacks: Taylor and Hudson
3. Political assassinations: Banks
4. Coups d'état: Banks
5. Internal or civil war: Ted Robert Gurr, *Why Men Rebel*, and Harry Eckstein, *The Evaluation of Political Performance: Problems and Dimensions*
6. Revolution: Banks and Taylor-Hudson[22]

Each of these six indicators is categorized as having few (0), moderate (1), or many (2) occurrences. The raw data for this section are averaged and assigned to these categories. To review how these assignments are made, see the Appendix.

Note that the aforementioned studies occasionally do not contain relevant information concerning the federations. To remedy the situation, this book has investigated individual country studies. Where data do not exist, as is often the case with the nineteenth-century federations, the federation is left out.

Long-Term Stability: Legitimacy or the Degree of Loyalty

One assumption of any working political system is that the loyalty of the citizens to the state, irrespective of regime or government in power, should be greater than their loyalty to another state that either exists or is in the making.[23] Furthermore, citizens must regard the in state as legitimate before they can accept the legitimacy of a particular regime. This is particularly important in the case of a democracy, which must guarantee civil liberties to all citizens. Democratic legitimacy, therefore, requires adherence to the rules of the game by both a majority of the voting citizens and those in positions of authority, as well as the citizens' trust in the government's commitment to uphold these rules.

Robert Dahl conceives of legitimacy as the extent to which power, policies, and political structures are considered to be right and proper by the members of the polity.[24] Dahl suggests that it is up to both the individual and the holders of power to decide what is right or proper to a political decision. Unlike those who subscribe to the "elite" approach, he argues that all members of a political system have a say in granting legitimacy. The elite approach, he argues, displays a lack of confidence in the capacity of the majority in a group or society to make the best decisions and, paradoxically, to choose voluntarily what deserves the label of legitimacy.

Harry Eckstein stresses that legitimacy produces a reservoir of support guaranteeing the cooperation of the members of the polity, even in the face of quite unpleasant policies. He says that sentiments of legitimacy should be traced by investigating a people's willingness to comply with value-depriving policies: "If we want to find out how strong legitimacy sentiments are among American whites . . . their patriotic professions are less significant than their reactions to policies relatively advantageous to blacks."[25]

In a state that is considered legitimate, the probability of compliance is rather high: a government would have to pass an extreme point before it would be confronted with noncompliance on the part of its citizens. Violent opposition to the government, for instance, might be the result of governmental offenses against the rules and procedures defining its legitimacy.[26] Eckstein finds that in a polity devoid of legitimacy, the authorities are permanently obliged either to produce costly benefits or to exercise coercion. In a legitimate political system, they may, now and then, take unpopular measures. Indeed, Wood shows that foremost among the political preconditions of secession is the absence or decline, at least in the perception of potential secessionists, of the legitimacy of the political system and/or incumbent central regime.[27]

It is, of course, the case that legitimacy is granted or withdrawn by each member of the society day in and day out. It does not exist outside the actions and attitudes of individuals. Regimes, therefore, enjoy more or less legitimacy just by existing. Gains and losses of support for governments, leaders, parties, and policies in a democracy are likely to fluctuate rapidly even though belief in the legitimacy of the system persists. There is clearly an interaction between support for a regime and support for the governing parties, which in the absence of other indicators leads to the use of electoral returns and public opinion responses as indirect evidence of the legitimacy of the system. Consequently, the lack of support for political actors by many citizens of a regime is likely to lead to a partial erosion of legitimacy, just as widespread support for a government is likely to contribute to the strength of legitimacy.[28]

Most citizens come to accept the legitimacy of a regime through force of habit. Individuals in a democratic state are not perpetually examining their conscience to see whether actions taken to gain concrete political ends infringe on the grand ideals of democracy. Taking their political end for granted, they pursue their goals through strategies that are largely determined by the patterns of behavior already existing inside the society.

To this point, the role of political legitimacy has been discussed only in democratic societies. This is because political allegiance in many communist or autocratic societies relies less on political legitimacy, or force of habit, than on coercion and repression. However, it is not asserted that autocratic regimes are never legitimate or stable, because some do enjoy varying levels of popular legitimacy and a great deal of stability. Indeed, the Mexican federation is characterized by considerable legitimacy and only a minimal level of repression. However, stability within certain of these regimes, such as the Soviet Union until recently, has been maintained only through intensive surveillance of citizens, overwhelming police power, and direct governmental control over the movement of citizens, trade, capital, and information flow. These restrictions on personal freedom are pervasive to an extent that is utterly unknown in the West and that citizens of the democratic Western polities would consider intolerable.

The dependent variables in this section differ from those in the previous section in terms of degree of violence. It is proposed that the dependent variables associated with the legitimacy of the regime are less violent or divisive than those in the previous category and do not threaten the actual political structure of the federation.

These dependent variables are defined in the following manner: The *durability* of a state refers to its years of existence or its ability to persist over time but not necessarily to its ability to adapt to change. Adaptation is a difficult concept to operationalize and is beyond the scope of this study. It is argued, however, that in concert with the other variables, durability can provide a valuable insight into legitimate politics. *Electoral violence* is interpreted as violence between rival factions during the electoral process. *Abuse of high office* is defined as evidence of corruption by the governing elite. *Small-scale terrorism* is regarded as guerrilla warfare and is defined as armed activity, sabotage, or bombings carried out by bands of citizens and directed toward the overthrow of the existing regime. *Mutiny,* or violence by authority figures, is defined as evidence that these figures no longer consider themselves subject to the decisions of the political authorities or senior officers. The aim of a mutiny is not the direct seizure of government. *Plots against the regime* are regarded as events in which an announcement or admission is made by the political elite that a plan to overthrow the government has been exposed. *Purges* are considered to be any systematic elimination of political opposition by jailing or execution. Finally, *general strikes* are defined as events involving organized disruptions of the economy by groups who refuse to work at their regular employment in order to bring pressure on political or economic authorities.

Following are these dependent variables and their data sources as of 1983:

1. Durability: individual case studies
2. Electoral violence: individual case studies
3. Abuse of high office by the political elite: individual case studies
4. Small-scale terrorism: Arthur Banks, *Cross-Polity Time-Series Data*
5. Mutiny (violence by police, military, or other authority figures): Harry Eckstein, *The Evaluation of Political Performance: Problems and Dimensions*
6. Plots against the regime: Eckstein
7. Purges: Banks
8. General strikes: Banks[29]

Furthermore, each of these six indicators is categorized as having few (0), moderate (1), or many (2) occurrences. To review how these assignments are made, see the Appendix.

Long-Term Stability: The Limitation of Violence—Collective Protests

Rosenthal and Gurr are but two of several writers who have hypothesized that nonviolent protest activity promotes, rather than threatens, governmental stability.[30] All argued that protests in contemporary societies are more likely to be successful when they are well controlled, when modest goals are pursued, and when little use is made of violence. Ekkart Zimmerman has noted that in factor analytic tests, protests almost invariably hinge on a single factor, independent of coups, conflict deaths, armed attacks, and so on.[31]

In an effort to derive theoretical reasons to support the idea that protests should be correlated with political stability, one can argue that protests, at least in democratic societies, do not threaten the legitimacy of the regime and therefore do not invite government repression. If it is the case that nonviolent protest activity implies latent supportive attitudes toward the political regime, then protest demonstrations express dissatisfaction with the incumbents rather than disaffection from the existing polity and its regime. That is, the incumbent authorities—not the nation's political structure—are held responsible for the nation's inadequacies. (It is worth noting that protests are, at least occasionally, permitted in nondemocratic societies, such as Tito's Yugoslavia, and are included in this study within the same theoretical rubric.)

Following Hudson, therefore, *protest demonstrations* are defined as nonviolent gatherings of people organized to criticize the policies, ideology, or actions of a regime, a government, or political leaders. They are not violent in the sense of causing major injury or destruction.[32] Thus, it is suspected that researchers are justified on empirical grounds in analyzing political protest as a distinct type of political conflict.

In this section, the impact of riots is also tested. Hibbs has hypothesized that riots and protests differ only in degree and should be investigated together. Powell, on the other hand, suggests that protests, unlike riots, require a substantial amount of citizen organization and coordination. It is obvious that the relevance of riots to federal political stability is most unclear. Indeed, riots are tested not only in this section but also in the section relating to long-term destabilizing potential.

The data for this section of the analysis are derived from the Banks and Taylor-Hudson studies as of 1983. Collective processes and riots are categorized in a trichotomous manner in which (0) represents few occurrences, (1) represents a moderate amount, and (2) represents many events. See the Appendix for the specific category assignments.

Short-Term Stability: Stability of the Chief Executive

One additional approach to political stability is to see it as the regular flow of political exchanges. According to this view, as long as individuals restrict themselves to the behavior patterns that fall within the limits imposed by political role expectations, there will be political stability.[33] Any act that deviates from these limits is an instance of political instability. The best example of this flow of political exchange might be associated with the continuity of governments, as indicated by the duration of terms of office or the turnover of personnel. That is, a system might be considered relatively stable or unstable depending on the rapidity of change of public officials.[34]

The stability of chief executive officers enters this analysis under the label of *political succession*.[35] Orderly political successions are regarded as high points of political institutionalization and reflect the state's political coming of age. However, political succession and continuity in office depend on the policies that the chief executives pursue and on related considerations (such as the personal qualities of the incumbent). This aspect of stability does not deal with the structure of authority, which is a component of the political regime. Rather, this component of stability is dependent on the turnover rate of the positions within this structure—if there is such a structure at all—as well as on a particular incumbent's effectiveness in maintaining power.

Historically, the stability of the chief executive is a precarious condition. The obstacles to orderly succession have included the following two:

1. The political authorities being confronted with different social groups and the articulation of different kinds of demands: it may happen that rewards for one group are punishments for another. Under such circumstances, the political authorities are never free from criticism and opposition. Even the most differentiated approach to the production of public policies would still be insufficient in this case.

2. Policy decisions not being the same as policy outcomes: questions arise, do people attribute policy effects to the political authorities? When do they make their assessments of profits and losses? Such questions indicate a number of serious complications for the political authorities. The gap between policy decisions and policy effects raises the possibility of rewarding policies turning into punishing effects—as well as the other way around, especially in the more modern federations. Furthermore, there is an increasing tendency to blame the political authorities for any misfortune but to consider the production of profitable policies "natural." This complicates the direct link between the political authorities and the population, the link that underlies the expectation of short-run political stability.

The method of succession is also a crucial indicator of political stability in autocratic systems. Regulation of political succession is considered to be one of the main characteristics of institutionalized politics in autocracies. Huntington, in *Political Order in Changing Societies*, is most notable in emphasizing the importance of orderly intergovernmental succession.[36]

The stability variables in this section of the chapter are defined in the following manner: *Executive effectiveness,* as defined by Powell, is the government's ability to maintain a legislative majority 75 percent of the time.[37] *Regular executive transfers* refer to those changes in the office of the national executive from one leader or ruling group to another that are accomplished through conventional legal or customary procedures and unaccompanied by actual or directly threatened physical violence.[38] *Irregular executive transfers* are those changes in the office of national executive from one leader or ruling group to another that are accomplished outside the conventional legal or customary procedures. *Unsuccessful irregular executive transfers* are failed attempts by an organized group to remove and replace the incumbent national executive outside the conventional procedures for transferring formal power. *Constitutional crises* are major challenges to the existing constitution, challenges that significantly alter the prerogative of the various branches of government. (Banks cites the substitution of presidential for parliamentary government or the replacement of monarchical by republican rule as examples.[39] It will be argued that this variable is related to the severe decline of a political regime's legitimacy.) *Major cabinet changes* refer to the number of times in a year that a new premier is named and/or that 50 percent of the cabinet posts are occupied by new ministers.[40]

In general, it is suspected that the greater the ability of the federal government to maintain effectiveness and regular executive transfers of power—while avoiding constitutional crises and major cabinet changes—the more likely the federation is to be stable today.

To review, those variables that are proposed to be related to the short-term stability or instability of chief executives and the data sources for these variables include:

1. Executive effectiveness: Powell
2. Regular executive transfers: Taylor-Hudson
3. Irregular executive transfers: Taylor-Hudson
4. Unsuccessful irregular executive transfers: Taylor-Hudson
5. Constitutional crises: Banks
6. Major cabinet changes: Banks

These variables or conditions are divided into four categories representing no (0), few (1), moderate (2), and many (3) events as of 1983. See the Appendix for the particular assignment of events.

It should be reiterated that where data relevant to this study are not available in these sources, individual country studies as of 1983 are used. (The country studies are listed in the Appendix.) Where country studies revealed no data on a particular question, the case is omitted from that particular analysis.

METHODOLOGICAL CONCERNS AND CONSIDERATIONS

One can encounter a great number of problems in cross-national research of this kind. Many analysts are very quick to draw causal inferences from simple statistical relations. However, macropolitical processes are typically too large and unwieldy for us to isolate cause and effect. Furthermore, mere statistical association does not reveal whether one feature is the cause of another or whether they are joint effects of some other antecedent. Given a sample of just forty-four cases, albeit the universe of cases, one can do no more than suggest that certain conditions seem to occur repeatedly with the presence or absence of federal stability. Nevertheless, the association does, at minimum, tell us that a federation is in trouble when it displays one or more features linked with instability regardless of whether the link is interpreted as causal or merely symptomatic.

As previously mentioned, this study focuses on federations that have existed over the past two hundred-odd years. A small nineteenth-century federation such as the Central American Federation (1824–39) or the Chilean Federation (1826–27) bears little resemblance to the modern-day United States or Soviet Union. Furthermore, five strikes in country A may or may not reflect as much instability as five strikes in country B. For these reasons, this study initially tests all of the federations but then examines only those in place since 1945. In addition, the last constitution or last period in the life of a given federation is weighted heavily, so that the lack of an overlapping history is minimized. Although all of the reported riots, purges, and other incidents of violence throughout the life of a federation are recorded, the most recent period is the one most heavily weighted.

A problem related to the incidence of unstable occurrences is that not all violent political conflicts have been reported, and incorrect data are often listed. These misrepresentations are due to censorship, distortion, lack of news value, and insufficient means of communication. As a result, the data may be somewhat biased. Because this absence of reliable data is most likely to be found in the older, failed federations, there is further reason to lay stress on the post–World War II federations.

Two final general methodological problems concern the time-dependent variables. If one of the stability dependent variables is operationalized as "not stable = no longer existing," then an eighteenth-century federation that lasted two hundred years and then became a unitary state, a constitutional monarchy, or whatever will still be regarded as unstable because it ended. A related difficulty in categorizing all presently existing federations as stable or partly stable is that such a federation might end tomorrow or might be at the midpoint of a thousand-year history of stability. Independent variables relating to this particular description of stability are thus biased to the more modern, presumably successful federations. One way around this problem, of course, is to operationalize the dependent variable in several ways. Nevertheless, it is still difficult to avoid bias toward the more recent federations.

NOTES

1. Uriel Rosenthal, *Political Order: Rewards, Punishments, and Political Stability* (The Netherlands: Sijthoff and Noordhoff, 1978).

2. Donald G. Morrison and Hugh Michael Stevenson, "Political Instability in Independent Black Africa: More Dimensions of Conflict Behavior within Nations," *Journal of Conflict Resolution* 15 (September 1971): 348.

3. Phillips Cutright, "National Political Development: Measurement and Analysis," *American Sociological Review* 28, no. 2 (April 1963): 253–67.

4. Ivo Fierabend and Rosalind Fierabend, "Aggressive Behaviors within Polities, 1948–1962: A Cross-National Study," *Journal of Conflict Resolution* 10 (September 1966): 249–71.

5. Rudolph J. Rummel, "Dimensions of Conflict Behavior within and between Nations," *General Systems Yearbook* 8 (1963): 1–50; Rudolph J. Rummel, "A Field Theory of Social Action with Application to Conflict within Nations," *General Systems* 10 (1965): 183–211.

6. Raymond Tanter, "Dimensions of Conflict Behavior within Nations, 1955–1960: Turmoil and Internal War," *Peace Research Society Papers* 3 (1965): 159–83; Raymond Tanter, "Dimensions of Conflict Behavior within and between Nations, 1958–60," *Journal of Conflict Resolution* 10, no. 1 (March 1966): 41–64.

7. Arthur S. Banks, "Patterns of Domestic Conflict 1919–39 and 1946–66," *Journal of Conflict Resolution* 16, no. 1 (March 1972): 41–50; D. P. Bwy, "Political Instability in Latin America: The Cross-Cultural Test of a Causal Model," *Latin American Research Review* 3 (1968): 17–66; Leo Hazlewood, "Concept and Measurement Stability in the Study of Conflict Behavior within Nations," *Comparative Political Studies* 6, no. 2 (July 1973): 171–195; Morrison and Stevenson, op. cit.

8. Morrison and Stevenson, op. cit.

9. Leon Hurwitz, "An Index of Democratic Political Stability," *Comparative Political Studies* 4, no. 1 (April 1971): 53–56, summarizes the conditions conducive to political stability as hypothesized by the aforementioned theorists as

1. the absence of violence;

2. a high degree of governmental longevity or duration;

3. the existence of a legitimate constitutional regime;

4. the absence of structural change; and

5. the presence of multifaceted societal attributes.

See also Leon Hurwitz, "Contemporary Approaches to Political Stability," *Comparative Politics* 5, no. 3 (April 1973): 449–63.

10. Morrison and Stevenson, op. cit., p. 266.

11. Gurr's classification of political instability is divided in the following manner:

    1. Turmoil: relatively spontaneous, unorganized political violence with substantial popular participation, including violent political strikes, riots, political clashes, and localized rebellions

    2. Conspiracy: highly organized political violence with limited participation, including organized political assassinations, small-scale terrorism, small-scale guerrilla wars, coups d'état, and mutinies

    3. Internal War: highly organized political violence with widespread popular participation, designed to overthrow the regime or dissolve the state and accompanied by extensive violence, including large-scale terrorism and guerrilla wars, civil wars, and revolutions

See Ted Robert Gurr, *Why Men Rebel* (Princeton: Princeton University Press, 1970), p. 11.

12. Samuel Huntington summarizes the argument in three "equations." See Samuel P. Huntington, *Political Order in Changing Societies* (New Haven: Yale University Press, 1968), p. 55.

13. Karl Deutsch, "Social Mobilization and Political Development," *American Political Science Review* 55 (September 1961): 493–514.

14. Rosenthal, op. cit.

15. William H. Riker and Jonathan Lemco, "The Relations between Structure and Stability in Federal Governments," in William Riker, ed., *The Development of American Federalism* (Norwell, Mass.: Kluwer, 1987).

16. Ted Robert Gurr, *New Error-Compensated Measures for Comparing Nations* (Princeton: Princeton University Center of International Studies, 1966), pp. 75–76.

17. John R. Wood, "Secession: A Comparative Analytic Framework," *Canadian Journal of Political Science* 14, no. 1 (March 1981): 108–34.

18. Michael Hudson, "Political Protest and Power Transfers in Crisis Periods," *Comparative Political Studies* 4, no. 3 (October 1971): 259–94; G. Bingham Powell, Jr., *Political Performance in Contemporary Democracies* (Cambridge: Harvard University Press, 1982); Douglas A. Hibbs, Jr., *Mass Political Violence: A Cross-National Causal Analysis* (London: John Wiley and Sons, 1973).

19. Powell, op. cit.

20. Hudson, op. cit.

21. Arthur S. Banks, *Cross-Polity Time-Series Data* (Cambridge: M.I.T. Press, 1971): xv.

22. Ibid.; Charles Lewis Taylor and Michael C. Hudson, *World Handbook of Political and Social Indicators*, 2d ed. (New Haven: Yale University Press, 1972); Gurr, *Why Men Rebel*; Harry Eckstein, *The Evaluation of Political Performance: Problems and Dimensions* (Beverly Hills: Sage, 1971), p. 62.

23. See especially Juan Linz, "Elements of Breakdown," in Juan Linz, ed., *Crisis, Breakdown, and Reequilibration*, 3d ed. (Englewood Cliffs: Prentice-Hall, 1978), pp. 60–61.

24. Robert A. Dahl, *Modern Political Analysis*, 3d ed.(Englewood Cliffs: Prentice-Hall, 1976), pp. 60–61.

25. Eckstein, op. cit.

26. Ibid.

27. Wood, op. cit., p. 118.

28. Linz, op. cit.

29. Banks, *Cross-Polity*, and Eckstein, *Political Performance*.

30. Gurr, *Why Men Rebel*, and Rosenthal, op. cit.

31. Ekkart Zimmerman, "Macro-Comparative Research on Political Protest," in Ted Robert Gurr, ed., *Handbook of Political Conflict: Theory and Research* (New York: Free Press, 1980).

32. Hudson, op. cit.

33. See especially Claude Ake, "A Definition of Political Stability," *Comparative Politics* 7, no. 2 (January 1975): 271–83.

34. Ibid.

35. Rosenthal, op. cit.

36. Huntington, op. cit.

37. Powell, op. cit.

38. Hudson, op. cit.

39. Banks, *Cross-Polity*.

40. Ibid.

3

THE RELATION BETWEEN STRUCTURE AND STABILITY IN FEDERAL GOVERNMENTS

In a 1987 book chapter, Riker and Lemco presented an argument that outlines the relationship between certain structural features of federal constitutions and federal political stability, with particular attention paid to political secession.[1] These conditions, it is suggested, are of particular importance for an understanding of federal stability in general. In this regard, they are investigated and tested in greater detail in the course of this study. More specifically, subsequent chapters take the independent variables in this chapter (i.e., degree of federal centralization, number of constituent units, existence of especially large units, level of wealth, degree of freedom, and level of language cleavage) and discuss and test them in detail for their relationship to federal stability. This chapter, however, serves as an overview of the role of these independent variables for political stability, and for political secession in particular. Hence, it provides a theoretical and conceptual point of reference for the remainder of the book.

In this chapter, the Riker-Lemco argument, the hypotheses so derived, and the findings of that study are discussed. It is asserted that one feature of federal constitutions that is particularly important to federal secession is their degree of centralization. Riker and Lemco have postulated that the greater the degree of political centralization in a federation, the greater the likelihood of political stability. Federations that appear to be no more than unitary forms of government, with subordinate units that are mere administrative units of the center, are

Portions of chapter 3 have been previously published in William H. Riker and Jonathan Lemco, "The Relations between Structure and Stability in Federal Governments," in William Riker, ed., *The Development of American Federalism* (Norwell, Mass.: Kluwer, 1987).

labeled as highly centralized. Decentralized or peripheralized federations, on the other hand, are loose associations or military alliances with many autonomous powers.[2] It is hypothesized that federations closer to the centralized end of the scale are more likely to be stable than those closer to the peripheralized extreme.

There are good reasons why centralization should be so important to a federation's stability. If external threat or military opportunity was the original impetus for a federal constitution in the first place, and a key reason for continued federal existence, then the more centralized the federation, the more likely is coherent military strategy.[3] In addition, if the formation of economic policy requires administrative coherence, then, it is argued, a centralized form of government is the most likely to provide that coherence. It should not be a surprise, therefore, that centralized federations are the most stable if they are best able to deal with military and economic matters. Finally, and most important, a centralized federation suggests that its constituent units are willing to cede certain powers to the central government. This is crucial to any viable federation.

Although centralization and the absence of political secession do seem to coincide most of the time, there are exceptions. Switzerland, a highly stable and quite decentralized federation, is the most notable example.

Furthermore, *centralization* is a highly ambiguous term. One should test certain other independent variables that may be related to stability and political secession.

POLITICAL STABILITY AND SECESSION

The variables to be tested in this chapter for their relevance to political stability and secession include:

1. The presence of exceptionally large constituent units
2. The number of constituent units
3. The presence of cultural or ethnic cleavages expressed in language differences
4. The degree of prosperity of the federation
5. The degree of political freedom in the federation and its units

These features have been selected because they have been precisely defined and are fairly easy to measure.

The Presence of Exceptionally Large Constituent Units

Throughout history, one of the main constitutional problems in federations has been the disproportionate size, in terms of population, of one or two constituent units (for our purposes, differences in wealth and military power are not explored). Although the constituent units of a federation are considered constitutionally equal, inequality in population size undermines their equality in political terms. One must acknowledge that a raison d'être for federalism is to accommodate such territorially based diversity: if the units were more alike, the federal structure might be unnecessary. Indeed, all federations have provincial disparities to varying degrees. The central problem is, however, that the constituent units of many federations differ greatly in size and population. Such disparities might threaten the stability of the nation. Surprisingly, only a small number of political theorists have addressed this problem.[4]

Large constituent units, because of their size and importance, naturally expect to have greater influence on decisions than small units. Indeed, they may be able to ensure that policy is formulated according to their own interests. Small units, on the other hand, often expect equality of influence. However, Ivo Duchacek notes:

> Even if the constitutional promise of divided power and cooperation among equals was initially based on a sincere decision to grant concessions to a group's desire for territorial identity and autonomy, no group can entirely rule out the possibility that the federation will in the long run be dominated by its most energetic, populous, or developed components. Such fear obstructed both the Dutch and the French attempts (but not quite the British) to transform their former colonial empires into federal structures guaranteeing a new partnership of equals.[5]

In the Canadian case, Ontario and Quebec seek influence commensurate with their size, whereas the smaller provinces expect an equal or near-equal vote in government decision making. Such a dispute, taken to an extreme, can threaten the existence of a federation. In the Canadian case, there is a struggle between the have and have-not provinces, the dominance of an overly large Ontario, and the secession potential of an overly large Quebec. (Exceptionally large or oversized constituent units are those that are twice the size, in terms of population, of all but other oversized constituent units.)

Since there are good theoretical reasons for the presence of oversized units to be closely associated with political instability, and particularly with secession, one should be able to verify the proposition that federations with one or two very large units are more unstable than those with units roughly equal in size.

The Number of Constituent Units

One of the threats to federal stability at inception is the presence of a limited number of constituent units. If a federation succeeds, it often grows by adding new units. When there are but a small number of units, usually less than ten, the existing ones have more reason to believe that, in the absence of external threat, they could succeed on their own. In addition, the greater the number of constituent units, it is suggested, the less likely is there to be any one unit strong enough to go it alone as a viable economic entity. In the Canadian case, the presence of only ten provinces ensures that each is relatively important and that ethnic differences are concentrated and reinforced rather than fragmented and subject to competition.

So, when there are many constituent units, there is reason to believe that the individual units will be much weaker (in both a military and economic sense) left on their own than if they are protected by many other units. In addition, the presence of many constituent units helps to ensure that the influence of an overwhelming unit or units will be minimized and that possibilities of continuous face-to-face internal conflict between potential powerful units will be lessened. In addition, inequalities will tend to be more pronounced in those federations made up of a smaller number of units.

Another reason for encouraging the creation of many constituent units in a federation is that a nation's population may be distributed among different regions, and if regional preferences vary, the fragmentation of the political system into a large number of constituent units will, almost of necessity, imply that within each unit, preferences will be more homogeneous than over the whole of the territory. If this is the case, then each unit will be better able to respond to the local concerns of its citizens, and in this way, one can argue that many units can be responsive to their citizens without posing a threat to the national government.[6] Ultimately, it is suggested that the ideal structural situation would have many small constituent units owing their first allegiance to a strong central government. Therefore, it is proposed that the fewer the number of constituent units, the more likely is federal instability.

Finally, there is a good theoretical reason to believe that political structure should be related to federal stability if one regards the benefits of federation as increased protection and the costs of federation as less autonomy. To break up the federation, then, is to renounce the crucial benefits of protection and security. If a constituent unit is, however, relatively strong, even in comparison with the federation itself, then the renunciation of ties is relatively inexpensive. The presence of only a small number of units, or of one or two overly large units, lowers the costs of dissolution.

The Presence of Cultural or Ethnic Cleavages Expressed in Language Differences

The two previously discussed properties of federations are part of their formal, written constitutions. It is argued that language differences, as well, are an important source of discord wherever they exist. Rabushka and Shepsle, for example, propose that when serious ethnic or language discord exists in a plural society, the possibilities for a peaceful resolution to their difficulties are quite limited. Political entrepreneurs in such societies are likely to take an issue such as language cleavage and build coalitions that counter the political elites. In this way, cleavages may become highly politicized movements allowing for few peaceful solutions.[7] Whether they are a cause of divisiveness or simply a reflection of discord, language differences are likely to be related to cleavage and, hence, also probably related to political secession.

Since language differences, it is argued, are related to political disunity, one would expect them to be related to instability in all kinds of government, federal or not. Indeed, many unitary governments are just as plagued with disputes over language as are many federations. Nevertheless, even though language disputes are not a specific disease of federalism, they might well be expected to exacerbate federal problems. It is very likely that federal constitutions are often adopted to moderate the intensity of disputes represented by language—such is sometimes said to be the case in Switzerland—and federalism may in fact so moderate.[8] One is led to conclude, however, that this does not preclude the possibility that language differences may be closely associated with secession.

The Degree of Prosperity of the Federation

Some scholars suggest that citizens of rich countries tend to be satisfied with the status quo and are less likely to seek to overthrow the existing political regime. On the other hand, it has been proposed that in a poor society, citizens feel that a change could only bring them some degree of prosperity. The converse propositions that rich societies are unstable and poor societies stable are just as defensible, however: prosperity may well encourage revolutionaries to believe that revolution is worthwhile, whereas poverty might convince potential revolutionaries that they must eat before they can change the political system. The empirical evidence is about as equivocal as the arguments: witness the vast and inconclusive literature on revolution and rising expectations. (In this regard, the most notable work is by Karl Deutsch, Ted Gurr, and Uriel Rosenthal.)[9] Nevertheless, since poverty or wealth has often been associated with federal stability or secession, there is the obligation to investigate these arguments.

The Degree of Political Freedom in the Federation and Its Units

A final assertion about stability, commonly encountered in the popular press but seldom in the professional literature, is that governments of free societies are more stable than oppressive governments (Lipset is especially notable for making this point).[10] However, casual inspection of political experience leads one to doubt this assertion. For every free country with a stable government, there seems to be an equally stable despotism. The converse is also the case. Since there seems to be little association between freedom and stability in governments generally, one should not expect to find it in the subclass of federations. Nevertheless, since the assertion is often made that freedom and stability are related, it will be tested here with respect to secession.

The following hypotheses are set forth in this chapter:

H2a: That centralization, many constituent units, and the absence of especially large units are positively correlated with federal stability and the absence of political secession in particular.

H2b: That the degree of wealth, the degree of language cleavage, and the degree of political freedom are not strongly associated with federal stability.

Three statistical works are excellent sources of reference for the tests performed in the chapter to come:

1.   John Aldrich and Charles F. Cnudde, "Probing the Bound of Conventional Wisdom: A Comparison of Regression, Probit,

and Discriminant Analysis," *American Journal of Political Science* 19, no. 3 (August 1975).

2. Eric Hanushek and John Jackson, *Statistical Methods for Social Scientists* (New York: Academic Press, 1977).

3. Richard McKelvey and W. Zavoina, "A Statistical Model for the Analysis of Legislative Voting Behavior" (paper presented at the annual meeting of the American Political Science Association, New York, 1969).

To examine these possible relations between institutional structure and stability, we need to measure the effect of structures on stability in a variety of federations. We have looked at both the forty-four federations that have existed, even briefly, from 1798 to the present and the thirty-two post–World War II federations.

Our other independent variables include:

1. The number of constituent units, as measured by counting units in each federation and dividing the federations into three groups: those with two to five constituent units (coded "1"), six to eleven units (coded "2"), and twelve to fifty units (coded "3"). A trichotomous rather than dichotomous categorization was used to minimize the influence of especially large or especially small federations on the entire analysis.

2. The presence or absence of oversized constituent units, as measured by whether one or two constituent units were large enough (in terms of population) to attempt to dominate the federation or secede from it. The dichotomous variable "oversized" (coded "1") or "not oversized" (coded "0") was defined precisely as oversized if one or two provinces had twice the population of the next-largest province.

3. Language cleavage, as measured by the existence of two or more significant language groups. This is also a dichotomous variable, defined as a cleavage (coded "1") if two or more languages are widely spoken, otherwise not (coded "0"). If a majority speaks one language, a second language is defined as "widely spoken" if 20 percent of the population uses it. If no language is spoken by a majority, then a language cleavage exists.

4. The degree of wealth of federations, as measured by defining a "rich" federation (coded "1") as one in the top half of the countries of the world ranked according to income at the time

the federation existed and by defining "not rich" (coded "0") as one in the bottom half of the same list. In part, the categorization for this dichotomous variable was derived from easily available data (e.g., G.N.P. as collected by the U.N.); but in part the categorization was also subjective and tentative. Evidence for the categorization of the United Netherlands, for example, was sketchy at best, although it was widely believed to be very wealthy in the seventeenth and eighteenth centuries.

5.   The degree of freedom, the final independent variable, as measured by the definition of freedom and the categorization of nations as "free" (coded "2"), "partly free" (coded "1"), or "not free" (coded "0") by Freedom House.[11] Since the annual survey by Freedom House covers only federations now in existence, the Freedom House methods to categorize federations that had failed were followed. A trichotomous variable was then derived.

Cross-Tabulations

The first technique of analysis was a simple cross-tabulation of each of the independent variables and stability. As is apparent from the data which follow, there is a positive association between each variable and stability.

Although the data concern an entire population rather than a sample, so that significance tests are inappropriate, still an informal way of appreciating the obviously high degree of association between centralization and stability is to note that were this a sample, the Kendall Tau B level of significance (or the probability that the apparent association occurred by chance) would be .00001.

Dependent Variable: Federal stability

Independent Variable: Centralization
Number = 44

	Centralized	Not Centralized
Stable	11	2
Partly stable	2	2
Not stable or ended	2	25

Number = 32

	Centralized	Not Centralized
Stable	11	2
Partly stable	2	2
Not stable or ended	2	13

Independent Variable: Constituent units

Number = 44
Kendall Tau C = Significant at .0054

	2 units thru 5	6 thru 11	12 thru 50
Stable	0	3	10
Partly stable	1	2	1
Not stable or ended	10	7	10

Number = 32
Kendall Tau C = Significant at .0028

	2 units thru 5	6 thru 11	12 thru 50
Stable	0	3	10
Partly stable	1	2	1
Not stable or ended	7	3	5

Independent Variable: Oversized units

Number = 44
Kendall Tau C = Significant at .0054

	No	Yes
Stable	8	5
Partly stable	0	4
Not stable or ended	5	22

Number = 32
Kendall Tau B = Significant at .0009

	No	Yes
Stable	8	5
Partly stable	0	4
Not stable or ended	1	4

Independent Variable: Language cleavage

Number = 44
Kendall Tau C = Significant at .2009

	No	Yes
Stable	8	5
Partly stable	0	4
Not stable or ended	11	16

Number = 32
Kendall Tau B = Significant at .0009

	No	Yes
Stable	8	5
Partly stable	0	4
Not stable or ended	5	10

Independent Variable: Rich

Number = 44
Kendall Tau C = Significant at .454

	No	Yes
Stable	5	8
Partly stable	2	2
Not stable or ended	18	9

Number = 32
Kendall Tau B = Significant at .0135

	No	Yes
Stable	5	8
Partly stable	2	2
Not stable or ended	12	3

Independent Variable: Freedom

Number = 44
Kendall Tau C = Significant at .05

	No	Partly	Yes
Stable	3	2	8
Partly stable	2	1	1
Not stable or ended	9	12	6

Number = 32
Kendall Tau B = Significant at .0240

	No	Partly	Yes
Stable	3	2	8
Partly stable	2	1	1
Not stable or ended	6	7	2

It is worth noting that Tau B or Tau C is significant at least at the .05 level for all the variables except language. Most important, our cross-tabulation of the number of units and stability in the forty-four-case sample revealed that ten of eleven of the federations with between two to five provinces failed entirely, whereas eleven of twenty-one with twelve to fifty units are stable or partly stable. Similar results were realized for our independent variable "oversized units." Federations that had no oversized constituent unit were far more likely to be stable than those with an oversized one.

The Multivariate Tests

It must be noted, however, that in such a pair-wise analysis as this, excessive bias is a real hazard. Some independent variables may appear to contribute to stability only because other variables, which might supersede them, are not included in the comparison. Hence, impressive as the cross-tabulations are, further statistical analysis seems appropriate. To reduce the inherent bias, we conducted a discriminant analysis on variables other than centralization. Discriminant analysis tests the ability of a set of independent variables to predict correctly the classification in the trichotomy (or groups) of the dependent variable for each of the forty-four countries. A canonical discriminant function, a multivariate analysis, revealed that the independent variables could discriminate to at least the .0057 level, explain 65 percent of the variable between groups, and classify 43 percent of the federal cases for the forty-four cases. For the thirty-two cases, the independent variables could discriminate to at least the .001 level, explain 65 percent of the variance between groups, and predict or classify 60 percent of the federal cases.

Standardized Canonical Discriminant Function Coefficients = (A)

Level of Significance of Wilks Lambda = (B)

Independent Variable	Number = 32		Number = 44	
	(A)	(B)	(A)	(B)
Constituent units (1)	-0.79101	.0103	-.51381	.6078
Oversized units (2)	0.59308	.0010	.50281	.9254
Language cleavage (3)	0.67757	.0676	-.81871	.1524
Rich (4)	0.01742	.0786	.17924	.1923
Freedom (5)	-0.20511	.0993	.00299	.6186

(1) Since the values for stability increased with instability (0, 1, 2) and the values for constituent units increased with the number of units, the negative sign means that the smaller the number of units, the greater the instability.

(2) Since values for oversized units were coded (0) or (1), the positive sign means that stability is associated with no oversized units.

(3) The positive sign represents an association between increasing instability and increasing number of languages.

(4) The negative sign represents the inverse relation between economic instability and becoming rich, i.e., prosperity and stability are associated.

(5) The negative sign represents an inverse relation between increasing instability and increasing freedom, i.e., stability and freedom are (slightly) associated.

The standardized canonical discriminant function coefficients are important because each coefficient represents the relative contribution of its independent variable to the discrimination into categories on the dependent variable. The interpretation is analogous to the interpretation of beta weights in multiple regression. It is clear that the number of constituent units and oversized units are the most important discriminating variables.

A test of significance—appropriate only for samples and not for entire populations—is Wilks Lambda, which we offer as an informal suggestion of the meaning of the association. It showed that on both our samples, our independent variables "constituent units" and "oversized units" could discriminate among groups to at least the .01 level.

Discriminant analysis does not isolate the effect of individual independent variables on stability, however. With that in mind, we conducted a regression analysis on the variables. An analysis of "centralization" alone resulted in this relationship:

$$\text{Stability} = \alpha + \beta x_1$$
$$\text{or } Y = 1.68 - 1.03x_1$$
$$(0.24) \quad \text{Standard Error}$$

Where Y = Stability on a scale from 0 (stable) to 2 (unstable):

$$x_1 = \text{centralization on a scale from 0 (not centralized)}$$
to 1 (centralized)
$$\beta = \text{the normalized coefficient of } x_1$$
$$\alpha = \text{a constant.}$$

Thus a unit change in x_1, for example, decentralizing by going from 1 (centralized) to 0 (peripheralized), would lead us to expect a 1.03 negative change in Y, that is, a change from stable (0) to partly stable (1) or from partly stable (1) to unstable (2). This inverse relationship is obviously very strong (almost one to one), and r^2, the correlation coefficient between the variables, is -.73. Were this an analysis of a sample rather than a universe, the association would be significant at the .001 level. Because centralization is so difficult to measure, however, we conducted a regression analysis on our remaining variables, some of which are doubtless features of centralization. We found a close association between stability and the number of constituent units (an association that would be significant at the .01 level) and between stability and oversized units (an association that would be significant at the .05 level). The remaining three independent variables were not closely associated with stability.

Number = 44
$r^2 = .27$

Independent Variable	Beta	F-Score	Significance
Centralization	+0.68891	43.650	.001

This equation related only centralization, and not the other independent variables, to stability.

Constituent units	+0.29975	4.154	.01
Oversized units	-0.25155	2.766	.05
Language cleavage	-0.05391	.128	Not Significant
Rich	-0.06946	.176	Not Significant
Freedom	+0.09739	0.353	Not Significant

If the analysis had been conducted on a sample rather than a whole population, an F-score of 2.85 would be significant at the .05 level.

Number = 32
$r^2 = .52$

Independent Variable	Beta	F-Score	Significance
Constituent units	.41150	7.563	.01
Oversized units	-.31057	3.749	.05
Language cleavage	.22265	2.310	Not Significant
Rich	.11885	.600	Not Significant
Freedom	.09899	.397	Not Significant

If the analysis had been conducted on a sample rather than a whole population, an F-score of 5.71 would be significant at the .01 level.

The evidence suggests, therefore, that the more centralized a federation and the more units it has, the more likely it is to be stable. Further, a federation without an exceptionally large province is more likely to be stable. Presumably, a small federation (in terms of units) with a large province is likely to be unstable. It is vital to stress, however, that this strong association is not necessarily a causal relationship.

There is, however, one extremely strong and important negative result: language cleavage, prosperity, and freedom are *not* directly related to a federation's stability as it is defined in this chapter and as it relates to political secession.

Finally, this study included several tests designed to detect multicollinearity and determine the degree of bias. The most notable test was a measure of the partial r_j^2 (where r_j^2 is defined as the squared multiple correlation coefficient of the jth independent variable on all other independent variables), a test intended to determine whether any pair of the several independent variables were measuring the same thing. Omitting centralization (which is, of course, a summary of many variables), we find that the remaining variables had partial r^2 ranging from .115 to .302, which by any standard are fairly low degrees of correlation and, hence, indicate low degrees of multicollinearity. Since none of the scores appear to distort the analysis severely, we infer that we did not measure the same thing with our several independent variables other than centralization.

Independent Variable	Number = 44 r_j^2	Number = 32 r_j^2
Constituent units	.302	.221
Oversized units	.287	.257
Language cleavage	.115	.182
Rich	.163	.288
Freedom	.156	.146

N-Chotomous Probit Analysis

Because the dependent variable is trichotomous and nonlinear, a regression analysis is not entirely appropriate. It implies that a given marginal change in probability, say changing P from .97 to .98, requires the same degree of change in x as changing P from .49 to .50. This is clearly an unrealistic assumption because a unit change when one is close to the limits (.97 to .98) is much less likely in the circumstances of this study than is a unit change at the median of the distribution. An alternative statistical model, Probit analysis, can account for this differing marginal change.

Probit analysis derives maximum likelihood estimates of the coefficients associated with the predictor variables, thus providing a test of significance. This is similar to the T-statistic used in regression analysis. The overall significance of the Probit analysis is measured by the chi-square statistic rather than the familiar F-test found in regression analysis.[12] The test indicates that the coefficients, taken together, have a considerable degree of significance for both the samples on the chi-square test. For the coefficients individually, the maximum likelihood estimators show significance for both samples regarding the degree of centralization, the existence of oversized units, and the number of constituent units.

Number = 44
Chi^2 = Significant at .05

Independent Variable	MLE/Standard Error	Significance
Oversized units	-2.054	.02
Constituent units	1.56	.06

Number = 32
Chi^2 = Significant at .001

Independent Variable	MLE/Standard Error	Significance
Oversized units	-2.241	.01
Constituent units	1.90	.03

Other "goodness of fit" tests have also been derived from the analysis. These include an r^2 statistic for both of the samples (.36 for the forty-four cases and .60 for the thirty-two cases). Within Probit analysis, this statistic represents the degree of variance between the actual value of the cases "regressed" on the predictor values.

The percentage of cases predicted correctly is similar to that found in discriminant analysis, that is, a raw score of accurate predictions. The model predicted 68 percent of the cases accurately on the sample of forty-four cases and 78 percent of the cases on the sample of thirty-two. This is clearly a marked improvement over the results of the discriminant analysis. Another useful test is Lambda B, which is the proportion by which error in predicting the value of the dependent variable is reduced from knowing the value of the independent variable (that is, how much better the prediction of the dependent variable is if one knows the value of the independent variable). These scores were .17 for the sample of forty-four cases and .61 for the sample of thirty-two cases.

Finally, the rank order correlation between the predicted versus the actual values was assessed. This statistic, much the same as a Tau B statistic, allows us to evaluate the strength of association between the outcome and the predictor values. A measure between .0 and .3 is "small," between .3 and .7 is "moderate," and between .7 and 1 is "high." The rank order correlation for the sample of forty-four is .39 and for the sample of thirty-two, .73. A test of the partial r^2s to detect levels of multicollinearity revealed only low levels of multicollinearity.

CONCLUSION

Clear-cut evidence of an association between federal stability and centralization, between stability and numerous constituent units, and between instability and oversized units has been derived. These results are especially illuminating in the case of Canada, which includes the exceptionally large provinces of Ontario and Quebec within a comparatively small number of total constituent units (ten). The evidence suggests further federal instability in the country.

The statistical investigation on the whole confirms the hypotheses. Centralization and stability/secession are indeed closely related, although the estimate of centralization is quite simplistic and will be explored in greater depth in chapter 5. To better address the problem, this study has investigated other independent variables believed to be related to federations. From these observations it has been demonstrated that the proximate cause of federal instability, at least with regard to political secession, is related to the federal structure.

There is a good theoretical reason to postulate that political structure is related to federal secession if one defines the benefits of federation as increased protection and the costs of federation as less autonomy. It is then clear that the structure of the federation is of great importance. To break up the federation is to renounce the benefits of protection and security. If a constituent unit is, however, relatively strong, even in comparison with the federation itself, then the renunciation is relatively inexpensive. It is exactly in these circumstances that it is relatively inexpensive to renounce. Other features of federal relationships, such as language differences, differences in wealth, and levels of freedom—all of which have been thought to be possible causes of secession—thus appear irrelevant to the decision to dissolve or resign from a federation. Centralization in general raises the costs of federal dissolution, and the presence of only a small number of constituent units or of a few overly large units lowers the costs of dissolution, whereas language or wealth is likely irrelevant to these costs. It should be noted that this theory is relevant to political instability as it applies to the decision to secede. It might well be the case that language cleavage, degree of wealth, etc., are related to the other stability dependent variables.

For a list of the federations, see the Appendix.

NOTES

1. William H. Riker and Jonathan Lemco, "The Relations between Structure and Stability in Federal Governments," in William Riker, ed., *The Development of American Federalism* (Norwell, Mass.: Kluwer, 1987).

2. Ibid.

3. See especially William Riker, *Federalism: Origin, Operation, Significance* (Boston: Little, Brown and Co., 1964), and William H. Riker, "Federalism," in Fred Greenstein and Nelson W. Polsby, eds., *Handbook of Political Science* (Reading: Addison-Wesley, 1975), 5: 93–172.

4. The most prominent have been John Stuart Mill in *Representative Government*; K. C. Wheare, *Federal Government*, 4th ed. (London: Oxford University Press, 1964); Ivo Duchacek, *Comparative Federalism* (New York: Holt, Rinehart and Winston, 1970); and Ronald May, "Decision-Making and Stability in Federal Governments," *Canadian Journal of Political Science* (March 1970).

5. Duchacek, op. cit., p. 101.

6. See Albert Breton and Anthony Scott, *The Design of Federations* (Montreal: Institute for Research on Public Policy, 1980), p. 16, for a fuller discussion of this point.

7. Alvin Rabushka and Kenneth Shepsle, *Politics in Plural Societies: A Theory of Democratic Instability* (Columbus: Charles E. Merrill, 1972).

8. See, for example, Hans Daalder, "On Building Consociational Nations: The Case of The Netherlands and Switzerland," in Kenneth McRae, ed., *Consociational Democracy: Political Accommodation in Segmented Societies* (Toronto: McClelland and Stewart, 1974), pp. 107–24, or Jurg Steiner, *Amicable Agreement Versus Majority Rule: Conflict Resolution in Switzerland* (Chapel Hill: University of North Carolina Press, 1974).

9. See, for example, Karl Deutsch, "Social Mobilization and Political Development," *American Political Science Review* 55 (September 1961): 493–514; Ted Robert Gurr, *Why Men Rebel* (Princeton: Princeton University Press, 1970); Uriel Rosenthal, *Political Order: Rewards, Punishments, and Political Stability* (The Netherlands: Sijthoff and Noordhoff, 1978).

10. Seymour Martin Lipset, *Political Man* (Garden City: Doubleday and Co., 1960).

11. Raymond Gastil, *Freedom in the World: Political Rights and Civil Liberties—1980* (New Brunswick: Transaction Books, 1980).

12. Eric Hanushek and John Jackson, *Statistical Methods for Social Scientists* (New York: Academic Press, 1977).

4

THE DEGREE OF POLITICAL FREEDOM AND FEDERAL STABILITY

In this chapter, the strength of association among freedom, democracy, and political stability is reviewed. The levels of freedom are defined according to Raymond Gastil's Freedom House study, examining measures of civil liberties, political rights, and the extent to which there is regime coercion.

For purposes of this investigation, freedom is equated with democracy. There exist no free nations, according to Gastil, that are not democratic. It is here hypothesized that, building on the results in the preceding chapter, the different measures of freedom will not be strongly associated with the measures of political stability. This is a far more comprehensive test of the freedom variable than in the last chapter, however, and there is a felt obligation to test its strength of association with the nonsecession stability variables.

In chapter 3, it was argued that nonsecessionist federations are not any more likely to be free than not free.[1] It was maintained that the conditions promoting political separation are unrelated to the forces resulting in political freedom. Bruce Berkowitz concurs, noting that "democracy is just a means for selecting policies that happen to work when people do not feel strongly about the issues at hand."[2] He is led to conclude that democracy is not a means of mediating conflict, as some scholars have suggested, and cannot reduce turmoil where no other mediating device is present.

However, one of the most important federal theorists, Daniel Elazer, argues that, ideally, federalism is designed to secure a good government based on liberty or to maintain an effective, stable government under conditions whereby the liberties of the partners to the federal bargain are maintained.[3] He argues that federations attempt to do this by restricting and dividing governing powers and, in part, by giving the partners to the federal compact a participatory role in the exercise of those powers. Yet they seek to do so not out of a desire to prevent governing but to allow governance to the maximum extent required. Certain theorists of federalism argue that this combination of ends—liberty, participation, and governance, and the relationship among them—is one of the defining characteristics of federal systems.[4] In reality, of course, many federations are not democratic and place great restrictions on liberty and participation.

In the previous chapter, no empirical association between political freedom and federal stability was demonstrated. The theoretical literature reveals rather mixed results, however. On the one hand, Douglas Hibbs and David Snyder and Charles Tilly have demonstrated a positive association between elections and political violence.[5] Harry Eckstein suggests that these findings reflect the possibility that the electoral process activates emotions appropriate also to other outlets. In addition, Hugh Davis Graham and Ted Robert Gurr find that democracies in their sample have more "civil conflict" than autocracies.[6]

Seymour Martin Lipset, on the other hand, has long argued that democracy and stability are positively related.[7] Lipset's thesis has been supported by several other studies, including those of Gabriel Almond and James Coleman and Karl Deutsch.[8] Hibbs employed Phillips Cutright's index of political development to show, at first glance, that democracies successfully eliminate or strongly reduce the probability of rebellion. This relationship disappears, however, if economic development is accounted for.[9] Hibbs, using elite electoral accountability and electoral turnover as indicators of democracy, an interaction term of both, and dependent variables including collective violence and civil war, finds no support for Lipset's thesis. Furthermore, in studying the period from 1800 to 1960, William Flanigan and Edwin Fogelman report a negative relationship between democracy and political violence at any level and at any rate of economic development.[10]

Leon Hurwitz also demonstrates a negative relationship between democracy and stability. His findings reveal that higher levels of democratic performance are weakly associated with greater instability.[11] Claude Ake, who looks at a different aspect of the problem, theorizes that maintaining a strong coercive capacity is one way regimes in transitional societies undergoing rapid social mobilization are able to neutralize the accompanying instabilities.[12] In turn, Gurr has suggested that the magnitude of systemic violence tends to vary inversely with the perceived capability for force in a political regime.[13] He further maintains that if governments have a high degree of coercive force, they can more readily resort to repression. A similar argument is made by Eckstein and by Amitai Etzioni, who propose that consistent authority patterns are very important correlates of political stability.[14]

Samuel Huntington is one of several theorists who propose that inflexible, repressive responses by government intensify the frustrations of dissidents and thus make them more prone to violence.[15] Such responses are, from the regime's perspective, counterproductive in that they tend to be associated with outbreaks of the very types of behaviors they are designated to prevent. Finally, theorists including Alexis de Tocqueville, James Davies, and Huntington suggest a curvilinear effect; that is, violence is most likely in societies with only moderately coercive capacity rather than very permissive or very repressive capacity.[16]

For purposes of this chapter, Gastil's Freedom House survey for the definitions of freedom, the available data, and the operationalization of the categories of freedom are all used.[17] Gastil and his coresearchers have examined most, if not all, of the nations of the world and have placed them on scales for "political rights," "civil liberties," degree of "political terror," and overall "political freedom." On the freedom scale, a rating of (1) is freest and (7) is least free. Standards are comparative and not based on an absolute scale. With respect to political rights, states rated (1) have a fully competitive electoral process, and those who are elected clearly rule. States rated with a (7) have political despots who seem to care little about popular opinion or popular tradition.

A (1) assigned to a country for civil liberties means that there is freedom of the press, high levels of protection of civil rights, etc. These states are the traditional democracies. A (7) implies that there is pervasive fear, no opposition to the government, and little individual expression. Gastil also provides estimates of political terror that represent the extent of a government's use of political force and the extent of its capacity for implementing political coercion. For a complete discussion of the basis on which numbers are assigned to states, see the 1980 edition of Gastil's study. The Gastil operationalization and data were chosen because the study's conclusions, on close inspection, are convincing and frequently cited.

Nonetheless, Gastil's data are relevant only for the existing federations. Where he did not account for the older and nonexistent federations, individual country summaries were investigated and assigned a numerical weight. (See the Appendix for a listing of the country studies.) It must again be stressed that because this subjective measure could be misleading or inaccurate to some extent, the federations were operationalized in two ways. First, they were divided into those that ended before 1945 and those that were created or existed after World War II. This is the total sample of forty-four cases. Second, only the postwar federations, numbering thirty-two cases, were tested. Although certain of these postwar federations no longer exist, those that do still exist have been accounted for by Gastil, and data are relatively easy to obtain for those that do not. To review:

> H3a: That the degrees of political freedom, political rights, civil liberties, and political terror are not significantly associated with federal stability

POLITICAL FREEDOM AND FEDERAL STABILITY

Cross-Tabulations

Several variables in this pair-wise analysis are strongly associated. The strength of association is presented between the significant variables and does not break down the cases into their specific categories. The variables for freedom include "political rights," "civil liberties," "political terror," and overall "political freedom."

> (+) represents a positive association (Kendall Tau C)
> (-) represents a negative association (Kendall Tau C)

Only the significant associations are presented. Blanks indicate no strong statistical association.

Number = 44

Independent Variable	Riots	Political Assassinations	Civil War	Abuse of High Office
Political rights	-.03		+.02	
Civil liberties			-.04	
Political terror	+.002		-.01	-.01
Political freedom			-.01	

Independent Variable	Small-Scale Terrorism	Purges	Executive Tenure	Reg. Exec. Transfers
Political rights			+.05	
Civil liberties				
Political terror		+.003		-.05
Political freedom	-.05			+.04

Number = 32

Independent Variable	Riots	Political Assassinations	Coups D'état	Civil Wars	Electoral Violence
Political rights		-.005			-.04
Civil liberties		-.02			-.03
Political terror	+.006	+.02	+.03	-.01	-.006
Political freedom		+.008		-.02	

Independent Variable	Abuses of Office	Small-Scale Terrorism	Mutinies	Plots	Purges	Reg. Exec. Transfers
Political rights		-.02				+.01
Civil liberties	-.05			-.03		+.02
Political terror	-.01	-.02	+.003	+.02	+.001	-.02
Political freedom	-.02				+.01	

Of the many pair-wise tests, only a few were significantly associated. The most important dependent variable, the federation's "absence of secession potential," was not significantly related to any of the freedom independent variables.

Discriminant Analysis

A discriminant analysis was conducted on the four freedom dependent variables, and not one proved to have a strong association of any kind with stability. Only a small percentage of the cases was grouped accurately on the first try, and only a low percentage of variance was explained.

Regression Analysis

The regression analysis, which is used only in a backup role, revealed no significant associations between the freedom variables and political stability. As a sample of the regression equations derived in this chapter, an analysis of the independent variable "political terror" and the dependent variable "absence of secession potential" revealed this relationship for the forty-four cases:

$$\text{Absence of secession potential} = \alpha + \beta x_1$$
$$\text{or } Y = 0.29 - 0.35x_1 + \Sigma$$
$$(0.23) \quad \text{Standard Error}$$

Where Y = Absence of secession potential on a scale from 2 (stable) to 0 (unstable):

x_1 = political terror on a scale from 1 (no political terror) to 5 (high level of political terror)
β = the normalized coefficient of x_1
α = a constant.

In a posttest, the structural variables "oversized units" and "constituent units" were tested with the freedom independent variables and the stability dependent variables. These two structural variables were significantly associated with stability, replicating the findings of the previous chapter. Because there is no theoretical reason to believe that the structural variables are related to freedom, however, this inclusion in this part of the analysis acts to misspecify the model. As a result, no great heed is paid to the result. (In chapter 3, the structural variables and "freedom," "rich," and "language cleavage" were hypothesized to be associated with the dependent variable "stability," but not necessarily related to one another. Indeed, the cross-tabulations and correlation coefficients between these other variables were not strongly associated.) There were also high levels of multicollinearity between all the freedom variables. To overcome this problem, this study first tested separately the variables, that is, they were individually tested with the structural variables and political stability, and then combined them into one freedom variable with the structural variables and the dependent variables. However, they remained weakly correlated with political stability.

N-Chotomous Probit Analysis

The Probit test indicates that, contrary to the findings of the regression analysis, certain of the independent variables have a significant association with certain of the dependent variables. This is inconsistent with the hypothesis that there are no strong associations and illustrates some of the theoretical problems of applying regression to such an analysis.

Long-Term Stability: Legitimate Politics

Dependent Variable: Electoral violence

Number = 44

Chi^2 = Not Significant

Independent Variable	MLE/Standard Error	Significance
Freedom		Not Significant
Political rights		Not Significant
Civil liberties	-1.675	.05
Political terror		Not Significant

Number = 32

Chi^2 = Significant at .05

Independent Variable	MLE/Standard Error	Significance
Freedom		Not Significant
Political rights		Not Significant
Civil liberties	-2.011	.02
Political terror		Not Significant

Goodness of Fit Tests

	Number = 44	Number = 32
r^2 =	.14	.32
% predicted correctly	55%	66%
Proportional reduction in error	.13	.35
Rank order correlation	.21	.43

The results confirm that the higher the degree of civil liberties, the lower the level of electoral violence.

Dependent Variable: Abuse of high office

Number = 44

Chi^2 = **Significant at .05**

Independent Variable	MLE/Standard Error	Significance
Civil liberties		Not Significant
Political terror	-2.480	.007

Number = 32

Chi^2 = Significant at .001

Independent Variable	MLE/Standard Error	Significance
Civil liberties	-2.607	.001
Political terror	-2.593	.005

The other independent variables were not significantly associated with stability.

Goodness of Fit Tests

	Number = 44	Number = 32
r^2 =	.20	.48
% predicted correctly	55%	66%
Proportional reduction in error	.13	.45
Rank order correlation	.32	.62

For the forty-four cases, the higher the level of political terror, the less the extent of abuse of high office. This relationship disappears with the thirty-two cases, however, where the findings confirm that the greater the degree of civil liberties in the postwar federations, the less likely the abuse of high office. The rank order correlation, similar to the Tau B score, was especially high.

Dependent Variable: Small-scale terrorism

Number = 44

Chi^2 = Significant at .10

Independent Variable	MLE/Standard Error	Significance
Freedom	-2.124	.02
Political rights	1.778	.04
Political terror	-1.883	.03

The other independent variables were not significantly associated with stability.

	Goodness of Fit Tests	
	Number = 44	
r^2 =	.25	
% predicted correctly	59%	
Proportional reduction in error	.05	
Rank order correlation	.22	

The only strong associations were demonstrated for the forty-four federations. The findings reveal that the higher the degree of political freedom overall, the less likely is small-scale terrorism. However, the more pervasive the level of political rights (one aspect of political freedom), the more widespread is small-scale terrorism. These are clearly contradictory results, and a resolution of this inconsistency will be attempted in the conclusion. Finally, the results reveal that governments practicing the most political terror experience the lowest degree of small-scale terrorism.

Short-Term Stability: Stability of Chief Executives

Dependent Variable: Regular executive transfers

Number = 44

Chi^2 = Significant at .05

Independent Variable	MLE/Standard Error	Significance
Political terror	-1.733	.04
Civil liberties		Not Significant

Number = 32
Chi^2 = Significant at .001

Independent Variable	MLE/Standard Error	Significance
Political terror		Not Significant
Civil liberties	2.03	.02

Goodness of Fit Tests

	Number = 44	Number = 32
r^2 =	.18	.94
% predicted correctly	59%	75%
Proportional reduction in error	.10	.20
Rank order correlation	.26	.51

The results show that, for the forty-four cases, the more the political terror, the less likely are regular executive transfers of power. For the thirty-two cases, on the other hand, the greater the extent of civil liberties in federations, the more likely are regular executive transfers of power. The rank order correlation for the thirty-two cases is again quite high.

Fairly high levels of multicollinearity between certain of the independent variables appeared in the Probit analysis (in the .5–.65 range). Even after the most collinear variables were deleted from the analysis, there still remained no more significant associations than before. The deletion of variables could severely alter the validity of the model, and great care was taken to avoid this problem.

CONCLUSION

The assumptions about the relationship between democracy and federal political stability were only partially confirmed. As expected, there is no strong association between democracy and stability when the two are defined in terms of long-term stability, destabilizing potential and long-term stability, and limitation of violence. However, certain variables believed to be related to long-term legitimacy and short-term stability in both of the federal samples were significantly related to political freedom.

It has been demonstrated that the higher the degree of civil liberties for both the federal samples, the lower the level of electoral violence. Where freedom exists, it seems there is less need for civil strife during electoral periods. One can assume that a high level of civil liberties is associated with a high degree of political legitimacy, and if the decisions disagreeable to substantial segments of the population are still adhered to in legitimate societies, then this finding should not be surprising.

It has also been demonstrated that the greater the extent of civil liberties for the thirty-two cases, the less likely is abuse of high office. This result is not too surprising, given that civil liberties imply a greater public role in the political process, which in turn acts as a check on executive corruption. It has also been shown that political terror is negatively associated with abuse of high office in both samples. This is a fairly unexpected result and might be explained in two ways. First, a highly coercive regime is less likely to be politically corrupt. It rules by forceful means and does not need to engage in extensive patronage. Another possible, and more persuasive, explanation is that coercive regimes are less likely to allow the reporting of executive corruption.

Political rights were positively associated with small-scale terrorism for the total sample of federations. This is consistent with Hibbs, Snyder and Tilly, and especially Eckstein, who, as has been discussed, suggested that participation in the electoral process may activate emotions appropriate also to other outlets. Note that civil liberties during electoral periods are not associated with violence, indicating that civil liberties and political rights are two very different independent variables.

Political terror is negatively associated with small-scale terrorism for the total sample of federations. It is suggested, following Ake, Gurr, and others, that small-scale terrorism is rarely tolerated in countries where coercion is widespread. Although this is not a significant association for the thirty-two cases, the results point in this direction.

Political freedom was negatively associated with small-scale terrorism for the entire sample. It is suggested that as political freedom is established and a regime comes to be regarded as legitimate, small-scale terrorism becomes a less attractive alternative for dissidents. This proposal is similar to the explanation for the negative relationship between civil liberties and electoral violence. Furthermore, it is proposed that overall freedom is more affected by civil liberties than by political rights, which are positively associated with small-scale terrorism.

One other related suggestion is that freedom is, to some extent, a compendium of the other three freedom variables, which, taken together, point in a negative direction. This finding is consistent with Lipset, Almond and Coleman, Deutsch, Cutright, and Flanigan and Fogelman.

Political terror is also negatively associated with regular executive transfers of power for the forty-four cases. This is an intuitive result, for those countries with high levels of terror are most likely to have dictatorships, which can be removed only through nondemocratic means. Although the same finding has not been demonstrated for the thirty-two cases, the results point in the same direction.

Finally, civil liberties are positively correlated with regular executive transfers of power for the thirty-two postwar federal cases. This is not a surprising finding: it stands to reason that countries with a high level of freedom are most likely to have an orderly succession of political executives. This is consistent with the findings derived from Gastil's sample.

All together, the federal theorists have been partially supported in these empirical tests. Although not related to political secession, certain elements of the freedom variables are clearly related to federal stability.

NOTES

1. This is contrary to the arguments proposed by several writers including:

   a. Alexander Hamilton, James Madison, and John Jay, *The Federalist Papers*, ed. Benjamin F. Wright (Cambridge: Harvard University Press, 1961), especially Nos. 46, 51, 53, 55, 63, 84, 85.

   b. Pierre-Joseph Proudhon, *The Principle of Federation* (Toronto: University of Toronto Press, 1979), pp. 43–49.

   c. Ursula K. Hicks, *Federalism: Failure and Success* (New York: Oxford University Press, 1978), pp. 175–77.

2. Bruce David Berkowitz, "Stability in Political Systems: The Decision to Be Governed" (Ph.D dissertation, University of Rochester, 1981), p. 305.

3. Daniel Elazer, "The Role of Federalism in Political Integration," in Daniel Elazer, ed., *Federalism and Political Integration* (Jerusalem: Turtledove Publishing Co., 1979), p. 44.

4. See especially ibid.

5. Douglas A. Hibbs, Jr., *Mass Political Violence: A Cross-National Causal Analysis* (New York: John Wiley and Sons, 1973), p. 118, Table 7.1; David Snyder and Charles Tilly, "Hardship and Collective Violence in France, 1830–1860," *American Sociological Review* 37, no. 5 (October 1972): 520–32.

6. Harry Eckstein, "Theoretical Approaches to Collective Political Violence," in Ted Robert Gurr, ed., *Handbook of Political Conflict* (New York: Free Press, 1980), especially pp. 149–52; Hugh Davis Graham and Ted Robert Gurr, eds., *Violence in America: Historical and Comparative Perspectives* (New York: Praeger, 1969).

7. Seymour Martin Lipset, *Political Man* (Garden City: Doubleday and Co., 1960). This is a central theme in this work.

8. Gabriel Almond and James Coleman, eds., *The Politics of the Developing Areas* (Princeton: Princeton University Press, 1960), pp. 532–76; Karl Deutsch, *Tides among Nations* (New York: Free Press, 1979).

9. Hibbs, op. cit., p. 118; Phillips Cutright, "National Political Development: Measurement and Analysis," *American Sociological Review* 28, no. 2 (April 1963): 253–67.

10. William H. Flanigan and Edwin Fogelman, "Patterns of Political Violence in Comparative Historical Perspective," *Comparative Politics* 3 (July 1970): 1–20.

11. Leon Hurwitz, "An Index of Democratic Political Stability," *Comparative Political Studies* (April 1971): 53–56.

12. Claude Ake, *A Theory of Political Integration* (Homewood: Dorsey Press, 1969); Claude Ake, "Political Integration and Political Stability: A Hypothesis," *World Politics* 19 (April 1967): 488–92.

13. Ted Robert Gurr, "A Comparative Study of Civil Strife," in H. D. Graham and Ted Robert Gurr, eds., *Violence in America: Historical and Comparative Perspectives,* 2d. ed. (Beverly Hills: Sage, 1979), pp. 544–605.

14. Harry Eckstein, "Authority Relations and Governmental Performance," *Comparative Political Studies* 2 (1969): 269–325; Amitai Etzioni, *Political Unification: A Comparative Study of Leaders and Forces* (New York: Holt, Rinehart and Winston, 1965).

15. Samuel P. Huntington, *Political Order in Changing Societies* (New Haven: Yale University Press, 1968).

16. Alexis de Tocqueville, *Democracy in America* (New York: Washington Square Press, 1964); James C. Davies, "Toward a Theory of Revolution," *American Sociological Review* 27 (1962): 5–19; Huntington, op. cit.; Ted Robert Gurr, *Why Men Rebel* (Princeton: Princeton University Press, 1970), pp. 41–42.

17. Raymond Gastil, *Freedom in the World: Political Rights and Civil Liberties— 1980* (New Brunswick: Transaction Books, 1980).

5

THE RELATION BETWEEN CENTRALIZATION AND STABILITY IN FEDERAL GOVERNMENTS

In chapter 3 it was demonstrated that a strong positive relationship exists between political centralization and the absence of federal secession. In this chapter, the independent variable "political centralization" is investigated in more detail. Political centralization will be operationalized as it relates to

1. the federal constitution;
2. the structure of political parties within the federation; and
3. the absence of crosscutting cleavages or the degree of federal "asymmetry."

It is hypothesized that certain variables associated with these general topics are positively related to federal stability. Furthermore, it is proposed that modern federations are more centralized than many nineteenth-century federations. With technological growth comes both the demand for increased coherence in policy-making in the central and the constituent governments and greater demand for government-sponsored social services. In addition, modern forms of transportation and communication have forced central governments to play increasingly important administrative roles. Nonetheless, why should one believe that political centralization as a concept should be related to political stability? The following reasons are proposed:

1. Centralized patterns of authority encompassing large systems such as federations do not tend to change rapidly. They are, in

the terminology of Fernand Braudel, part of "social history, with [its] slow but perceptible rhythms."[1]

2. If centralization implies the monopoly of power, which can both act as a threat or induce compliance, then stability is, in this sense, the result of coercion and oppression, as well as of more subtle uses of power.[2]

3. Centralization is conducive to stability insofar as it provides coordination, effectiveness, and overall efficiency to the political system on the one hand and enhances the development of coherent military strategy and economic policy on the other. These factors are political centralization's greatest contribution to the policy-making process in federations.

In sum, one can say that stability is enhanced when new federations (and possibly new states as a whole) develop the capacity to check violence by establishing differentiated, autonomous centralized organizations that are powerful enough to enforce order.[3] For example, it has been suggested in another context by Riker and Lemco that Canada might be a stronger nation if its provinces could be broken up into smaller and more numerous constituent units. Each constituent unit would then need the central government to form more coherent economic policies and, possibly, coherent military strategies. The many small units would then owe their first allegiance to a strong central government rather than to their respective constituent governments.[4]

However, Youssef Cohen et al. argue that the centralizing process itself in modernizing countries contributes to political violence because it intrudes into preexisting structures of rights and obligations—that is, the centralizing process, at least in modernizing states, can disrupt the existing patterns of authority. "To the degree that this power accumulation is necessary for the imposition or maintenance of order, collective violence is also indicative of movement towards political order on a new scale . . . violence is a usual feature of the process of primitive accumulation of power."[5]

In this study, the last or most recent period of each federation is heavily weighted. The centralization process itself is of less importance. Following Cohen et al., however, there is the implication that some of the failed nineteenth-century federations may owe their demise, at least in part, to the centralizing process itself. Our results will give us some indication of this. (It should be noted that the Cohen study applies to modernizing states. Many of the federations in this sample have or had progressed beyond this level, and Cohen's work may not apply to them.)

POLITICAL CENTRALIZATION AND THE FEDERAL CONSTITUTION

If the bulk of constitutional powers is granted to the central government, then it will presumably be the dominant partner in the federal bargain. The federation can thus be recognized as being "centralized." If the preponderance of powers is granted to the constituent units, then it can be said that the federation is "peripheralized" or "decentralized." It cannot be asserted, however, that there is necessarily a causal relationship here. Some states with highly centralized constitutions (the Central American Federation or the first Mexican Federation) exhibited important divisive strains that eventually caused the federations to dissolve. Conversely, there have been decentralized federal constitutions associated with highly centralized federal unions (India and, depending on one's interpretation, the Soviet Union are examples). Following the earlier findings, however, it is suggested that, in general, the more centralized the federal constitution, the more likely is there to be political stability.

The relationship between the degree of constitutional centralization and the level of stability is tested in two ways. In the first method, the federations are divided into those that can be considered

1. empires (these include some of the eighteenth- and nineteenth-century federations);
2. highly centralized federations (these are almost unitary in their constitutional structure);
3. mixed federations (those that have powers fairly equally divided between the two levels of government); or
4. peripheralized federations (these resemble confederations in their constitutional structure).

The independent variables for this test are the degree of constitutional centralization, the number of constituent units, and the existence of especially large or oversized constituent units. To review:

H4a: That a centralized constitution is positively correlated with federal stability

The countries with federal constitutions were classified into the following categories:

	Number = 44	Number = 32
Empires	4 (0 presently existing)	2
Highly centralized federations	14 (4 presently existing)	12 (4 presently existing)
Mixed federations	22 (13 presently existing)	18 (13 presently existing)
Peripheral federations (near-confederations)	4 (0 presently existing)	0

Cross-Tabulations

The structural variables "constituent units" and presence of "oversized units" are correlated with secession to a significant level. The number of constituent units is associated to at least the .005 level for both the forty-four and the thirty-two cases. Oversized units is negatively associated to political secession to at least the .005 level for both samples. Mixed federations is negatively related to a significant degree to the potential for political secession in the sample of thirty-two. There is no significant bivariate relationship between any aspect of centralization and secession for the sample of forty-four.

The Multivariate Tests

The discriminant analysis reveals a strong significant association between all of the independent variables and political secession. Similar results were demonstrated in the regression analysis. As a sample of the regression equations derived in this chapter, an analysis of the independent variable "form of constitution" and the dependent variable "absence of secession potential" revealed this relationship for the forty-four cases:

$$\text{Absence of secession potential} = \alpha + \beta x_1$$
$$\text{or } Y = 0.097 - 0.11x_1 + \Sigma$$
$$(0.16) \quad \text{Standard Error}$$

Where Y = Stability on a scale from 2 (stable) to 0 (unstable):

$$x_1 = \text{form of constitution on a scale from 0 (empire) to 3 (peripheralized federation)}$$
$$\beta = \text{the normalized coefficient of } x_1$$
$$\alpha = \text{a constant.}$$

The most important test, however, was Probit analysis, and only the structural variables proved to be significantly associated with secession. A summary of the results follows.

Number = 44
Chi^2 = **Significant at .02**

Independent Variable	**MLE/Standard Error**	**Significance**
Constituent units	1.053	.03
Oversized units	-1.933	.02

Number = 32
Chi^2 = Significant at .001

Independent Variable	**MLE/Standard Error**	**Significance**
Constituent units	2.159	.015
Oversized units	-2.253	.01

Other "goodness of fit" tests from the analysis are also derived. These include an r^2 statistic for the samples (.32 for the forty-four cases and .59 for the thirty-two cases). In addition, the model predicted 66 percent of the cases accurately for the total sample and 69 percent of the cases for the sample of thirty-two. The Lambda B scores were .12 for the sample of forty-four cases and .41 for the sample of thirty-two cases. Finally, the rank order correlation for the sample of forty-four was .32, which is moderately low, and for the sample of thirty-two it was .53, which is moderate.

The independent variables were significantly related with the other stability dependent variables in cross-tabulations, but no statistical significance was demonstrated in the multivariate tests. Therefore, for the sake of brevity, these results are not discussed.

It has been demonstrated that the structural variables are important constitutional features with respect to political secession. The form of constitution, with respect to its degree of centralization as defined here, appears to be less important. The next part of this section discusses this issue more thoroughly.

THE CANADA WEST STUDY

The second method for testing the relationship between centralized federal constitutions and federal stability is an adaptation of a classification of federal states by the Canada West Foundation.[6] In that study, a comparative index is developed regarding the manner in which personnel are appointed to central institutions. This factor is singled out because it is proposed that government staffing is a key determinant of the direction the institution will take. The key political institutions specified in federal constitutions and identified by the Canada West Foundation include:

1. The head of state
2. The head of government
3. The lower house or first chamber of the legislature
4. The upper house or second chamber of the legislature
5. The central court of the federal system

The selection agency is coded in decreasing levels of centralization as follows:

1. A "1" is assigned to the national government, the most centralized agency
2. A "2" is assigned to the national legislature
3. A "3" is assigned to election by national electorate, constituency, or constituent unit electorate
4. A "4" is assigned to the provincial legislature
5. A "5" is assigned to the provincial cabinet, the most decentralized selection agency

The Canada West Foundation used a sample of just seven modern, democratic federations. However, its criteria are perfectly applicable to the total sample of forty-four cases. The federations are first presented with their centralization scores as per the Canada West Foundation criteria. Then "centralization" is tested as operationalized here, with the stability dependent variables. It is expected that the more centralized constitutions are likely to be the most stable. It must be acknowledged that this is a rough measure, with many possible important variables omitted. Nevertheless, the relationship between a centralized federal constitution and political stability should become clearer.

Measures of centralization have been assigned to the sample of forty-four countries. The lowest scores represent the greatest level of decentralization, and the highest scores represent the highest degree of centralization. Sources for the data include the Canada West study,[7] Herman's *Parliaments of the World* study,[8] and individual country studies.[9]

Federation	Centralization Score (as of 1983)
1. Argentina (1853–)	18
2. Australia (1901–)	12
3. Austria-Hungary (1867–1918)	3
4. Austria (1919–38)	3
5. Austria (1945–)	12.5
6. United States of Brazil (1891–1934)	6
7. Brazil (1946–)	11
8. British West Indies (1958–62)	10
9. Burma (1948–62)	8
10. Cameroons (1961–72)	10
11. Canada (1867–)	9
12. Central African Federation (1953–63)	4
13. Central American Federation (1824–39)	13.5
14. Chile (1826–27)	2
15. Grand Colombia (1819–30)	13
16. Colombia (1853–86)	19
17. Congo (1960–69)	12
18. Czechoslovakia (1969–)	12
19. Ethiopia (1952–62)	5
20. German Empire (1867–1919)	10
21. Germany—Weimar Republic (1919–38)	13
22. German Federal Republic (1949–)	15
23. India (1950–)	9
24. Indonesia (1949–50)	14
25. Federation of Iraq and Jordan (1958)	3
26. Libya (1951–63)	7
27. Malaya (1957–63)	11
28. Malaysia (with Singapore) (1963–65)	11
29. Malaysia (without Singapore) (1965–)	11
30. Mali Federation (1959–60)	10
31. Mexico (1824–36)	13.5
32. Mexico (1917–)	13
33. Nigeria (1960–70)	5
34. Nigeria (1970–)	13
35. Pakistan (1947–)	10
36. Switzerland (1848–)	12
37. Uganda (1962–67)	10.5
38. U.S.S.R. (1922–)	15
39. United Arab Republic (1958–61)	4
40. United Netherlands (1579–1798)	11
41. United States (1787–1861)	13.5
42. United States (1865–)	13.5
43. Venezuela (1864–)	16
44. Yugoslavia (1946–)	15

Cross-Tabulations

The cases were tested in a bivariate analysis with the secession variable. As expected, the more centralized federations (those with higher numbers or scores) were strongly associated with the most stable category. The forty-four cases were significant to the .008 level and the thirty-two cases significant to the .0005 significance level.

Discriminant Analysis

The canonical discriminant function revealed that the independent variable could discriminate to at least the .0082 level for the forty-four cases and classify 55 percent of the federal cases. For the thirty-two cases, the independent variable could discriminate to the .0005 level and predict 53 percent of the federal cases. The Wilks Lambda test showed that the independent variable could discriminate to at least the .008 level.

Regression Analysis

Dependent Variable: Absence of secession potential

Number = 44

$r^2 = .21$

Independent Variable	Beta	F-Score	Significance
Centralization	0.46	11.09	.01
Constituent units			Not Significant
Oversized units			Not Significant

Number = 32

$r^2 = .41$

Independent Variable	Beta	F-Score	Significance
Centralization	0.64	20.46	.001
Constituent units			Not Significant
Oversized units			Not Significant

These findings reveal that the most centralized federations are strongly associated with the absence of a secessionist threat.

N-Chotomous Probit Analysis

As mentioned, because the dependent variable is trichotomous and nonlinear, regression is not entirely appropriate for this analysis.

Number = 44
Chi^2 = Significant at .001

Independent Variable	MLE/Standard Error	Significance
Centralization	3.074	.001

Number = 32
Chi^2 = Significant at .001

Independent Variable	MLE/Standard Error	Significance
Centralization	3.145	.001

Other "goodness of fit" tests are derived from the analysis. These include an r^2 statistic for both of the samples (.42 for the forty-four cases and .59 for the thirty-two cases). The model predicted 66 percent of the cases for the sample of forty-four and 72 percent for the sample of thirty-two. This is clearly a marked improvement over the results of the discriminant analysis. The Lambda B scores were .07 for the forty-four cases and .47 for the thirty-two cases. Finally, the rank order correlation between the predicted versus the actual values was assessed. The rank order correlation (similar to Tau B) was .32 for the forty-four cases and .63 for the thirty-two cases; both scores are moderately high. The other stability variables were not significantly related to the centralization measure. Furthermore, the structural variables were not strongly associated with political stability. A test of the partial r^2s detected only low levels of multicollinearity.

This particular test presents clear-cut evidence of an association between stability/secession and centralization as it relates to the federal constitution. It is interesting to note that centralization was not significantly related to political stability/secession in the analysis relating to the degree of centralization as classified in the first part of the chapter but was significantly related in the second. Thus the method of personnel selection and the general centralization definition in chapter 3 seem to be of the greatest relevance with respect to the centralized constitution–federal stability relationship. Whether the federation is an empire, highly centralized, mixed, or peripheral is not as critical in this relationship.

POLITICAL CENTRALIZATION AND THE FEDERAL PARTY SYSTEM

A good measure of the degree of centralization in federal governments is the extent to which their party systems are centralized. If the base of support for political parties and their leaders is at the center, the party system is centralized. Similarly, if the base of support is in the regions or provinces, the party system is decentralized. Political parties are especially crucial in the federal integration process, a concept that is closely related to political centralization. Political parties facilitate political participation and inter-regional bargaining. The absence or ineffectiveness of statewide parties and a statewide party system may both indicate and increase the likelihood of secession. In Nigeria before 1966, national parties lost influence while regional parties with few links or interests outside their own respective regions gained ascendancy. In Pakistan, the results of the December 1970 election similarly presaged political disintegration as the Awami League and the Pakistan People's Party each won seats exclusively in their own regions.[10] In Quebec, the emergence of the separatist Parti Québécois in the 1970s was an obvious indication of the absence of strong, centralized, highly integrated, and nationally based political parties in Canada. In such troubled societies, a zero-sum scramble develops in which demands for regional rights and autonomy in decision making escalate into secessionist demands while the interests of the nation as a whole are largely forgotten.

In a number of cases, political coalition breakdown is accompanied by such an increase in mass political participation and expectation in the potentially secessionist region that existing political institutions are unable to accommodate demands. Particularly where a political "dark age" seems to terminate rapidly (Quebec after Duplessis or East Pakistan after Ayub Khan), an upsurge of political participation by a repressed cultural or regional group may result in new forms of militancy. The legitimacy crisis deepens when, as Deutsch explains, in the case of small states, the central government lacks the capacity to act or, in large states, the capacity to pay attention to this growing militancy.[11]

There are several ways of considering the question of how important centralized political parties are for federal stability. Perhaps the most effective way to address the question is to use the "structural approach" to federal party systems. This approach is most closely associated with the study of party systems; the work of two important theorists, Maurice Duverger and Giovanni Sartori, falls into this category.[12] The most obvious structural characteristic of party systems—the number of parties—has been the basis for the oldest, but still fashionable, classification of one-party, two-party, and multiparty systems, which Duverger termed "classic" party systems. Sartori has used that same criterion for further refining multipartyism into limited and extreme pluralism.[13]

Several studies have used this numerical criterion in conjunction with other structural characteristics to develop somewhat more complex typologies. Jean Blondel and Kenneth Janda, for example, use the number of parties and their electoral strength to categorize party systems.[14] Sartori includes ideological distance as a second criterion in his typology and also the relative size of parties in the system by introducing predominant party systems.

Although the number of parties criterion is the dominant classification in structural studies of party systems, it is by no means universally accepted. Neither are the other structural variables suggested in the literature. One approach has been to substitute for number the fractionalization of a system, which takes into account both the number of political parties and their sizes. Douglas Rae first introduced this concept and measure to political science.[15] Others have preferred to leave it out altogether. Joseph LaPalombara and Myron Weiner, for example, use competitiveness and ideological distance to form their fourfold typology: hegemony vs. turnover and ideology vs. pragmation.[16]

There seems to be no widespread agreement on which aspects of the party system are relevant to federal stability. Most analysts devise their own methods with different dimensions and groupings, so that the classification effort historically has not been integrative. Nevertheless, G. Bingham Powell has undertaken what is perhaps the most effective conceptualization of party systems based on their democratic performance.[17] Powell concludes that the most durable governments are single-party majority governments, "for they have control of the legislature for policy purposes, yet do not have to share their offices or seats with any other party."[18] Similarly, Leon Hurwitz hypothesized that there is a negative relationship between the degree of multipartyism and stability (i.e., those countries with a multiparty system tend to be less stable than countries with a two-party system).[19]

It is important to note that centralized federations do not necessarily have centralized political parties. The sample is too small to make such an assertion. Following Morton Grodzins, it is proposed instead that the two conditions seem to go together.[20]

The independent variables employed in this section of the chapter, therefore, are related to the number and structure of political parties in the federation. Gastil's operationalization is again adapted, using the following classification scheme. The sample will first be divided into

1. one-party dictatorships;
2. one-party dominant systems (such as India);
3. two-party systems; or
4. multiparty systems.

The party systems are then explored in more detail following the Gastil model. This category is divided into:

1. nonparty, nonmilitary governments (these are very primitive federations, such as the early Chilean federation);
2. nonparty, military federations (such as Argentina);
3. nationalist one-party governments;
4. one-party communist federations (U.S.S.R., Czechoslovakia);
5. one-party socialist governments;
6. dominant-party governments (these allow the forms of democracy but structure the political process so that the opposition groups do not have a realistic chance of achieving power);
7. centralized multiparty systems (the central government organizes lower levels of government for reasons of efficiency); or
8. decentralized multiparty systems (these are considered to be the most democratic federations).[21]

This section discusses one more centralization variable. Following Riker, a test is conducted to explore whether the party in control of the national government also controls the constituent governments. "If the nationally controlling party cannot win in state and provincial elections, then it can hardly hope to bring about a centralized party structure or a centralized constitution."[22]

If the degree of centralization is related to a national party's success on the constituent level, then how successful such parties are may reveal a good deal about the relationship between centralization and stability. This category is operationalized as a simple dichotomous independent variable. That is, if the national party is successful, a "1" is assigned, and if unsuccessful, a "0." To review:

H5a: That the higher the level of political party centralization, the more likely is federal stability

The Statistical Results

Only the N-Chotomous Probit test is considered in this section. There were a great many strong bivariate associations in this part of the analysis, but with one exception, these associations were not replicated in the multivariate analyses and, for the sake of brevity, are not included.

Centralized political parties were not significantly associated with the most important stability variable, "political secession." However, the independent variable concerning the ability of a national party to win elections on the constituent level was significantly and positively associated with the executive tenure dependent variable. That is, for both samples, the more effective the national party on the state level, the more likely it is to retain a legislative majority at least 75 percent of the time. The specific results follow.

Independent Variables: Political party simple (1–4), Political party complex (1–8), National party success on constituent levels

Dependent Variable: Executive tenure

Number = 44
Chi^2 = Significant at .05

Independent Variable	**MLE/Standard Error**	**Significance**
National party success	1.837	.03

Number = 32
Chi^2 = Significant at .02

Independent Variable	**MLE/Standard Error**	**Significance**
National party success	2.123	.02

The r^2 statistic for both of the samples includes a .23 for the forty-four cases and a .34 for the thirty-two cases. The percentage of cases predicted correctly is 61 percent for the total sample and 56 percent for the thirty-two cases. The Lambda B results are .26 for the forty-four cases and .10 for the thirty-two cases. Finally, the rank order correlations are .27 for the total sample and .50 for the thirty-two cases. The former is fairly low, whereas the latter is in the moderate range.

These results are not unexpected. Although the independent and dependent variables are not causal, they are obviously closely related. What is puzzling, however, is the unimportance of the other independent variables. It must be concluded that, at least with respect to this particular sample, the form of party structure within the political spectrum is not significantly related to federal stability.

POLITICAL CENTRALIZATION AND FEDERAL ASYMMETRY

The last category of centralization in this study investigates the relationship between asymmetric federations and political stability. It is argued that asymmetric federations are the opposite of federations with crosscutting cleavages. In the former, cleavages are restricted to specific regions or constituent units rather than existing across the federation as a whole. Because these cleavages are concentrated in specific areas and are not crosscutting, they are mutually reinforcing. Therefore, the fundamental premise of asymmetric federalism is that the distribution of powers and responsibilities is not uniform between central and individual governments.[23] Indeed, some of the subunits may be willing to give up more power to the central government than others. However, in the extreme case of asymmetry, the federation is unable to moderate its cleavages to any significant degree and thus dissolves. In such a case, the multiplication of groups with narrow, parochial interests induces conflicting demands that are difficult to accommodate.

It is also proposed that high degrees of cultural heterogeneity can lead to political separatism on the part of disadvantaged cultural minorities, which, in turn, often results in higher levels of political violence. On the other hand, if social, economic, and other cleavages cut across regional boundaries, that is, are "symmetric," then there is a greater chance for political stability. Indeed, Ramesh Dikshit acknowledges that crosscutting cleavages contribute to political centralization.[24]

One could not, of course, expect a federation to be perfectly symmetric. Ivo Duchacek makes this point quite explicitly in his discussion of "integral ethnoterritorial federalism."[25] Indeed, one rationale for the creation of many federal, as opposed to many unitary, states lies in the very existence of diversity and inequality among constituent units. However, it is proposed that the greater the degree of crosscutting cleavages in the federal sample, the more likely there is to be political stability.

In this section, the operative independent variables representing stability include:

1. The presence (2), partial presence (1), or absence (0) of language and regional correspondence. If a particular language is found in only one constituent unit, it is coded (2). Conversely, if one or more languages are spoken throughout the federation, it is coded (0).

2. Religion and region correspondence. This is coded in the same way as language and region concentration.

3. Race and region correspondence.

4. The structural variables' relationship to centralization. The number of constituent units is coded as follows: (0) 0 to five units, (1) six to eleven units, and (2) twelve to fifty units.

5. The presence of oversized units, which is coded (0) no, (1) yes. On a superficial level, oversized units and asymmetric constituent units are quite similar. Both imply provinces of unequal size and importance. However, the former does not imply the existence of homogeneous interests within each constituent unit.

To review:

H6a: That crosscutting cleavages are positively correlated with federal stability

H6b: That language-region, race-region, and religion-region correspondences are negatively correlated with federal stability

Cross-Tabulations

Dependent Variable: Absence of secession potential

Number = 44

Independent Variable		**Significance**
Language-region correspondence	Tau C	.3992
Religion-region correspondence	Tau C	.03
Race-region correspondence	Tau C	.4
Oversized units	Tau C	.02
Constituent units	Tau B	.02

Number = 32

Independent Variable		**Significance**
Language-region correspondence	Tau C	.11
Religion-region correspondence	Tau C	.0004
Race-region correspondence	Tau C	.12
Oversized units	Tau C	.004
Constituent units	Tau C	.01

The "constituent units" variable has a positive association with the absence of political secession. The other independent variables are negatively related to the absence of political secession.

Discriminant Analysis

The discriminant analysis revealed that for the total sample, only oversized units had a Wilks Lambda significance level of at least .01. For the postwar federations, religion-region correspondence had a Wilks Lambda significance level of .001. The Wilks Lambda significance level for oversized units was .006.

The independent variables for the total sample could discriminate to the .07 level, explain 94 percent of the variance between groups, and classify 43 percent of the federal cases. For the postwar federations, the independent variables could discriminate to at least the .07 level, explain 96 percent of the variance between groups, and predict or classify 66 percent of the federal cases.

Regression Analysis

For the total sample, only the number of constituent units was statistically significant (at a .001 level with a positive Beta of .35). There was a total r^2 of all the independent variables of .28. The postwar sample had three statistically significant associations. Language-region correspondence was negatively associated with a .05 level of significance. Religion-region correspondence was negatively associated with a .001 level of significance. The number of constituent units was positively associated with the absence of secession to a .001 level of significance. The independent variables all had an r^2 of .65.

N-Chotomous Probit Analysis

Number = 44

Chi^2 = Significant at .05

Independent Variable	MLE/Standard Error	Significance
Constituent units	1.94	.02

Number = 32

Chi^2 = **Significant at .001**

Independent Variable	MLE/Standard Error	Significance
Religion-region correspondence	-2.655	.004
Constituent units	2.63	.004

The total sample had a r^2 of .38 and the postwar sample an r^2 of .76. The model predicted 68 percent of cases for the total sample and 75 percent of the cases for the postwar sample. Lambda B scores were .18 for the former sample and .67 for the latter. Finally, the rank order scores were .37 for the total sample and .53 for the postwar sample. These are both in the moderate range of the Weisberg-Bowen scale.

The same independent variables were tested against the other stability dependent variables. Several of the bivariate tests revealed strong associations, but for the sake of brevity, just the significant Probit results are presented. The only significant relationship in the total sample was between religious-region correspondence and political assassination. In the postwar sample, a significant relationship existed between language-region and abuse of high office, and race-region and abuse of high office.

Long-Term Destabilizing Potential

Dependent Variable: Political assassination

Number = 44

Chi^2 = Significant at .02

Independent Variable	MLE/Standard Error	Significance
Religion-region correspondence	-2.34	.01

Long-Term Legitimacy

Dependent Variable: Abuse of high office

Number = 32

Chi^2 = Significant at .05

Independent Variable	MLE/Standard Error	Significance
Language-region correspondence	1.521	.06
Race-region correspondence	1.669	.05

The total sample had an r^2 of .23, could predict 61 percent of the cases accurately, had a Lambda D score of .29, and had a rank order correlation of .43. The postwar sample had an r^2 of .25, could predict 69 percent of the cases accurately, had a Lambda B score of .38, and had a rank order correlation of .49.

CONCLUSION

The important findings in this section of the chapter include the strong relationship between the number of constituent units and the absence of political secession. This supports the earlier findings in this chapter and in chapter 3. In addition, religion-region correspondence was revealed to be negatively associated with the dependent variable, thus confirming the thesis that asymmetry contributes to political instability. Furthermore, there was a negative relationship between religion-region correspondence and political assassination for the total sample. Positive relationships were distinguished between language-region and race-region correspondence and were demonstrated with abuse of high office for the postwar sample. With respect to the former, a review of the older federations reveals a dearth of reported assassinations. It is difficult to determine whether this particular dependent variable has gone unreported while the other dependent variables have been adequately reported or whether, in fact, there is a relationship between religion-region correspondence and political assassination. (One might argue that a near-homogeneous religious concentration contributes to political quietude, but it has been shown that religion-region correspondence is negatively associated with the absence of political secession.)

The other result is quite expected, for it is not difficult to believe that these two examples of asymmetry contribute to the abuse of high office. Where cleavages are concentrated in particular regions, it can be argued, the ruling elite will take any measures necessary to circumvent a threat to its power. Such measures might include the use of extensive patronage and corrupt practices to retain power. It is also worth noting that the postwar federations did not emerge as any more centralized than federations in the total sample of cases. This counterintuitive result is largely due to the small number of total cases and may be just an artifact. Altogether, the hypotheses have been only partially confirmed.

NOTES

1. Fernand Braudel, *The Mediterranean World in the Age of Philip II* (New York: Harper Torchbooks, 1975), 1:20–21.

2. Gorcen Therborn, *What Does the Ruling Class Do When It Rules?* (London: New Left Books, 1978), pp. 219–44.

3. Youssef Cohen, Brian Brown, and A. F. Organski, "The Paradoxical Nature of State-Making: The Violent Creation of Order," *American Political Science Review* 75, no. 4 (December 1981): 901–10.

4. William H. Riker and Jonathan Lemco, "The Relations between Structure and Stability in Federal Governments," in William Riker, ed., *The Development of American Federalism* (Norwell, Mass.: Kluwer, 1987).

5. Cohen, Brown, and Organski, op. cit., p. 909.

6. David Elton, F. C. Engelman, and Peter McCormick, *Alternatives: Towards the Development of an Effective Federal System for Canada* (Banff, Alberta: Canada West Foundation, 1978), pp. 10–13.

7. Ibid., pp. 10–13.

8. Valentine Herman, *Parliaments of the World* (London: Macmillan Press, 1976).

9. See the relevant country studies in the Appendix.

10. John R. Wood, "Secession: A Comparative Analytic Framework," *Canadian Journal of Political Science* 14, no. 1 (March 1981): 119.

11. Karl Deutsch, *Tides among Nations* (New York: Free Press, 1979), p. 194.

12. Maurice Duverger, *Political Parties*, trans. B. North and R. North (New York: Methuen and Co., 1967), p. 203; Giovanni Sartori, *Parties and Party Systems*, vol. 1, (Cambridge: Cambridge University Press, 1976), especially chapters 5, 6, and 9.

13. Sartori, op. cit.

14. J. Blondel, "Party Systems and Patterns of Government in Western Democracies," *Canadian Journal of Political Science* 1, no. 2 (1968): 180–203; K. Janda, "Retrieving Information for a Cooperative Study of Political Parties," in W. Crotty, ed., *Approaches to the Study of Party Organizations* (Boston: Allyn and Bacon, 1968).

15. Douglas Rae, *The Political Consequences of Electoral Laws* (New Haven: Yale University Press, 1967), and Douglas Rae, "A Note on the Fractionalization of Some European Party Systems," *Comparative Political Studies* 1, no. 3 (1968): 413–18.

16. J. LaPalombara and M. Weiner, eds., *Political Parties and Political Development* (Princeton: Princeton University Press, 1966), chapter 1.

17. G. Bingham Powell, Jr., *Political Performance in Contemporary Democracies* (Cambridge: Harvard University Press, 1982), chapter 7.

18. Ibid.

19. Leon Hurwitz, "Democratic Political Stability: Some Traditional Hypotheses Reexamined," *Comparative Political Studies* 4 (January 1972): 479.

20. Morton Grodzins, "American Political Parties and the American System," *Western Political Quarterly* 13 (1960): 974–88.

21. Raymond Gastil, *Freedom in the World: Political Rights and Civil Liberties— 1980* (New Brunswick: Transaction Books, 1980), pp. 40–45.

22. William H. Riker, "Federalism," in Fred Greenstein and Nelson Polsby, eds., *Governmental Institutions and Processes* (Reading: Addison-Wesley, 1975), 5:137.

23. Charles D. Tarlton, "Symmetry and Asymmetry As Elements of Federalism: A Theoretical Speculation," *Journal of Politics* 27 (November 1965): 861–74.

24. Ramesh Dutta Dikshit, *The Political Geography of Federalism* (New Delhi: Macmillan Co., 1975).

25. Ivo Duchacek, "Antagonistic Cooperation: Territorial and Ethnic Communities," *Publius* 7, no. 4 (Fall 1977): 15.

6

POLITICAL CLEAVAGE AND FEDERAL STABILITY

One of the most common assertions about political instability is that ethnic, language, racial, or religious cleavages are causes of unrest. In chapter 3, however, it was demonstrated that language differences are not significantly related to political secession, and in chapter 5 it was revealed that certain aspects of ethnic cleavage are quite salient when they are territorially based. In this chapter, the role of political cleavage is explored in more depth. Federal asymmetry or crosscutting cleavages, although still important with respect to one of the independent variables to be tested, are of less interest.

According to Walker Connor,[1] religious, ethnic, racial, linguistic, and other communal ties (Clifford Geertz refers to them as "primordial attachments")[2] represent one of the most important classes of the determinants of instability. Many quantitative, comparative studies provide substantial evidence that the greater the extent or intensity of cleavages among ethnic, religious, and other communal groups in a country, the greater the extent of turmoil (Switzerland is a notable exception to this). Studies that give particular attention to cleavages include W. L. Barrows, Ted Robert Gurr and R. Duvall, Hibbs, Morrison and Stevenson, Powell, and F. R. Von der Mehden.[3]

Throughout the world, federations comprise numerous linguistic groups and tribal units, many of which have histories of bitter antagonism toward one another. India, for example, has been unable to resist demands that its internal state boundaries be drawn along linguistic lines, a development that could place severe strains on its ultimate national unity. Among the federations that have failed, Pakistan was historically divided into two sections that differed in language and in level of economic development.

Burma has had at least five different communally based separatist movements struggling for autonomy or independence. The West Indies Federation, Central African Federation, the various Arab federations, and the Congo Federation are other examples of failed federations with enormous cultural diversity. This is not to claim that such cleavages are necessarily causally related to the dissolution of the federation. Indeed, it has already been demonstrated that certain other conditions are related to federal stability. Nevertheless, cultural and ethnic diversity might well play an important role.

It is logical to assume that the key elements of ethnicity—race, language, religion—may be strongly related to the conditions for instability, especially where cleavages among groups are clear-cut and cumulative. But ethnicity, as Paul Brass, Ronald Cohen, and Nelson Kasfir have all demonstrated, is also a highly fluid concept. "Ethnic" individuals may have multiple identities, and ethnic groups may expand or contract their social boundaries.[4] Ethnic identities can be artifacts, manipulated by ethnic leaders or government policy.

This last point is particularly important. Ideology by itself does not explain the rise of a dissident or secessionist movement. Much is to be gained by examining the political entrepreneurship of secessionist leaders who, in effect, turn secessionist predilections into actual movements. According to Alvin Rabushka and Kenneth Shepsle, "The successful political entrepreneur . . . is the person who manipulates natural social cleavages, who makes certain of those cleavages politically salient, who exploits, uses, and suppresses conflict."[5] Playing on cultural or economic fears and aspirations, secessionist entrepreneurs create and encourage discontent while fostering an image of an independent state where group interests will be safe. René Lévesque and Mujibur Rahman are two recent entrepreneurs of this kind.

Furthermore, Rabushka and Shepsle argue that when cleavages become too intense, they will be impossible to resolve in a democratic fashion. Indeed, they go so far as to argue that stable democracy in plural societies is inherently impossible, and they claim that scholars who think otherwise are led astray by their democratic commitments. "Many scholars display a bias for democratic political arrangements which has led, we think, to some wishful and as yet unsuccessful attempts to demonstrate that stable democracy can be maintained in the face of cultural diversity."[6]

One can suggest several examples of relatively stable, democratic, plural countries in the world today (Switzerland, the Netherlands, Belgium), countries that partially refute Rabushka and Shepsle's argument. These countries, however, employ what some have called consociational practices, rather than the zero-sum bargaining strategies that are of particular interest to Rabushka and Shepsle.

This chapter investigates the relationship between political cleavage and federal stability, using an operationalization adapted, in part, from a study conducted by Marie Haug and one by Rabushka and Shepsle.[7] The categories of cleavage follow:

1. The first measure of political cleavage is whether or not a federation can be considered plural. Some might argue that the plural-nonplural distinction is meaningless because most federations today are heterogeneous. There are a number of examples of homogeneous federations, however, including Austria. Therefore, this device is clearly meaningful. The "plural" measure is operationalized in the following manner: a "0" is assigned to a plural federation, and a "1" is assigned to a nonplural federation. The data for this section are derived from the Rae-Taylor index, Kurian's "homogeneity index," assorted world almanacs, and in the case of the nineteenth-century federations, individual country studies.[8]

2. The second measure of political cleavage is whether, in Rabushka and Shepsle's terms, a federation can be considered to be fragmented (1); to have a dominant minority (2); to have a dominant majority (3); or to have balanced competition (4).[9] Nondemocratic federations are inappropriate in the Rabushka and Shepsle model and are therefore excluded from this analysis. This classification thus includes:

    a. "Fragmented" societies, which are characterized by many small ethnic communities (not one of which is dominant) and the inability of these communities to form political coalitions. Such societies are extremely likely to become nondemocratic or to collapse altogether; examples include the Congo and the first Nigerian federation. This categorization is significantly different from the previous analysis of federations characterized by many small constituent units that owe their first allegiance to a strong central government. In the earlier discussion of the structural basis of federal stability, there is an assumption of centralized, crosscutting cleavages with small constituent units. In such federations a strong ethnic group is not concentrated in a large unit; thus, the costs of secession far outweigh the benefits. In the Rabushka and Shepsle categorization, on the other hand, ethnic communities are assumed to be centralized and, most important, territorially based.

b. The category "dominant minority," which refers to a minority group's domination of a whole society's political structure. Severe restrictions are placed on democratic action in such a federation (best represented by the failed Central African Federation of Rhodesia and Nyasaland).

c. The category "dominant majority," which refers to a situation in which one ethnic group overwhelms all others by force of sheer numbers. Few ethnic coalitions are able to form in such a configuration. This category is very similar to the "institutionalized dominance" discussed by Milton Esman.[10]

d. The category "balanced competition," which refers to a federation that comprises a small number of ethnic groups—not one of which is dominant. It is suspected that such countries are the most likely to be stable, democratic federations.

These categories are not investigated separately against the dependent variables. This is because the categories of "balanced competition" and "fragmentation" have the most cases and the strongest association with the dependent variables. Furthermore, it is suspected that if one investigates the categories in terms of degree, such that "balanced competition" is most democratic and "fragmentation" is least democratic, the results will be especially revealing. In this sense, the categories are a reflection of both pluralism and democracy.

3. The third measure of political cleavage focuses exclusively on the relationship between language and federal stability. For a variety of reasons, the competition between cultures usually takes place in the form of linguistic conflict. Language is perhaps the most salient characteristic of culture: in its capacity for variety, feeling, and imagination, it gives the protection of culture a frame of reference.

Ursula Hicks and others have argued, however, that there is no inherent reason why language differences in and of themselves should be divisive.[11] Indeed, Switzerland has four official languages, Canada has two, and India and Nigeria have hundreds. One can argue that trouble comes, however, when the government attempts to impose one language on the whole, as is the case in India, Pakistan, and Quebec in Canada, and when, as mentioned, political entrepreneurs encourage the politicization of language. Unfortunately, it is very difficult to find solid evidence, one way or another, for governmental intervention in the linguistic institutions of many of the federations: information is terribly sketchy for many of the older federations, and what evidence does exist may well be distorted. As a result, this analysis does not test a governmental intervention variable but instead operationalizes "language" in a form similar to that of Haug. This classification is adapted in the following manner:

a. A "2" is assigned to a federation in which at least 70 percent of the population speaks the same primary language and in which no substantial minorities speak any other single language. In such a federation, there is a totally dominant linguistic group. This resembles one aspect (language) of the Rabushka and Shepsle "dominant majority" variable.

b. A "1" is assigned to a federation in which at least 70 percent of the population speaks the same primary language but in which a substantial minority speaks another language.

c. A "0" is assigned to a federation that is linguistically heterogeneous—that is, no one group speaks a dominant language. This variable has elements of the Rabushka and Shepsle "balanced competition" category. The data are derived from the Kurian study, assorted world almanacs, and individual country studies.

4. The fourth measure of political cleavage concerns the role of racial differences and political instability. A "1" is assigned to a federation in which 85 percent or more of the state is of one racial group; a "0" is assigned to a federation in which less than 85 percent of the population shares a single racial background. It is suspected that this independent variable will not prove to be particularly significant.

5. The fifth measure of political cleavage concerns the impact of religious differences on federal stability and is divided into two parts. The first, part a, considers the role of religious cleavage as a whole for federal stability. The second, part b, concerns the role of the Catholic church with regard to federal disunity.

a. Along with the other aspects of ethnicity, religion may provide a noninstrumental basis for promoting or sustaining national consciousness. It may represent a convenient means of differentiation through labeling that has no real substantive foundation. In other respects, religious differences may reflect genuine incompatibilities among peoples. For example, a religious group whose existence is threatened by the missionary zeal of another or by some secular ideology may feel compelled to struggle for survival. Furthermore, the potential for conflict is greater when religions compete on the basis of exclusive claims to truth. When the religious division is also reflected in economic or status discrepancy in a society, the conflict is most likely to assume overtones of nationalism.

One may also offer an alternate explanation and suggest that homogeneous religious interests act as rivals to existing political elites for popular support. The struggle between political and religious institutions may result in great internal divisiveness. Racial and linguistic interests, on the other hand, cannot usually mobilize support with the same intensity, although the failed Central African Federation and the present Canadian federation may be exceptions.

For purposes of this study, religion is operationalized in the following manner. A "1" is assigned to a federation in which at least 85 percent of the population shares one religion. Conversely, a "0" is assigned to a federation in which less than 85 percent of the population shares the same religious faith.

b. The second part of this investigation of a religious cleavage–federal stability link concerns the role of the Catholic church. This is of particular importance because the Catholic church is, or was, predominant in the Latin American and Western European federations. Hurwitz has hypothesized that there is a negative relationship between political stability and the presence of Roman Catholicism as the dominant religious belief system in a country (i.e., Catholic countries will tend to be less stable).[12] Several other writers have also suggested that such a relationship might exist (Raymond Aron; A. Gide; S. M. Lipset).[13] These writers suggest that the Catholic church acts as a rival to existing constitutional structures and so encourages political divisiveness. Hurwitz concludes: "It is not Catholicism as such that causes instability. Instead, it acts as an added load on the system and forms the basis for social and political cleavages—cleavages which would not be present if the dominant religion were not Catholicism."[14]

Michael Novak makes an excellent point when he states that, with respect to many Latin American countries, the Catholic church's ignorance regarding economic matters has resulted in increased poverty and internal political dissension. For three centuries the church has accepted no responsibility for trade, commerce, and industry. "They seem to imagine that loans and aid should be tendered them independent of economic laws, and that international markets should operate without economic sanctions."[15] This ignorance of the economic world by such an important force in Latin American politics, it is argued, has resulted in a great deal of dissatisfaction with the ruling elites (and with the foreign and domestic powers that support these elites).

One can suggest the alternative argument, however, that the presence of a fairly homogeneous body such as the Catholic church serves to stabilize an otherwise conflict-ridden society. The presence of a common faith, common symbols, and common authority figures might help citizens in divisive societies to find a common ground, particularly in times of rapid modernization. This is clearly an independent variable worth testing against the stability dependent variables.

The sample was divided in the following fashion: "4" was assigned to federations that were at least 99 percent Catholic; "3" was assigned to federations whose population was between 90 and 98 percent Catholic; "2" was assigned to federations whose population was between 75 and 89 percent Catholic; "1" was assigned to federations whose population was between 50 and 74 percent Catholic; finally, "0" was assigned to federations whose population was less than 50 percent Catholic.

The data for this section on religious cleavage and federal stability were collected from Kurian's *Book of World Rankings*, assorted world almanacs, and studies of individual countries as of 1983.

POLITICAL CLEAVAGE AND FEDERAL STABILITY

For clarity, and because the statistical model is sufficiently robust, the independent variables are tested together against the individual dependent variables. Only the strongly associated variables are discussed. This is a particularly revealing series of independent variables because several of them are significantly associated in the multivariate analyses. The first tests include those that relate to the "absence of secession" dependent variable.

Cross-Tabulations

Number = 44

Independent Variable		Kendall Score	Significance
Religion	Tau C		Not Significant
Catholicism	Tau C		Not Significant
Language	Tau B		Not Significant
Race	Tau C		Not Significant
Balanced competition	Tau C		Not Significant
Plural	Tau C		Not Significant

Number = 32

Independent Variable		Kendall Score	Significance
Religion	Tau C	.35938	.03
Catholicism	Tau C	.50684	.0006
Language	Tau B	.26748	.0543
Race	Tau C		Not Significant
Balanced competition	Tau C		Not Significant
Plural	Tau C		Not Significant

Three of the ethnic variables for the postwar cases are positively associated with absence of secession.

Discriminant Analysis

Number = 44

Independent Variable	Stand. Can. Coef.	W/L Significance
Religion	Not Significant	
Catholicism	Not Significant	.64825
Language	Not Significant	.80947

Number = 32

Independent Variable	Stand. Can. Coef.	W/L Significance
Religion		Not Significant
Catholicism	7.868	.002
Language	3.413	.05

The other independent variables for both samples were not significant.

Canonical Discriminant Functions

	Number = 44	Number = 32
% of variance explained	62%	55%
Chi^2 =	Significant at .19 level	Significant at .01 level
% grouped accurately	45%	66%

Regression Analysis

An analysis of "plural" alone resulted in this relationship:

$$\text{Absence of secession potential} = \alpha + \beta x_1$$
$$\text{or } Y = 0.15 - 0.33 x_1$$
$$(0.43) \quad \text{Standard Error}$$

Where Y = Absence of secession potential on a scale from 2 (stable) to 0 (unstable):

$$x_1 = \text{plural on a scale from 0 (plural)}$$
$$\text{to 1 (nonplural)}$$
$$\beta = \text{the normalized coefficient of } x_1$$
$$\alpha = \text{a constant.}$$

Number = 44
$r^2 = .15$

Independent Variable	Beta	F-Score	Significance
Plural	-.36902	3.021	.05
Religion			Not Significant
Catholicism			Not Significant
Language			Not Significant
Race			Not Significant
Balanced competition			Not Significant

Number = 32
$r^2 = .41$

Independent Variable	Beta	F-Score	Significance
Plural			Not Significant
Religion			Not Significant
Catholicism	-.49323	8.118	.001
Language			Not Significant
Race			Not Significant
Balanced competition			Not Significant

There was very little multicollinearity for the sample of forty-four (between .2 and .49). However, language had a partial r^2 of .65 and explained only .007 percent of the variance for the thirty-two cases. It was removed from this part of the analysis.

N-Chotomous Probit Analysis

For the forty-four cases, the only independent variable significantly associated with secession was "plural." Plural was negatively associated with the absence of secession—that is, the more homogeneous the federation, the more likely it is to have the absence of secession or its potential. Plural had an MLE/Standard Error score of -1.743, a Chi^2 significance level of .04, and an r^2 of .20. Seventy percent of the cases were grouped accurately, the proportional reduction in error (or Lambda score) was .24, and the rank order correlation score was .44, which is moderate.

For the postwar federations, the only significantly associated independent variable was "Catholicism"—that is, the presence of political secession or its potential is enhanced in the most Catholic countries. Catholicism had a MLE/Standard Error score of 2.81, a Chi^2 significance level of .0025, and an r^2 of .48. In addition, 69 percent of the cases were grouped accurately, the proportional reduction in error was .30, and the rank order correlation, now to be referred to as the rank score, was .30, which is low to moderate.

This confirms the suspicion that, for the total sample, the more homogeneous or nonplural the federation, the more likely it is to remain unified. Note that "plural" is categorized differently from the other variables, with "plural" = 1 and "nonplural" = 0. One could argue that the most ethnically homogeneous federal states are the most likely to be near-unitary or highly centralized. It is also worth noting that the writers mentioned in this chapter are supported by the finding that the prevalence of Catholicism is positively related to political secession. The rest of the results refer to the significant dependent variables. For the sake of brevity, only the Probit results will be discussed.

Long-Term Destabilizing Potential

Dependent Variable: Riots

Number = 44

Independent Variable	MLE/Standard Error	Significance
Religion	-2.29	.01
Catholicism		Not Significant
Language		Not Significant
Race	-2.15	.02
Balanced competition		Not Significant
Plural	-2.09	.02

Number = 32

Independent Variable	MLE/Standard Error	Significance
Religion		Not Significant
Catholicism		Not Significant
Language	-2.01	.02
Race		Not Significant
Balanced competition		Not Significant
Plural	-2.148	.02

The forty-four cases had a Chi^2 significance level of .01, had an r^2 of .75, had 80 percent of the cases grouped accurately, had a proportional reduction in error or Lambda score of 0, and had a rank score of .20, which is considered low.

The thirty-two cases had a Chi^2 significance level of .10, had an r^2 of .95, had 84 percent of the cases grouped accurately, had a proportional reduction in error of .17, and had a rank score of .45, which is considered moderate.

Religion is negatively associated with riots for the whole sample. If one believes that religious homogeneity contributes to political instability, then riots, in this case, must be regarded as an element of long-term stability—that is, riots must be regarded here as contributing to federal stability in the same way that collective peaceful protests are believed to contribute to federal stability. As expected, plural was negatively associated with riots. Note again that plural is operationalized differently from the other variables, and this result reveals that homogeneity is positively associated with the absence of riots. Language and race are negatively associated with riots for the samples of thirty-two and forty-four cases, respectively. This is an expected result and further affirms the proposal that ethnic homogeneity is related to political quietude. Indeed, one could extend the assertion and say that ethnic homogeneity is most likely to be associated with political centralization.

Dependent Variable: Political assassinations

Number = 44

Independent Variable	MLE/Standard Error	Significance
Catholicism	3.022	.001

Number = 32

Independent Variable	MLE/Standard Error	Significance
Catholicism	2.053	.02

The other independent variables were not significantly associated with political assassinations.

For the forty-four cases, the Chi^2 was significant at .01, the r^2 was .35, the percentage of cases grouped accurately was 59 percent, the Lambda or the proportional reduction in error was .25, and the rank score was .51, which is moderate.

For the thirty-two cases, the Chi^2 was significant at .10, the r^2 was .24, the percent grouped accurately was 66 percent, the proportional reduction in error was .08, and the rank score was .38, which is moderate.

Catholicism was positively associated with political assassinations for both of the samples, as expected. This analysis of political assassinations indicates that Catholic leaders rival the existing political elites for popular support.

Dependent Variable: Coups d'état

Number = 44

Independent Variable	MLE/Standard Error	Significance
Religion	1.755	.04
Catholicism	1.233	Not Significant
Balanced competition	-2.560	.005

Number = 32

Independent Variable	MLE/Standard Error	Significance
Religion	2.639	.004
Catholicism	2.000	.02
Balanced competition	-2.709	.003

The remaining independent variables were not significantly associated with coups d'état.

For the forty-four cases, the Chi^2 was significant at .01, the r^2 was .37, the percent grouped accurately was 70 percent, the proportional reduction in error was .29, and the rank score was .50, which is moderate.

For the thirty-two cases, the Chi^2 was significant at .01, the r^2 was .63, the percent grouped accurately was 78 percent, the proportional reduction in error was .3, and the rank score was .78, which is very high.

For both samples, the higher the degree of balanced competition, the fewer coups d'état. This is an expected result following the assumptions presented. Religion and Catholicism are positively associated with coups d'état, which further supports the assertion that religious homogeneity is associated with political instability.

Long-Term Legitimacy

Dependent Variable: Electoral violence

Number = 44

Independent Variable	MLE/Standard Error	Significance
Catholicism	2.369	.009

Number = 32

Independent Variable	MLE/Standard Error	Significance
Catholicism	.902	Not Significant

The remaining independent variables were not significantly associated with electoral violence.

For the forty-four cases, the Chi^2 was significant at .02, the r^2 was .17, the percent grouped accurately was 59 percent, the proportional reduction in error was .17, and the rank score was .33, which is moderate.

It is clear, at least with regard to the total sample, that Catholic federations are the most likely to experience electoral violence.

Dependent Variable: Mutiny

Number = 44

Independent Variable	MLE/Standard Error	Significance
Religion	.84	Not Significant
Catholicism	1.95	.03
Balanced competition	-1.485	Not Significant

Number = 32

Independent Variable	MLE/Standard Error	Significance
Religion	1.80	.04
Catholicism	1.20	Not Significant
Balanced competition	-2.24	.01

The remaining independent variables were not significantly associated with mutiny.

For the forty-four cases, the Chi^2 was significant at .05, the r^2 was .27, the percent grouped accurately was 68 percent, the proportional reduction in error was .26, and the rank score was .43, which is moderate.

For the postwar cases, the Chi^2 was significant at .05, the r^2 was .39, the percent grouped accurately was 72 percent, the proportional reduction in error was .10, and the rank score was .36, which is moderate.

Balanced competition is negatively associated with mutiny. Since no one communal group is dominant, and all have a relatively equal voice in the federal political structure, it is not surprising that the agents of the government would be less dissatisfied and less likely to mutiny. As expected, religion and Catholicism are positively related to mutiny.

Dependent Variable: General strikes

Number = 44

Independent Variable	MLE/Standard Error	Significance
Catholicism	2.269	.01

Number = 32

Independent Variable	MLE/Standard Error	Significance
Catholicism	2.78	.003

The remaining independent variables were not significantly associated with general strikes.

For the forty-four cases, the Chi^2 was significant at .02, the r^2 was .17, the percent grouped accurately was 61 percent, the proportional reduction in error was .18, and the rank score was .18, which is quite low.

For the thirty-two cases, the Chi^2 was significant at .01, the r^2 was .35, the percent grouped accurately was 72 percent, the proportional reduction in error was .10, and the rank score was .47, which is moderate.

Catholicism is positively associated with general strikes. This lends further support to the arguments of the mentioned writers.

Short-Term Stability

Dependent Variable: Regular executive transfers of power

Number = 44

Independent Variable	MLE/Standard Error	Significance
Language	.99	Not Significant
Race	2.74	.003
Balanced competition	1.82	.03

Number = 32

Independent Variable	MLE/Standard Error	Significance
Language	1.68	.05
Race	1.49	.07
Balanced competition	2.26	.01

The remaining independent variables were not significantly associated with regular executive transfers of power.

For the forty-four cases, the Chi^2 was significant at .01, the r^2 was .45, the percent grouped accurately was 84 percent, the proportional reduction in error was .11, and the rank score was .60, which is moderately high.

For the thirty-two cases, the Chi^2 was significant at .05, the r^2 was .40, the percent of cases grouped accurately was 69 percent, the proportional reduction in error was 0.0, and the rank score was .18, which is quite low.

Balanced competition and regular executive transfers of power were positively associated. This result is an affirmation of the proposal that balanced competition is correlated with democracy and stability. It may also reflect the existence of consociational strategies used by the elites of multiethnic federations. Language and race are positively associated in a significant manner with regular executive transfers for the thirty-two cases. Race is significantly associated for the postwar sample. This finding confirms the suspicion that ethnic homogeneity is positively associated with the different measures of political stability.

Dependent Variable: Unsuccessful executive transfers of power

Number = 44

Independent Variable	MLE/Standard Error	Significance
Catholicism	1.198	Not Significant

Number = 32

Independent Variable	MLE/Standard Error	Significance
Catholicism	2.597	.005

The other independent variables were not significantly associated with unsuccessful executive transfers of power.

For the forty-four cases, the Chi^2 was significant at a .07 level, the r^2 was .71, the percent grouped accurately was 78 percent, the proportional reduction in error was .50, and the rank score was .51, which is moderate.

For the thirty-two cases, the Chi^2 was significant at a .01 level, the r^2 was .22, the percent grouped accurately was 59 percent, the proportional reduction in error was .05, and the rank score was .31, which is low-moderate.

The prevalence of Catholicism is clearly related to unsuccessful executive transfers of power. This result supports the contention that Catholicism acts as a rival to established political elites within the federal postwar states.

Dependent Variable: Constitutional crises

Number = 44

Independent Variable	MLE/Standard Error	Significance
Balanced competition	-2.757	.03

Number = 32

Independent Variable	MLE/Standard Error	Significance
Balanced competition	-1.826	.03

The other independent variables were not significantly associated with constitutional crises.

For the forty-four cases, the Chi^2 was significant at a .02 level, the r^2 was .71, the percent grouped accurately was 55 percent, the proportional reduction in error was .20, and the rank score was .35, which is moderate.

For the thirty-two cases, the Chi^2 was significant at a .10 level, the r^2 was .17, the percent grouped accurately was 44 percent, the proportional reduction in error was .05, and the rank score was .31, which is low-moderate.

Balanced competition is negatively associated with constitutional crises. This is consistent with the suggestion that democratic, plural groups of equal size are most likely to enjoy political stability.

Dependent Variable: Major cabinet changes

Number = 44

Independent Variable	MLE/Standard Error	Significance
Religion	1.661	.05
Catholicism	-1.039	Not Significant
Language	1.633	.05
Race	.315	Not Significant
Balanced competition	-1.786	.04
Plural	.225	Not Significant

Number = 32

Independent Variable	MLE/Standard Error	Significance
Religion	3.003	.001
Catholicism	-1.317	Not Significant
Language	-.222	Not Significant
Race	-.974	Not Significant
Balanced competition	-2.490	.006
Plural	-.762	Not Significant

For the forty-four cases, the Chi^2 was significant at a .20 level, the r^2 was .33, the percent grouped accurately was 61 percent, the proportional reduction in error was 0.0, and the rank score was .17, which is low.

For the thirty-two cases, the Chi^2 was significant at a .01 level, the r^2 was .71, the percent grouped accurately was 78 percent, the proportional reduction in error was .50, and the rank score was .51, which is moderate.

Balanced competition is negatively associated with major cabinet changes. On the one hand, it is not surprising that the most democratic countries are least likely to experience major disruptions of the chief executive office. On the other hand, the sample of federations with a cabinet of any kind was fairly low (thirty-six cases). One must therefore be suspicious of this particular result.

Conversely, language is positively (and significantly) associated with major cabinet changes for the total sample. It is not significant for the postwar federal sample, however. This is an odd result, but it could reflect the fact that many nineteenth-century federations were not democratic and so had no cabinet to change. The proposal gains credence when one notes that there is a negative association, as would be suspected, for the postwar sample.

Religion is also positively associated with major cabinet changes. As expected, religious homogeneity seems to contribute to major cabinet changes, as it does to other forms of political instability.

CONCLUSION

All together, the findings reveal that linguistic and racial homogeneity, where significant, is usually positively related to political stability. Religious homogeneity, by contrast, seems to interfere with existing political structures and political elites, often resulting in civil strife. These results are inconsistent with the original hypothesis, discussed in chapter 3, that religious, language, and racial cleavage would not be significantly related to stability. The distinction between the absence of secession potential and the other stability dependent variables, with respect to their associations with the independent variables, is therefore quite clear. Finally, and as previously hypothesized, balanced competition is positively associated with the greatest degree of federal stability.

NOTES

1. Walker Connor, "Nation-Building or Nation-Destroying?" *World Politics* 24 (1972): 339–55.

2. Clifford Geertz, "The Integrative Revolution: Primordial Sentiments and Civil Politics in the New States," in Clifford Geertz, ed., *Old Societies and New States: The Quest for Modernity in Asia and Africa* (New York: Free Press, 1963).

3. W. L. Barrows, "Ethnic Diversity and Political Instability in Black Africa," *Comparative Political Studies* 9 (1976): 139–70; Ted Robert Gurr and R. Duvall, "Introduction to a Formal Theory of Conflict within Social Systems," in L. A. Coser and O. N. Larsen, eds., *The Uses of Controversy in Sociology* (New York: Free Press, 1976); Douglas A. Hibbs, Jr., *Mass Political Violence: A Cross-National Causal Analysis* (New York: John Wiley and Sons, 1973); Donald Morrison and H. M. Stevenson, "Integration and Instability: Patterns of African Political Development," *American Political Science Review* 66 (1972): 902–27; G. Bingham Powell, Jr., *Political Performance in Contemporary Democracy* (Cambridge: Harvard University Press, 1982); Fred Von der Mehden, *Comparative Political Violence* (Englewood Cliffs: Prentice-Hall, 1973), p. 173.

4. Paul R. Brass, "Ethnicity and Nationality Formation," *Ethnicity* 3 (1976): 225–41; Ronald Cohen, "Ethnicity: Problem and Focus in Anthropology," *Annual Review of Anthropology* 7 (1978): 379–403; Nelson Kasfir, "Explaining Ethnic Political Participation," *World Politics* 32 (1979): 365–88.

5. Alvin Rabushka and Kenneth Shepsle, *Politics in Plural Societies: A Theory of Democratic Instability* (Columbus: Charles E. Merrill, 1972), p. 60.

6. Alvin Rabushka and Kenneth Shepsle, "Political Entrepreneurship and Patterns of Democratic Instability in Plural Societies," *Race* 12, no. 4 (April 1971): 462, 467, 470.

7. Marie Haug, "Social and Cultural Pluralism As a Concept in Social System Analysis," *American Journal of Sociology* 73, no. 3 (November 1967): 294–304; Rabushka and Shepsle, *Politics in Plural Societies*.

8. Douglas Rae and Michael Taylor, *An Analysis of Political Cleavages* (New Haven: Yale University Press, 1970); George Thomas Kurian, *The Book of World Rankings* (New York: Facts on File, 1979).

9. Rabushka and Shepsle, *Politics in Plural Societies*.

10. Milton J. Esman, "This Management of Communal Conflict," *Public Policy* 21 (Winter 1973): 49.

11. Ursula K. Hicks, *Federalism: Failure and Success* (New York: Oxford University Press, 1978), p. 12.

12. Leon Hurwitz, "Democratic Political Stability: Some Traditional Hypotheses Reexamined," *Comparative Political Studies* 4 (January 1972): 476–90.

13. Raymond Aron, *France: Steadfast and Changing* (Cambridge: Harvard University Press, 1960); A. Gide, *Journals*, vol. 4 (New York: Alfred A. Knopf, 1954); Seymour Martin Lipset, *Political Man* (Garden City: Doubleday and Co., 1960).

14. Hurwitz, op. cit., p. 479.

15. Michael Novak, "Why Latin America Is Poor," *Atlantic Monthly* 249 (March 1982): 69.

7

MODERNIZATION, SOCIAL MOBILIZATION, RELATIVE DEPRIVATION, AND FEDERAL STABILITY

This chapter investigates how modernization, social mobilization, and relative deprivation affect federal political stability. One of the predominant themes in the political instability literature concerns the social conditions that are associated with the structural and psychological strains within society. Modernization, as a process of large-scale social change, is commonly thought to introduce such strains by uprooting and dislocating long-standing social, cultural, economic, and political institutions.

Émile Durkheim is especially noted for his proposal that the disruption of established communal life leads to the growth of both industrial civilization and anomie (rootlessness and normlessness).[1] He asserted that anomie, discontent, and unrest among those who have been dislocated from their native communities and from their families, the development of rising but unsatisfied expectations, and unemployment and under-employment in the industrial sectors are all effects of sociodemographic change during the modernization process. Durkheim's discussion of dis-location and anomie is closely related to what were later known as the products of rapid social mobilization. His mention of rising but unsatisfied expectations is the core idea behind what Ted Robert Gurr later referred to as "relative deprivation." Finally, Durkheim contends that unemploy-ment and underemployment are conditions that promote relative depriva-tion and possibly social mobilization.

One popular assertion is that modernization enhances social disor-ganization by weakening the hold of long-established values and traditions and so produces a new set of expectations to which people have to adjust. Moreover, it is likely that conditions associated with modernization create

tension and competition among diverse cultural elites or between traditional and modern elites. Political changes associated with modernization
include the spread of mass political participation and the induction of
various social groups into more or less commonly accepted institutional
frameworks. More frequent interactions among different groups and
classes with potentially conflicting interests may well increase social and
political tensions and may also alienate various groups from the political
system. Such conflicts may even challenge the very existence of political
institutions. Thus, modernization brings about the disruption and disor-
ganization of old patterns and frequently is accompanied by anomie,
discontent, disorientation, rising expectations, and value conflicts—all of
which are ultimately expressed in an outburst of violence.

SOCIAL MOBILIZATION AND FEDERAL STABILITY

Social mobilization, in Karl Deutsch's terms, subsumes several interre-
lated processes of social change, processes that affect the quality of life as
well as residential, occupational, and social settings and attitudinal and
behavioral patterns.[2] The concept of *social mobilization* is defined as "the
process in which major clusters of old social, economic and psychological
commitments are eroded and broken and people become available for new
patterns of socialization and behaviors."[3] It incorporates two distinctive
stages of social change: (1) the stage of "uprooting or breaking away from
old settings, habits and commitment;" and (2) the induction of "mobilized
persons into some relatively stable new patterns of group membership,
organization and commitment."[4]

Deutsch believes that social mobilization brings about a change in the
quality of politics because rising aspirations and expectations engendered
by social mobilization require a greater scope of government services and
functions, especially those relating to the quality of life (such as living
conditions and social welfare). Moreover, social mobilization inevitably
weakens the hold of traditional values and organizations and accordingly
requires new patterns of organization that can provide a dependable social
setting for individuals uprooted or alienated from their traditional communities. However, rapid social mobilization is considered politically
destabilizing because it intensifies demands for change. Such demands
challenge the viability of the political system and generate critical communication problems between government and uprooted individuals.[5]

What are the specific consequences of social mobilization for the
political system? First, mobilized populations have different experiences
and expectations than unmobilized populations, as a result of their in-

creased contact with a variety of social groups and life-styles. New social problems are created at the same time that older institutions, such as the family, are losing their capacity to handle the problems. The concentration of populations in specific areas, such as cities or university campuses, makes them available either for mobilization into new organizations with new leaders or for mobilization into more anomic crowd behavior. All of these changes increase existing stresses on the political system.

In addition, social mobilization increases the load on governments because it diffuses political resources. Social mobilization involves the expansion of intellectual, organizational, and communications skills in a polity and the enjoyment of these skills by a larger number of people. The growth of an economy focused on secondary and tertiary occupations entails a corresponding growth in either voluntary or enforced leisure. As the needs described earlier are crystallized into unions, new groups enter the political system or become indispensable to its operation. In all of these cases, more people have the time and ability to engage in politics and to compel the attention of the nation's rulers. To relieve some of these pressures, Samuel Huntington argues, the governing elites must devise a stable development policy that strengthens or creates institutions—particularly political parties that are durable and flexible enough to absorb the newly mobilized groups.[6] Countries may be destroyed if they fail to respond adequately to the new demands. Indeed, even responsive nations might find that governing a mobilized society involves almost impossible feats of coordination.

How can federal states, in particular, respond to increased degrees of mobilization? Cynthia Enloe argues that when the mobilization needs of the federal states as a whole—as determined by the central elite—reach a point that federalist fragmentation becomes an unacceptable obstacle to the federal state's ends, one of two changes is likely to be initiated:

> The central elite may try to graft consociational democracy onto federalism in such a way that sub-unit elites are co-opted. They become more eager to serve central mobilization programs rather than to protect their own local constituencies against central penetration. Alternatively, the central elite will create a centrally controlled political party which can monopolize the most sought after resources. This will be easiest in those countries where federal sub-units are not coterminous with ethnic group concentrations.[7]

It was demonstrated in chapter 5 that where there is a political cleavage–territory correspondence, the problems of instability and secession are

greatly exacerbated. Empirical evidence concerning the relationship between social mobilization and political stability is quite contradictory.
Working with a sample of eighty-four nations, Ivo Fierabend, Rosalind
Fierabend, and Betty Nesvold conclude, on the basis of cross-tabulations,
that there is a positive linear relationship between a composite measure of
social change and political instability.[8] The Fierabends come to much the
same conclusion in their study for the period from 1948 to 1960.[9] In their
investigation of ten affluent nations, on the other hand, Peter Schneider
and Anne Schneider find a moderately positive relationship between social
mobilization and political violence, but they demonstrate that the relationship disappears when the effects of political institutionalization and
economic development are controlled.[10] Hibbs provides even less support
for the idea that political violence is a function of social change. He
regresses two dimensions of political violence (collective protest and
internal war) on social change (measured by change in urbanization rate)
and population size, but the contribution of change in urbanization proves
to be negligible.[11] By contrast, Lee Sigelman and Syng Nam Yough's
study of sixty-one less developed nations reveals a negative relationship
between a composite measure of social mobilization rate and three
dimensions of political violence (collective protest, internal war, and
power transfers). However, Sigelman and Yough find that the negative
impact of rapid social change is uniformly modest and that the strength
of these relationships varies across the three types of political violence.[12]

The first variables to be tested here relate to the level of modernization
in the federations. That is, the federal samples are divided into countries
that have or had traditional social, economic, and political structures in
their most recent period. These federations are coded "0." Federal states
that are in the process of modernizing are coded "1." Finally, federal
countries that are modern are coded "2." The data are based on levels of
GNP, urbanization, and military capacity.

The rationale for dividing the samples into forty-four and thirty-two
cases is clearest in this section. To compare a long-ended nineteenth-century federation with a modern-day superpower would be terribly misleading. Therefore, special attention is paid to the postwar sample. The
remaining independent variables that are hypothesized to be related to
social mobilization are clustered under the following headings:

1. Social mobilization: general
   The independent variables associated with this category include
   the federation's population size, its population growth rate, and
   its geographic size.

2. Social mobilization: political institutionalization
   The independent variables associated with this category include the age of the most recent national constitution, the effectiveness of the federation's legislature, and the age of the oldest of its existing or most recent political parties, if any.

3. Social mobilization: inequality
   The independent variables associated with this category include the presence of extreme regional economic inequalities, the presence of extreme class economic inequalities, and the percentage of income earned by the top 5 percent of the federation's population.

4. Social mobilization: particular aspects of modernization
   The independent variables associated with this category include the number of newspaper readers per population of one thousand, the number of radios owned per population of one thousand, the percentage of the population that is literate over the age of fifteen, the number of university students per population, the percentage of the population in cities of more than fifty thousand, and the percentage of the labor force in nonagricultural occupations.

SOCIAL MOBILIZATION: GENERAL

Many writers have discussed the relevance of population size and population growth rates to political stability. Gurr et al. found significant positive relationships between the growth of the total population and the dependent variables of man-days of participation and magnitude of protest.[13] Hibbs found rapid population growth (average annual percentage change in population, 1955–65) to be a positive and significant determinant of both collective protest and internal war. In Hibbs's final model specifications, however, population growth loses its explanatory power.[14] S. Welch and A. Booth studied the relationship between population density and two forms of political violence and reported that "this variable is strongly related to both incidence and intensity of political violence."[15]

On the other hand, if it is impossible, or even extremely difficult, for nations with rapidly growing populations to develop, then the rise in wealth and power of nations such as Brazil, South Korea, Taiwan, or the United States in previous generations would be inexplicable. After all, these countries and others experienced some of the postwar world's fastest rates of population growth: until the turn of the nineteenth century, America's rate of population growth was faster than Bangladesh's today. Population growth did not prevent the economic and political rise of the West in the eighteenth and nineteenth centuries (when its rate of natural increase was two or three times faster than the rest of the world's); nor has the "achievement" of zero population growth forestalled the political and economic eclipse of the once-mighty nation of Great Britain.

The connection between population growth and political stability is not clear-cut. If population growth means more mouths to feed, then it also means more hands to work. If it means more demands on the economy, then it also means growing markets. If it means straining the ability of the earth to produce enough natural resources, then it also opens up opportunities for resource-saving, and productivity-increasing, innovations. If it means greater challenges to the government, then it may encourage as well the sorts of flexible, creative responses that characterize the successful governing elites of the world.

In almost every discussion of the population explosion, one essential point is entirely forgotten. The populations of less-developed countries are growing rapidly not because they have suddenly started breeding like rabbits but because they have finally stopped dying like flies.[16] In sum, it is not clear from the evidence whether population growth helps, hurts, or has no effect on federal political stability. As such, this test will be of special interest.

The independent variable "population size" is coded "0" for federations with populations of less than five million, "1" for federations with populations between five and fifteen million, and "2" for federations with more than fifteen million. Population growth rate scores are derived by analyzing population growth and change during the course of the federation's existence.

A related independent variable concerns the relationship between the geographical size of the federations and political stability. It can be argued that small federations are more stable because fewer demands are placed on their political institutions. Robert Dahl and Edward Tufte argue that the larger the country, the greater the number of organizations and interest groups. This inhibits the efficiency of the policy-making process.[17] In addition, one might argue that the largest federations would provide the greatest obstacles to securing adequate transportation and communication facilities. On the other hand, many of the largest countries of the world are quite stable federations (the United States, Australia, and Brazil are obvious examples). It is clear that stable countries can correspond to both sides of the theoretical dialogue. As a result, though it is probable that this independent variable will be less revealing than the others, it is still worth investigating.

The federations are divided into the largest, next largest, and smallest in geographic size and are tested with the dependent variables. Data for these topics were derived from the *United Nations Demographic Yearbook*, the Taylor-Hudson study, Kurian's *Book of World Rankings*, and individual studies. See the Bibliography for these references.

Cross-Tabulations

Dependent Variable: Absence of secession potential

Number = 44

Independent Variable		Kendall Score	Significance
Modernization	Tau B	.62584	.00001
Population size	Tau B	.31770	.01
Population growth rate	Tau C		Not Significant
Largest geographic size	Tau C		Not Significant

Number = 32

Independent Variable		Kendall Score	Significance
Modernization	Tau B	.61487	.0001
Population size	Tau B	.30426	.03
Population growth rate	Tau C	-.24902	.06
Largest geographic size	Tau C		Not Significant

Discriminant Analysis

Number = 44

Independent Variable	W/L	F-Score	Significance
Modernization	.557	16.30	.00001
Population size	.857	3.42	.04
Population growth rate			Not Significant
Largest geographic size			Not Significant

Number = 32

Independent Variable	W/L	F-Score	Significance
Modernization	.587	10.19	.0004
Population size	.85328	2.493	.1
Population growth rate			Not Significant
Largest geographic size			Not Significant

Canonical Discriminant Functions

	Number = 44	Number = 32
% of variance explained	96%	96%
$Chi^2 =$	Significant at .001	Significant at .02
% grouped accurately	66%	66%

Regression Analysis

An analysis of "modernization" alone resulted in this relationship:

$$\text{Absence of secession potential} = \alpha + \beta x_1$$
$$\text{or } Y = 0.278 - 1.0x_1 + \Sigma$$
$$(0.21) \quad \text{Standard Error}$$

Where Y = Absence of secession potential on a scale from 2 (stable) to 0 (unstable):

x_1 = modernization on a scale from 0 (traditional) to 2 (modern)

β = the normalized coefficient of x_1

α = a constant.

Number = 44

$r^2 = .46$

Independent Variable	Beta	F-Score	Significance
Modernization	.70354	22.84	.001

Number = 32

$r^2 = .46$

Independent Variable	Beta	F-Score	Significance
Modernization	.61862	10.987	.001

The other independent variables were not significantly associated with the absence of secession.

Multicollinearity, as measured by the partial r^2s, was quite low for both samples (.01–.42 for the whole sample and .18–.42 for the postwar sample). As a separate test, the independent variables were tested without modernization, but not one was significant, and the total r^2 was low.

N-Chotomous Probit Analysis

The independent variables included in this test were "modernization," "population size," "population growth rate," and "largest geographic size." The dependent variable was the "absence of secession potential."

For the forty-four cases, the only independent variable significantly associated with secession was "modernization." Modernization was positively associated with the absence of secession—that is, the more modern the federation, the less likely it is to experience secession or its potential. Modernization has a MLE/Standard Error score of 3.423, a Chi^2 significance level of .0003, and an r^2 of .81. Eighty percent of the cases were grouped accurately, the proportional reduction in error or Lambda score was .47, and the rank order correlation score was .68, which is high.

For the postwar federations, the only significantly associated independent variable was again "modernization." Modernization had a MLE/Standard Error score of 2.808, a Chi^2 significance level of .001, and an r^2 of .64. In addition, 69 percent of the cases were grouped accurately, the proportional reduction in error was .3, and the rank score was .55, which is moderate.

Long-Term Destabilization

Dependent Variable: Political assassinations

Number = 44

Independent Variable	MLE/Standard Error	Significance
Population size		Not Significant

Number = 32

Independent Variable	MLE/Standard Error	Significance
Population size	1.627	.05

The other independent variables for both samples were not significant.

The thirty-two cases had a Chi^2 significance level of .20, had an r^2 of .26, had 66 percent of the cases grouped accurately, had a proportional reduction in error of .09, and had a rank score of .35, which is low-moderate.

Long-Term Legitimacy

Dependent Variable: Electoral violence

Number = 44

Independent Variable	MLE/Standard Error	Significance
Modernization	-1.809	.04

All other independent variables for both samples were not significant.

The forty-four cases had a Chi^2 significance level of .10, had an r^2 of .11, had 48 percent of the cases grouped accurately, had a proportional reduction in error of .04, and had a rank score of .11, which is very low.

Dependent Variable: Mutinies

Number = 44

Independent Variable	MLE/Standard Error	Significance
Modernization	-2.568	.005

All other independent variables for both samples were not significant.

The forty-four cases had a Chi^2 significance level of .01, had an r^{2}of .23, had 64 percent of the cases grouped accurately, had a proportional reduction in error of .16, and had a rank score of .31, which is low-moderate.

Dependent Variable: Plots

Number = 32

Independent Variable	MLE/Standard Error	Significance
Modernization	-2.408	.008
Population size	3.372	.0004

All other independent variables for both samples were not significant.

The thirty-two cases had a Chi^2 significance level of .001, had an r^2 of .53, had 66 percent of the cases grouped accurately, had a proportional reduction in error of .39, and had a rank score of .47, which is moderate.

Dependent Variable: Purges

Number = 32

Independent Variable	MLE/Standard Error	Significance
Population size	2.923	.002

All other independent variables for both samples were not significant.

The thirty-two cases had a Chi^2 significance level of .01, had an r^2 of .37, had 69 percent of the cases grouped accurately, had a proportional reduction in error of .29, and had a rank score of.48, which is moderate.

Short-Term Stability

Dependent Variable: Irregular executive transfers of power

Number = 44

Independent Variable	MLE/Standard Error	Significance
Modernization	-2.545	.005

All other independent variables for both samples were not significant.

The forty-four cases had a Chi^2 significance level of .01, had an r^2 of .27, had 61 percent of the cases grouped accurately, had a proportional reduction in error of .15, and had a rank score of .32, which is low-moderate.

Dependent Variable: Constitutional crises

Number = 32

Independent Variable	MLE/Standard Error	Significance
Population size	1.61	.05

All other independent variables for both samples were not significant.

The thirty-two cases had an insignificant Chi^2 level, had an r^2 of .10, had 38 percent of the cases grouped accurately, had a proportional reduction in error of .09, and had a rank score of .29, which is low-moderate.

Two independent variables proved to be significant factors of political stability: degree of "modernization" in the total federal sample, which was expected, and "population size" in the postwar federations, which was not anticipated. It is easy to believe that the most modern states are the most likely to be stable, whereas those that are traditional or modernizing experience the highest degree of divisiveness. It is something of a surprise, however, to discover that population size is negatively correlated with certain aspects of political stability. It might have been expected that rapid population growth rates would be negatively correlated with political stability, but instead, this analysis indicates that the most heavily populated federations are the most likely to experience certain forms of instability. It is worth noting, however, that population size is not related to political secession. Federal states with small populations may be more likely to be run efficiently. In this way, the Dahl-Tufte conclusions relating large geographic size to political instability may be relevant here.

SOCIAL MOBILIZATION: POLITICAL INSTITUTIONALIZATION

Many of the modernization writers consider political development to be a process of building institutions capable of handling the problems that accompany social change. Nonetheless, many diverse views have been presented concerning the meaning of this popular concept. Some scholars focus on increasing government efficiency and capability to meet changing demands (A.F.K. Organski, Lucien Pye, K. Von Vorys).[18] Others give more emphasis to structural differentiation and continuity (S.N. Eisenstadt, Fred Riggs, Michael Hudson).[19] Still others are more interested in functional differentiation (Talcott Parsons, Gabriel Almond and James Coleman, Gabriel Almond and G. Bingham Powell).[20]

The concept of political institutionalization has gained currency in the literature of comparative politics largely through Huntington's influential work on political development and decay.[21] According to Huntington, the strength of political organizations depends on the scope of their external support and on their level of institutionalization, which is defined as "the process by which organizations and procedures acquire value and stability."[22] Huntington stresses in particular the stability, differentiation, and effectiveness of political organizations—aspects of institutionalization that can be measured in terms of adaptability, complexity, coherence, and autonomy. According to Huntington, a nation's persistence, which can be measured by the simple chronological age of national political institutions, acts as a test of adaptability. Complexity refers to both structural differentiation of political organizations and a relatively stable pattern of interaction among subsystems. Coherence refers to a system's degree of legitimacy. Autonomy involves functional differentiation between political organizations on the one hand and social forces on the other.

Many scholars have commented on the difficulties involved in studying—and particularly in measuring—this challenging concept.[23] As a result, its operationalization has varied considerably from study to study. (For examples of these studies, see R. Duvall and M. Welfling, Hibbs, Hudson, and Schneider and Schneider.)[24]

In this study, the institutionalization of civilian political processes and structures is measured in terms of three indicators: the age of the oldest major national political parties and the age of the most recent national constitution, both of which are employed by Hibbs as the measures of institutional coherence, and a legislative effectiveness score assigned by Arthur Banks.[25] The latter score, according to Banks, summarizes the functional autonomy of legislatures. These conditions are tested against the stability dependent variables. In addition to the aforementioned sources, data for this section are taken from assorted world almanacs and studies of individual countries.

Cross-Tabulations

Independent Variables: Age of most recent constitution (Agecon), Legislative effectiveness (Effect), Age of the oldest of two parties (Agepar)

Dependent Variable: Absence of secession potential

All of the bivariate associations have a Kendall Tau C score.

Number = 44

Independent Variable	Kendall Score	Significance
Agecon	.39514	.0008
Effect	.33781	.004
Agepar	.25878	.02

Number = 32

Independent Variable	Kendall Score	Significance
Agecon	.65	.00001
Effect	.36	.01
Agepar	.45	.001

Discriminant Analysis

Number = 44

Independent Variable	W/L	F-Score	Significance
Agecon	.78	5.7	.006
Effect	.82	4.5	.02
Agepar			Not Significant

Number = 32

Independent Variable	W/L	F-Score	Significance
Agecon	.46	17.3	.00001
Effect	.82	3.3	.05
Agepar	.69	6.4	.005

Canonical Discriminant Functions

	Number = 44	Number = 32
% of variance explained	91%	96%
Chi^2 =	Significant at .07	Significant at .003
% grouped accurately	57%	78%

Regression Analysis

Number = 44

r^2 = .30

Independent Variable	Beta	F-Score	Significance
Agecon	.39528	4.06	.01

Number = 32

r^2 = .57

Independent Variable	Beta	F-Score	Significance
Agecon	.73988	35.059	.001

There were low levels of multicollinearity for the sample of forty-four (.09–.59). "Agepar" was highly correlated with "agecon" in the postwar sample and explained little of the variance. It was therefore deleted from this section of the analysis.

N-Chotomous Probit Analysis

For the forty-four cases, the only independent variable significantly associated with the absence of secession was "agecon." Agecon was positively associated with the absence of secession—that is, the older the constitution, the more likely there is to be no secession or its potential. Agecon had an MLE/Standard Error score of 2.1, a Chi^2 significance level of .01, and an r^2 of .44. Seventy percent of the cases were grouped accurately, the proportional reduction in error was .24, and the rank score was .48, which is moderate.

For the thirty-two cases, the only independent variable significantly associated with the absence of secession was "agecon." Agecon had an MLE/Standard Error score of 3.38, a Chi^2 significance level of .001, and an r^2 of .65. In addition, 78 percent of the cases were grouped accurately, the proportional reduction in error was .47, and the rank score was .74, which is high.

Long-Term Destabilizing Potential

Dependent Variable: Political assassinations

Number = 32

Independent Variable	MLE/Standard Error	Significance
Agecon	-1.685	.05

The remaining independent variables for both samples were not significant.

The thirty-two cases had a Chi^2 significance level of .02, had an r^2 of .43, had 69 percent of the cases grouped accurately, had a proportional reduction in error of .23, and had a rank score of .54, which is moderate.

Long-Term Legitimacy

Dependent Variable: Small-scale terrorism

Number = 44

Independent Variable	MLE/Standard Error	Significance
Agepar	-1.864	.03

The remaining independent variables for both samples were not significant.

The forty-four cases had a Chi^2 significance level of .10, had an r^2 of .14, had 61 percent of the cases grouped accurately, had a proportional reduction in error of .24, and had a rank score of .51, which is moderate.

Dependent Variable: Plots

Number = 44

Independent Variable	MLE/Standard Error	Significance
Effect	-1.541	.06

The remaining independent variables were not significant.

The forty-four cases had a Chi^2 significance level of .20, had an r^2 of .08, had 59 percent of the cases grouped accurately, had a proportional reduction in error of .10, and had a rank score of .24, which is moderately low.

Long-Term Limitation of Violence

Dependent Variable: Protests

Number = 32

Independent Variable	MLE/Standard Error	Significance
Agepar	2.21	.01

The thirty-two cases had a Chi^2 significance level of .10, had an r^2 of .41, had 75 percent of the cases grouped accurately, had a proportional reduction in error of .39, and had a rank score of .67, which is moderately high.

The age of the most recent constitution is positively correlated with the absence of secession and negatively associated with political assassinations, whereas the age of the oldest political party is positively correlated with collective protests and negatively associated with small-scale terrorism. These results support the Hibbs and Huntington thesis that the age of national political institutions is positively related to political institutionalization and, therefore, to stability. Interestingly, though, this analysis indicates that legislative effectiveness is not as important to political stability as the other independent variables because it is related only to the number of plots against the political regime.

SOCIAL MOBILIZATION: INEQUALITY

Extreme Regional Inequality

According to Bruce Russett, there is a positive correlation between inequality of land ownership and some measures of political violence.[26] J. Nagel's research confirms these results.[27] Regional inequality (as measured by inequality of land ownership and average income in the different regions or constituent units) may have a negative association with political stability for the federal samples and is well worth testing as a dichotomous variable, with "0" representing extreme regional inequality and "1" representing the absence of extreme inequality. Data for this section are derived from Kurian's study, Shail Jain's "Gini" index, and individual country studies. See the Bibliography for references.

Extreme Class and Income Inequality

Some argue that social inequality is a main source of political instability. Inequality helps to determine class consciousness and thereby encourages collective action. However, some writers have mentioned that political violence gradually lessens in postindustrial societies with the appearance of greater equality.

The impact of economic and technological progress on economic equality has been approached in several ways. Clark Kerr and his associates argue that economic growth creates a large, relatively homogeneous middle class by expanding the division of labor.[28] Gerhard Lenski contends that economic inequality is reduced through the production of a large surplus, which alleviates scarcity.[29] Lipset believes that the collective bargaining power of working-class organizations helps to obtain more material wealth for the working class.[30]

According to this perspective, greater equality reduces differences in status, outlook, and life-style and thereby undermines class consciousness. Where rigid class distinctions do not divide society, the interests of various groups are more harmonious. Thus, the lower class has a stake in preserving and reforming the political system and manifests higher levels of system support than in highly stratified systems. Members of the large middle class find themselves caught between a desire for upward mobility for themselves and their children and the relatively privileged status they enjoy. The upper class remains more moderate politically when it is clear that its continued prosperity is not fundamentally threatened. Thus, it is proposed that the growth of social affluence reduces political violence by integrating all classes into the existing framework of politics. Political competition develops within the framework of the political system rather than against it.

Powell, for his part, supports the thesis that income inequality is unrelated to political violence.[31] Furthermore, Erich Weede finds that income inequality does not seem to affect domestic violence if population and average income effects are controlled but if other possible determinants of violence are not controlled.[32] On an intuitive level, however, the evidence is not convincing that income inequality fails to be negatively correlated with the absence of political stability. As a result, these associations are well worth testing with the federal sample. Note that class inequality is coded in the same way as the regional inequality independent variable, and the data are derived from the same sources.

A related variable concerns the proportion of income received by the richest 5 percent of the population. Federations in which the wealthiest 5 percent hold at least 35 percent of the national income are coded "2." Federations in which the richest 5 percent hold 25 to 34 percent of the national income are coded "1." Federations in which the wealth held by the top 5 percent is less than 25 percent of the national income are coded "0." The predominant source for this data is Kurian's *Book of World Rankings*. World Bank studies and individual country studies are also used as references.

Cross-Tabulations

Independent Variables: Regional inequality, Class inequality, % of income held by top 5% of population (Top)

Dependent Variable: Absence of secession potential

All of the bivariate associations have a Kendall Tau C score.

Number = 44

Independent Variable	Kendall Score	Significance
Regional inequality		Not Significant
Class inequality	-.206	.05
Top		Not Significant

Number = 32

Independent Variable	Kendall Score	Significance
Regional inequality		Not Significant
Class inequality		Not Significant
Top		Not Significant

Discriminant Analysis

Not one of the independent variables for either sample was significantly associated with the absence of secession.

Regression Analysis

Not one of the independent variables for either sample was significantly associated with the absence of secession.

N-Chotomous Probit Analysis

Not one of the independent variables was significantly related to the absence of secession, and the rank scores were only low-moderate.

Long-Term Destabilizing Potential

Dependent Variable: Political assassinations

Number = 44

Independent Variable	MLE/Standard Error	Significance
Class inequality	1.791	.04

The forty-four cases had a Chi^2 significance level of .10, had an r^2 of .21, had 55 percent of the cases grouped accurately, had a proportional reduction in error of .07, and had a rank score of .49, which is moderate.

Short-Term Stability

Dependent Variable: Unsuccessful executive transfers

Number = 44

Independent Variable	MLE/Standard Error	Significance
Class inequality	1.689	.05

The forty-four cases had a Chi^2 significance level of .05, had an r^2 of .30, had 68 percent of the cases grouped accurately, had a proportional reduction in error of .39, and had a rank score of .45, which is moderate.

Class inequality is positively related to two of the dependent variables for the total sample of forty-four cases. Perhaps class inequality contributed to instability in the traditional and modernizing federations of the nineteenth and the early twentieth centuries, but became less significant after World War II.

SOCIAL MOBILIZATION: PARTICULAR ASPECTS OF MODERNIZATION

Increased Mass Media Exposure and Federal Stability

It has often been stated that modernization starts with new communication processes. As Huntington explains, "Urbanization, increases in literacy, education, and media exposure all give rise to enhanced aspirations and expectations which, if unsatisfied, galvanize individuals and groups into politics."[33] The empirical evidence for the effects of mass media exposure, however, is inconclusive. M. Parvin reports a positive relationship between the number of radios per capita and political violence.[34] C. L. Taylor, on the other hand, finds no relationships between level and rate of communications development and the dependent variables "turmoil," "internal war," and "political instability" (which is defined in terms of changes in government).[35] Gurr et al. report negative or negligible relationships between expansion of the mass media and measures of political violence.[36] Finally, Von der Mehden found little correlation in his sample between communications and the presence of violence.[37]

In this section, the number of newspaper readers and radios owned per population of one thousand is tested with the dependent variables. Particular attention is paid again to the postwar sample (because radios, for example, were made popularly available in the United States only in the 1930s).

Data for this section are taken from Arthur Banks's investigation and studies of individual countries. The categories of federal cases for this section and the two to follow are coded in terms of degree, with most newspaper readers, for example, being assigned the highest number. Because these cases cluster differently, they are divided into as few as three and as many as six categories.

The Role of Education for Political Stability

Gurr finds a positive relationship between the number of educated males and the magnitude of rebellion in his sample.[38] Morrison and Stevenson also report positive relationships between educational facilities and various indicators of political violence.[39] However, evidence presented by A. J. Sofranko and R. C. Bealer, as well as by Von der Mehden, does not support these results.[40] In this section, social mobilization–modernization, the proportion of university students, and the percentage of literate citizens in the federal samples (based on Banks's reported cases) and in individual country studies are tested. The evidence is quite contradictory and therefore of special interest.

Urbanization and Federal Political Stability

William Kornhauser contends that rapid urbanization and industrialization have politically destabilizing effects because they atomize large segments of the population. This atomization follows from the destruction of intermediate organizations and institutions that bind people to the existing social order—a process that produces the conditions of "mass politics," in which "large numbers of people engage in political activity outside of the procedures and rules instigated by a society to govern action" (see also Mancur Olson and S. N. Eisenstadt).[41] Unrest, anomie, and alienation also provide a favorable condition for extremist movements that challenge the existing social order.[42] In this section, the percentage of the population in cities of more than fifty thousand and the percentage of the labor force in nonagricultural occupations are tested with the dependent variables. It is suggested that these two independent variables help explain the association between urbanization and federal political stability. The data for this section are derived from the *United Nations Demographic Yearbook*, the United Nations Statistical Yearbook, and studies of individual countries.

Cross-Tabulations

Independent Variables: Newspaper readers per 1,000 (News), Radios owned per 1,000 (Radios), % literate over age 15 (Lit), University students (Univ), % of population in cities over 50 thousand (Cities), % in Nonagricultural occupations (Nonag)

Dependent Variable: Absence of secession potential

All of the bivariate associations have a Kendall Tau C score.

Number = 44

Independent Variable	Kendall Score	Significance
News	.333	.005
Radios	.11	.20
Lit	.39	.001
Univ	.395	.0009
Cities	.497	.00001
Nonag	.384	.0015

Number = 32

Independent Variable	Kendall Score	Significance
News	.63	.00001
Radios	.61	.0001
Lit	.52	.0005
Univ	.54	.0003
Cities	.50	.0008
Nonag	.53	.0005

Discriminant Analysis

Number = 44

Independent Variable	W/L	F-Score	Significance
News	.92	1.76	.18
Radios	.82	4.6	.02

Number = 32

Independent Variable	W/L	F-Score	Significance
News	.52	13.42	.0001
Radios	.53	12.9	.0001

The remaining variables for both samples were not significantly associated.

Canonical Discriminant Functions

	Number = 44	Number = 32
% of variance explained	61%	84%
Chi^2 =	Significant at .0008	Not Significant
% grouped accurately	57%	72%

Regression Analysis

There were no independent variables significantly associated with the absence of secession, but "news," "lit," and "radios" were highly correlated and will be considered one variable.

N-Chotomous Probit Analysis

There were no independent variables significantly associated with the absence of secession for either of the samples.

Long-Term Legitimacy

Dependent Variable: General strikes

Number = 44

Independent Variable	MLE/Standard Error	Significance
Cities	3.4	.0003

The remaining independent variables for both samples were not significant.

The forty-four cases had a Chi^2 significance level of .01, had an r^2 of .43, had 69 percent of the cases grouped accurately, had a proportional reduction in error of .23, and had a rank score of .58, which is moderate.

Surprisingly, relatively few of the independent variables were associated with federal stability. It is likely that as rapid urbanization took place in all of the federations, general strikes were a common outlet for political dissatisfaction. One might also have expected that nonagricultural workers would express similar degrees of dissatisfaction, but this was not a significant relationship.

RELATIVE DEPRIVATION AND FEDERAL POLITICAL STABILITY

Many theorists maintain that extensive social change increases discontent and frustration among "politically relevant strata" because, although it generates a new set of attitudes, expectations, and aspirations, there is likely to be a wide gap between the real social and political conditions and this "revolution of rising expectations."[43] This gap is the most important element of *relative deprivation*, a term coined by Gurr.

Gurr defines *relative deprivation* as an actor's perceptions of the discrepancy between his value expectations (the goods and conditions that he believes he is entitled to) and his value capabilities (the amount of goods and conditions that he thinks he is able to get and keep).[44] To Gurr, a negligible chance for social mobility is an important source of relative deprivation. This is the most important difference between social mobilization and relative deprivation. The growing opportunities for upward mobility may decrease antisystem frustrations, because "the impoverished masses in a highly stratified system may be less frustrated if there is a meaningful chance for them to improve their lot between the foreseeable future."[45] Gurr's relative deprivation model is remarkably similar to the first of Huntington's famous three equations.[46] That is, relative deprivation resembles Huntington's argument that when economic development lags behind social mobilization in modernizing states, social frustration is likely.

Throughout the theoretical literature, it has been persuasively argued by Davies, Fierabend and Fierabend, Gurr, and Huntington—and vigorously disputed by Charles Tilly—that relative deprivation is a major determinant of political protest and violence.[47] Unfortunately, positive and negative evidence roughly balance each other, at least at the cross-national level of analysis, and uncomfortable ambiguity prevails. (See especially D. Snyder who makes this point in greater detail.)[48] Given this discrepancy, the following independent variables that are elements of relative deprivation are tested with the stability dependent variables:

1. The presence of one or two constituent units prosperous enough to entice others to join the federation
2. The percentage of national income earned by the top 5 percent of the population
3. The presence or absence of rapid economic growth
4. The level of urbanization in the federation
5. The federation's literacy rate
6. The level of communication in the federation, as measured by the extent of mail service and the number of telephones
7. The form of political-economic system as discussed and categorized by Raymond Gastil[49]

Note that the urbanization, education-literacy, and inequality variables overlap with their social mobilization counterparts. These independent variables are related to both concepts (i.e., dissatisfied, literate, and urban citizens are also likely to feel relatively deprived), and their presence does not distort either model.

The Presence of Constituent Units Prosperous Enough to Entice Others to Join

Karl Deutsch has argued that at least some constituent units in a federation must be "sufficiently well off to attract the others into what will seem to them a rewarding relationship of collaboration."[50] Some expectation of economic growth, it is proposed, is necessary for new provinces to consent to join the union. First, federations that have or had one or more prosperous states that enticed others to join are identified. The sample is then tested against the dependent variables to see if, in fact, this independent variable is associated with federal stability. This variable is dichotomous, with "0" assigned to the absence of prosperous constituent units and "1" assigned to the presence of such units.

Rapid Economic Growth and Federal Stability

The theoretical literature often emphasizes the influence of rapid economic change on political stability. According to Neil Smelser and Pitirim Sorokin, rapid transformation of socioeconomic and cultural systems is a major source of internal disturbances and structural strains.[51] More specifically, Ralf Dahrendorf has argued that rapid economic change leads to political instability, and Barrington Moore and Myron Weiner have focused on the destabilizing effects of rapid urbanization.[52] Explicit in all these formations is the notion that discontinuities and dislocations accompanying extensive social change are the primary conditions leading to political violence.

More detailed explanations are extremely diverse. Olson is particularly notable for proposing that rapid economic change leads to "social dislocation," which in turn leads to alienation and a susceptibility to political radicalism among large portions of the population.[53] Huntington's mobilization-institutionalization hypothesis is a modified version of Olson's argument.[54] Tilly has also mentioned that rapid change is associated with political violence.[55]

In their study of fourteen nations that experienced successful revolutions during 1955–60, R. Tanter and M. Midlarsky reveal a negative relationship between economic growth and revolutions in Latin America but a positive relationship in the Middle East and Asia.[56] Douglas Bwy supports the Latin American result but argues that a different relationship among the variables holds for less-developed countries. He concludes that the levels of both organized and anomic violence vary inversely with the annual rate of growth of GNP per capita (1950–59).[57] Flanigan and Fogelman's longitudinal analysis for the period from 1800 to 1960 also reveals that domestic violence varies negatively with the rate of economic growth.[58] In addition, the Fierabends and B. A. Nesvold report a high negative association between the rate of economic development and instability.[59] Furthermore, H. R. Alker and B. M. Russett find in their study of thirty-three nations that levels of political unrest are strongly and negatively associated with rates of change in GNP per capita (from 1950 to 1960).[60] Hibbs finds different relations between rapid economic change and different types of political violence.[61] He is also unable to find any significant relationship between rapid economic growth and both collective protest and internal war. Finally, Gurr and C. Ruttenberg, in their study of 119 nations, find no relationship between civil violence and growth rate in per capita income (1953–62).[62]

In sum, the empirical research literature on the relationship between socioeconomic change and political violence reveals contradictory conclusions: some researchers report a positive linear relationship, others contend that the relationship is negative, and still others find no appreciable relationship in either direction. As such, the role of rapid economic change for federal political stability is of particular interest. Data are derived for this independent variable by averaging the GNP growth rates of the federations based on Banks's and Kurian's reported findings and studies of individual countries. It is worth noting that data were collected for national revenue, national expenditure, and national gross domestic product. Per capita figures for these variables were also derived. Unfortunately, levels of multicollinearity between these variables were so high (.8–.95), as one would expect, that these variables were deleted from the analysis.

Communications and Federal Stability

Communication networks are often identified as a relevant condition for political stability. It is often argued that rapid increases in the sources of information bring a demand for resources that the government often cannot yet provide. As rising expectations are not fulfilled, political violence becomes widespread. L. Pye argues that it was the pressure of communications development that brought the downfall of stable, traditional societies and that gave rise to unstable, transitional ones.[63] Lerner, Deutsch, the Fierabends, Gurr, Davies, and Taylor all address similar aspects of this problem.[64]

On the other hand, poor communications can be a divisive force in federations. In federations whose lines of communication are long and unreliable, it is extremely difficult to keep the constituent units in touch. It then becomes all too easy for misunderstandings and suspicions to arise. This problem was experienced in Pakistan—which was split in two with a slice of India in between—in East Malaysia, in Western Australia, and in the West Indies Federation and may be found in a Canada without Quebec.

To further examine this phenomenon, this study tests the role of communications (as operationalized by mail and telephones per capita). Telephones are relevant only to the postwar sample, of course, although their importance for the whole sample is investigated. The data from this section of the analysis are derived from Banks's study.

Gastil's Political-Economic Variables

The final relative deprivation independent variables to be examined are Raymond Gastil's classification of political-economic systems.[65] A "0" is assigned to socialist federations, which strive to place the nation's economy under government control. A "1" is assigned to capitalist-socialist federations, which provide social services on a large scale through governmental or other nonprofit institutions. Private control over property is sacrificed to egalitarian purposes. A "2" is assigned to capitalist-statist federations, which have large government productive enterprises either because of an elitist development philosophy or because of major dependence on a key resource. A "3" is assigned to capitalist federations, which rely on the operation of the free market and on private provision for industrial welfare. Several of the older federations are too primitive to fit easily into this classification system and are not included. Here again, the postwar sample is of particular interest.

Cross-Tabulations

Independent Variables: Prosperous constituent units (Wealth), % of income held by top 5% of population (Top), Rapid economic growth (Rapid), Urban, Education, Telephones, Mail, Gastil's political-economic categories (Gastil)

Dependent Variable: Absence of secession potential

All of the bivariate associations have a Kendall Tau C score.

Number = 44

Independent Variable	Kendall Score	Significance
Wealth		Not Significant
Top	-.274	.01
Rapid	-.623	.00001
Urban		Not Significant
Education	.315	.007
Telephones		Not Significant
Mail		Not Significant
Gastil		Not Significant

Number = 32

Independent Variable	Kendall Score	Significance
Wealth		Not Significant
Top		Not Significant
Rapid	-.58	.0002
Urban	.41	.005
Education	.52	.0006
Telephones	.46	.001
Mail		Not Significant
Gastil		Not Significant

Discriminant Analysis

Number = 44

Independent Variable	W/L	F-Score	Significance
Rapid	.56219	15.6	.00001

Number = 32

Independent Variable	W/L	F-Score	Significance
Rapid	.74	5.1	.01

The remaining independent variables were not significant.

Canonical Discriminant Functions

	Number = 44	Number = 32
% of variance explained	96%	89%
Chi^2 =	Significant at .0009	Significant at .15
% grouped accurately	64%	50%

Regression Analysis

Number = 44

r^2 = .44

Independent Variable	Beta	F-Score	Significance
Rapid	-.63	26.15	.001

Number = 32

r^2 = .30

Independent Variable	Beta	F-Score	Significance
Rapid	-.505	6.71	.001

The remaining independent variables for both samples were not significant.

There was little multicollinearity for both samples (.03–.32).

N-Chotomous Probit Analysis

For the forty-four cases, the only independent variable significantly associated with the absence of secession was "rapid." Rapid economic growth was negatively associated with the absence of secession: the faster the economic growth in the federal sample, the greater the secession potential. Rapid had an MLE/Standard Error score of -2.746, a Chi^2 significance level of .02, an r^2 of .57, 75 percent of the cases grouped accurately, a proportional reduction in error of .35, and a rank score of .56, which is moderate.

For the thirty-two cases, the only independent variable significantly associated with the absence of secession was again "rapid." Rapid had an MLE/Standard Error score of -2.489, a Chi^2 significance level of .10, an r^2 of .63, 66 percent of the variance explained, a proportional reduction in error of .23, and a rank score of .46, which is moderate.

The independent variable "rapid" proved to be significantly related, in a negative direction, with most of the dependent stability variables. To determine whether the other independent variables might have been overwhelmed by the importance of this variable, "rapid" was deleted from the list of independent variables, and new Probit tests were conducted. As is clear from a perusal of the results, no one independent variable assumes a great deal of importance. It is likely, however, that in the absence of the variable "rapid," some of the other independent variables may be important to stability.

Long-Term Destabilizing Potential

Dependent Variable: Political assassinations

Number = 44

Independent Variable	MLE/Standard Error	Significance
Education	-1.645	.05
Mail	-1.882	.03
Gastil	-1.987	.02

The forty-four cases had a Chi^2 significance level of .02, had an r^2 of .48, had 64 percent of the cases grouped accurately, had a proportional reduction in error of .06, and had a rank score of .34, which is low-moderate.

Dependent Variable: Revolutions

Number = 44

Independent Variable	MLE/Standard Error	Significance
Gastil	-1.570	.06

The forty-four cases had a Chi^2 significance level of .20, had an r^2 of .23, had 66 percent of the cases grouped accurately, had a proportional reduction in error of .13, and had a rank score of .29, which is low.

Dependent Variable: Riots

Number = 32

Independent Variable	MLE/Standard Error	Significance
Urban	2.452	.007

The thirty-two cases had a Chi^2 significance level of .02, had an r^2 of .25, had 53 percent of the cases grouped accurately, had a proportional reduction in error of 0, and had a rank score of .27, which is low.

Long-Term Legitimacy

Dependent Variable: Mutinies

Number = 44

Independent Variable	MLE/Standard Error	Significance
Education	-2.21	.01

The forty-four cases had a Chi^2 significance level of .10, had an r^2 of .23, had 61 percent of the cases grouped accurately, had a proportional reduction in error of .11, and had a rank score of .27, which is low.

Dependent Variable: Plots

Number = 44

Independent Variable	MLE/Standard Error	Significance
Education	-2.323	.01

The forty-four cases had a Chi^2 significance level of .01, had an r^2 of .71, had 66 percent of the cases grouped accurately, had a proportional reduction in error of .25, and had a rank score of .42, which is moderate.

Short-Term Stability

Dependent Variable: Executive tenure

Number = 44

Independent Variable	MLE/Standard Error	Significance
Mail	1.910	.03

Number = 32

Independent Variable	MLE/Standard Error	Significance
Mail	2.205	.02

The forty-four cases had a Chi^2 significance level of .20, had an r^2 of .10, had 46 percent of the cases grouped accurately, had a proportional reduction in error of .08, and had a rank score of .32, which is low-moderate.

The thirty-two cases had a Chi^2 significance level of .10, had an r^2 of .16, had 44 percent of the cases grouped accurately, had a proportional reduction in error of .10, and had a rank score of .33, which is low-moderate.

Dependent Variable: Irregular executive transfers

Number = 32

Independent Variable	MLE/Standard Error	Significance
Gastil	-2.002	.02

The thirty-two cases had a Chi^2 significance level of .05, had an r^2 of .16, had 69 percent of the cases grouped accurately, had a proportional reduction in error of 0, and had a rank score of .31, which is low-moderate.

CONCLUSION

Rapid economic development emerges as the most important element of relative deprivation as it relates to federal secession and other indicators of instability. This is consistent with Smelser, Sorokin, Dahrendorf, Olson, etc. It is also worth noting that the capitalist systems, as defined by Gastil, seem to coincide with certain aspects of political stability, as do the extent of mail delivery and the level of educational attainment. Finally, riots are related to urbanization, since they not only are likely to take place when housing conditions and other basic amenities may not be readily available but also require concentrations of population to mobilize in the first place.

NOTES

1. Emile Durkheim, *The Division of Labor in Society*, trans. George Simpson (New York: Free Press, 1964).

2. Karl Deutsch, "Social Mobilization and Political Development," *American Political Science Review* 55 (September 1961): 493–514.

3. Ibid., p. 494.

4. Ibid.

5. See especially Ibid.; Samuel P. Huntington, *Political Order in Changing Societies* (New Haven: Yale University Press, 1968); K. Von Vorys, "Use and Misuse of Development Theory," in J. Charles, ed., *Contemporary Political Analysis* (New York: Free Press, 1967), pp. 350–66.

6. Huntington, *Political Order*.

7. Cynthia Enloe, "Internal Colonialism, Federalism, and Alternative State Development Strategies," *Publius* 7, no. 4 (Fall 1977): 155.

8. Ivo Fierabend, Rosalind Fierabend, and B. A. Nesvold, "Social Change and Political Violence: Cross-National Patterns," in H. D. Graham and Ted Robert Gurr, eds., *Violence in America* (New York: Signet, 1969) pp. 608–68.

9. Ivo Fierabend and Rosalind Fierabend, "Aggressive Behaviors within Polities, 1948–1962: A Cross-National Study," *Journal of Conflict Resolution* 10 (September 1966): 249–71.

10. Peter Schneider and Anne Schneider, "Social Mobilization, Political Institutions, and Political Violence: A Cross-National Analysis," *Comparative Political Studies* 4 (April 1971): 69–90.

11. Douglas A. Hibbs, Jr., *Mass Political Violence: A Cross-National Causal Analysis* (London: John Wiley and Sons, 1973).

12. Lee Sigelman and Syng Nam Yough, "Left-Right Polarization in National Party Systems: A Cross-National Analysis," *Comparative Political Studies* 11 (October 1978): 355–79.

13. Ted Robert Gurr, *World Patterns and Correlates of Conflict* (Beverly Hills: Sage, 1983).

14. Hibbs, op. cit.

15. S. Welch and A. Booth, "Crowding As a Factor in Political Aggression: Theoretical Aspects and an Analysis of Some Cross-National Data," *Social Science Information* 13 (1974): 155.

16. This argument is adapted from Eric Breindel and Nick Eberstadt, "Paradoxes of Population," *Commentary* 70, no. 2 (August 1980): 42.

17. Robert A. Dahl and Edward R. Tufte, *Size and Democracy* (Stanford: Stanford University Press, 1973), p. 40.

18. A.F.K. Organski, *The Stages of Political Development* (New York: Alfred A. Knopf, 1965); Lucien Pye, *Aspects of Political Development* (Boston: Little, Brown and Co., 1966); Von Vorys, op. cit.

19. S. N. Eisenstadt, *Modernization: Protest and Change* (Englewood Cliffs: Prentice-Hall, 1966); S. N. Eisenstadt, "Breakdowns of Modernization," *Economic Development and Cultural Change* 12 (July 1964): 345–67; S. N. Eisenstadt, "Initial Institutional Patterns of Political Modernization," *Civilization* 12 (1962): 461–72; Fred Riggs, "The Dialectics of Developmental Conflict," *Comparative Political Studies* 1 (July 1969): 197–226; Michael Hudson, *Conditions of Political Violence and Instability: A Prelimi-*

nary Test of Three Hypotheses, Sage Professional Papers in Comparative Politics, no. 01–005 (Beverly Hills: Sage, 1970).

20. Talcott Parsons, "A Sociological Approach to the Theory of Organizations," *Administrative Science Quarterly* 1 (July 1956): 225–39; Gabriel Almond and James Coleman, eds., *The Politics of the Developing Areas* (Princeton: Princeton University Press, 1960); Gabriel Almond and G. Bingham Powell, Jr., *Comparative Politics: A Developmental Approach* (Boston: Little, Brown and Co., 1966).

21. Samuel Huntington, "Political Development and Political Decay," *World Politics* 17 (April 1965): 386–430; Huntington, *Political Order.*

22. Huntington, *Political Order*, p. 12.

23. M. Kesselman, "Overinstitutionalization and Political Constraints," *Comparative Politics* 3 (October 1970): 21–44; G. Ben-Dor, "Institutionalization and Political Development: A Conceptual and Theoretical Analysis," *Comparative Studies in Society and History* 17 (July 1975): 309–25.

24. R. Duvall and M. Welfling, "Determinants of Political Institutionalization and Conflict in Black Africa: A Quasi-Experimental Analysis," *Comparative Political Studies* 5 (January 1973): 387–415; Hibbs, op. cit.; Hudson, op. cit.; Schneider and Schneider, op. cit.

25. Hibbs, op. cit.; Arthur S. Banks, *Cross-Polity Time-Series Data* (Cambridge: MIT Press, 1971).

26. Bruce Russett, "Inequality and Instability: The Relation of Land Tenure to Politics," *World Politics* 16 (April 1964): 442–54.

27. Jack Nagel, "Erratum," *World Politics* 28 (January 1976): 315.

28. Clark Kerr, John T. Dunlop, Frederick H. Harbison, and Charles A. Myers, *Industrialism and Industrial Man* (New York: Oxford University Press, 1964).

29. Gerhard Lenski, *Power and Privilege: A Theory of Social Stratification* (New York: McGraw-Hill Book Co., 1966).

30. Seymour Martin Lipset, *Political Man* (New York: Doubleday, 1960).

31 G. Bingham Powell, Jr., *Political Performance in Contemporary Democracies* (Cambridge: Harvard University Press, 1982), chapter 3, p. 34.

32. Erich Weede, "Income Inequality and Domestic Violence," *Journal of Conflict Resolution* 25, no. 4 (December 1981): 651.

33. Huntington, *Political Order*, p. 47.

34. M. Parvin, "Economic Determinants of Political Unrest: An Econometric Approach," *Journal of Conflict Resolution* 17 (1973): 271–96.

35. Charles L. Taylor, "Communications Development and Political Instability," *Comparative Political Studies* 1 (1969): 557–63.

36. Gurr, *World Patterns.*

37. Fred Von der Mehden, *Comparative Political Violence* (Englewood Cliffs: Prentice-Hall, 1973), p. 98.

38. Gurr, *World Patterns.*

39. Donald Morrison and H. M. Stevenson, "Measuring Social and Political Requirements for System Stability: Empirical Validation of an Index Using Latin American and African Data," *Comparative Political Studies* 7 (1974): 252–63.

40. A. J. Sofranko and R. C. Bealer, *Unbalanced Modernization and Domestic Instability: A Comparative Analysis*, Sage Professional Papers in Comparative Politics, no. 01–036 (Beverly Hills: Sage, 1972); Von der Mehden, op. cit., p. 98.

41. William Kornhauser, "Rebellion and Political Development," in Harry Eckstein, ed., *International War* (New York: Free Press, 1964), p. 24; Mancur Olson, "Rapid Growth As a Destabilizing Force," *Journal of Economic History* 23 (December 1963): 529–52; Eisenstadt, *Modernization.*

42. Olson, op. cit.; Myron Weiner, "Political Integration and Political Development," *Annals* 358 (March 1965): 52–64; Neil J. Smelser, *The Theory of Collective Behavior* (New York: Free Press, 1963).

43. Daniel Lerner, *The Passing of Traditional Society* (New York: Free Press, 1958); Deutsch, op. cit.; James C. Davies, "The J-Curve of Rising and Declining Satisfactions As Cause of Some Great Revolutions and Contained Rebellions," in H. D. Graham and Ted Robert Gurr, eds., *Violence in America* (New York: Signet, 1969); James C. Davies, "Toward a Theory of Revolution," *American Sociological Review* 27 (February 1962): 5–19; Durkheim, op. cit.

44. Ted Robert Gurr, *Why Men Rebel* (Princeton: Princeton University Press, 1970).

45. Ted Robert Gurr, "A Causal Model of Civil Strife: A Comparative Analysis Using New Indices," *American Political Science Review* 62 (December 1968): 1104–24.

46. Huntington, *Political Order*, p. 55.

47. Davies, "Toward a Theory of Revolution"; Ivo Fierabend and Rosalind Fierabend, "Aggressive Behaviors within Polities, 1948–1962: A Cross-National Study," *Journal of Conflict Resolution* 10 (September 1966): 249–71; Gurr, *Why Men Rebel*; Gurr, "A Causal Model of Civil Strife"; Huntington, *Political Order*; L. Tilly and R. Tilly, *The Rebellious Century* (Cambridge: Harvard University Press, 1975); Charles Tilly, *From Mobilization to Revolution* (Reading: Addison-Wesley, 1978).

48. D. Snyder, "Collective Violence: A Research Agenda and Some Strategic Considerations," *Journal of Conflict Resolution* 22 (1978): 499–534.

49. Raymond Gastil, *Freedom in the World: Political Rights and Civil Liberties— 1980* (New Brunswick: Transaction Books, 1980).

50. Karl Deutsch, *Nationalism and Its Alternatives* (New York: Alfred A. Knopf, 1969), p. 106.

51. Smelser, op. cit.; Pitirim Sorokin, *Social and Cultural Dynamics* (Boston: Horizon Books, 1957).

52. Ralf Dahrendorf, *Class and Class Conflict in Industrial Society* (Stanford: Stanford University Press, 1959); Barrington Moore, *The Social Origins of Dictatorship and Democracy* (Boston: Beacon Press, 1966); Weiner, op. cit.

53. Mancur Olson, "Rapid Growth As a Destabilizing Force," *Journal of Economic History* 23 (1963): 529–52.

54. Huntington, *Political Order*.

55. Charles L. Tilly, "Does Modernization Breed Revolution?" *Comparative Politics* 5 (1973): 425–47.

56. Raymond Tanter and M. Midlarsky, "A Theory of Revolution," *Journal of Conflict Resolution* 11 (1967): 264–80.

57. D. P. Bwy, "Political Instability in Latin America: The Cross-Cultural Test of a Causal Model," *Latin American Research Review* 3 (1968): 17–66.

58. William H. Flanigan and Edwin Fogelman, "Patterns of Political Violence in Comparative Historical Perspective," *Comparative Politics* 3 (1970): 1–20.

59. Fierabend, Fierabend, and Nesvold, op. cit.

60. H. R. Alker and B. M. Russett, "The Analysis of Trends and Patterns," in Bruce Russett et al., eds., *World Handbook of Political and Social Indicators* (New Haven: Yale University Press, 1964).

61. Hibbs, op. cit.

62. Ted Robert Gurr, with C. Ruttenberg, *The Conditions of Civil Violence: First Test of a Causal Model*, Research Monograph no. 28 (Princeton: Center of International Studies, 1967).

63. Pye, op. cit.

64. Lerner, op. cit.; Karl Deutsch, *Nationalism and Social Communication: An Inquiry into the Foundations of Nationality*, 2d ed. (Cambridge: M.I.T. Press, 1966); Fierabend and Fierabend, op. cit.; Gurr, *Why Men Rebel*; Davies, "The J-Curve"; Taylor, op. cit.

65. Gastil, op. cit.

8

THE FEDERAL THEORISTS AND
THEIR CONDITIONS FOR
POLITICAL STABILITY

In this chapter, several of the conditions associated with the stability dependent variables as suggested by the federalism theorists in chapter 1 are tested. In addition, two of the more ambiguous conditions—the presence of external threat and the existence of some prior association between constituent units—are discussed in some depth. For many years, the presence or absence of some or all of these conditions has been assumed to be related to federal stability, but no rigorous statistical test has ever been conducted to determine if in fact there is empirical support for these assumptions. The conditions, and the theorists associated with these conditions, follow.

Conditions associated with the origins of federations:

1. The presence of a territorial or spatial division of power (Elazer, Lijphart)
2. The presence of a written, flexible constitution (Watts, Elazer)
3. The presence of a bicameral form of government (Watts, Lijphart)
4. The presence of an external threat or the hope of military expansion (Riker, Wheare, Maddox, Dikshit)
5. The existence of a popular hope for an improved economic position by federating (Wheare, Deutsch)
6. The experience of a previous political association (Wheare, Watts)
7. The existence of similar political and social institutions before and after federation (Wheare)
8. Geographical neighborhood among constituent units (Wheare, Maddox)

9. The presence of flexible elites during the federating process (Deutsch, Lijphart)

10. The existence of evidence of administrative efficiency before federation (Watts)

11. The presence of a general community of outlook (Watts)

12. The existence of role models (Watts)

Conditions associated with the maintenance of federations:

1. The existence of a continued external threat (Wheare, Maddox, Riker, Dikshit)

2. The existence of a hope for continued economic advantage with federation (Deutsch, Wheare, Dikshit)

3. The presence of two-party or multiparty systems (Riker, Dikshit)

4. The presence of political freedom in the federation (Lipset)

5. The presence of crosscutting cleavages (Watts, Lipset, Dikshit)

6. The presence of easy communication across political spheres (Deutsch)

7. The presence of easy transportation across constituent units (Deutsch)

8. The presence of flexible elites (Deutsch, Lijphart)

9. The presence of major constitutional change (Wheare, Dikshit)

Although it is difficult to derive objective data for some of these independent variables, objectively collected data do exist for the majority of them. These include nos. 1, 2, 3, 4, 6, 7, 8, and 12 in the "origin" section and nos. 1, 3, 4, 6, 7, and 9 in the "maintenance" section. The other variables were less objectively analyzed, and data were derived from individual country studies in a largely subjective fashion.

The federal cases are coded "1" where the relevant condition is present and "0" where that condition is absent. Before the actual testing, however, it is worth discussing two of the least straightforward of these conditions—the presence of external threat and the existence of a previous political association—in greater depth.

EXTERNAL THREAT AND FEDERAL STABILITY

Several scholars have presented evidence to show that political violence is closely linked to foreign conflict (see Georg Simmel, Lewis Coser, and James

Rosenau).[1] Explicit in this view is the assumption that group consciousness and the identification of a common enemy often bind the members of a group together into a cohesive whole. Thus, conflict with other nations strengthens internal cohesion and national unity while reducing internal stress. It is also possible that if conflict with other nations can accelerate internal cohesion, a nation experiencing internal stress could engage in foreign conflict in hopes of temporarily alleviating its internal problems. This is not a new proposition by any means. As far back as Jean Bodin in 1576, political theorists have suggested that the best way to preserve a state is to "find an enemy against whom (citizens) can make common cause."[2]

An alternative hypothesis, however, is that if a society lacks basic solidarity, foreign conflicts and threats from other nations may lead to breakdown rather than cohesion. In a divided society, external threat may encourage internal divisiveness or confusion. Rummel, by contrast, argues that foreign conflict behavior is completely unrelated to domestic conflict behavior.[3]

A related problem, particular to federations, is that if external threat is indeed related to internal cohesion, it must not be so strong as to lead to a general desire for unitary government. This is, of course, if one values federations for their own sake. A number of federations have turned into unitary states in the face of external threat (Indonesia, Colombia, and Chile are examples). All together, the effects of external threat for federal stability are most unclear in the literature and are well worth testing.

THE EXISTENCE OF SOME POLITICAL
ASSOCIATION BEFORE THE FEDERATING PROCESS

K. C. Wheare argues that one of the basic requirements of federalism is that the federating units should have had a previous existence both as distinct colonies or states and as constituent governments that were in harmony with local group solidarities.[4] Higley et al. show that in all cases in which what they call "consensual unified elites" govern from the attainment of independence, the previous dependent regime had active representative institutions affording experience to indigenous elites in limited representative government.[5] Where such institutions are lacking, as they were in the colonies preceding the early Latin American federations, there is little chance of a native consensual elite forming and preserving itself politically in the initial years of independence. The result, based on the available evidence, is that a praetorian or military regime installs a series of military-unitary governments. Finally, Riker notes that some previous association "is a perfect correlate with at least the contemporary federations."[6] He does stress, however, that he knows no theoretical reason why this should be the case and that, therefore, previous association cannot be regarded as a necessary condition for successful federations.

Clearly, it is worth testing to see how many of the federations have had some previous association before union and how stable they have been in the ensuing years. If most of the successful federations have had a previous political association, one obviously cannot argue that the two are causally related. One can suggest, however, that the two variables coincide to a statistically significant degree.

Note that the existing objective data are derived from the Banks, Taylor-Hudson, and Kurian studies. The remaining data are collected from individual country studies.

The Statistical Results

For the sake of brevity, only the N-Chotomous Probit results in this chapter were chosen, although a sample regression equation is included here. An analysis of "bicameral government" alone resulted in this relationship:

$$\text{Absence of secession potential} = \alpha + \beta x_1$$
$$\text{or } Y = 0.340 - 0.34x_1$$
$$(0.348) \quad \text{Standard Error}$$

Where Y = Absence of secession potential on a scale from 2 (stable) to 0 (unstable):

x_1 = bicameral government on a scale from 0 (not bicameral) to 1 (bicameral)

β = the normalized coefficient of x_1

α = a constant.

In all the tests, the levels of multicollinearity are low.

THE ORIGINS OF FEDERATIONS

N-Chotomous Probit Analysis

The significant associations with respect to the origins of federal countries include the following:

Dependent Variable: Absence of secession potential

Number = 44

Independent Variable	MLE/Standard Error	Significance
External threat	2.186	.01
General community of outlook	2.508	.006

Number = 32

Independent Variable	**MLE/Standard Error**	**Significance**
General community of outlook	1.952	.03

The remaining independent variables were not significantly associated with the absence of secession.

For the forty-four cases the Chi^2 significance level was .01, the r^2 was .46, the percent of cases grouped accurately was 66 percent, the proportional reduction in error was .12, and the rank score was .30, which is low-moderate.

For the thirty-two cases the Chi^2 significance level was .01, the r^2 was .43, the percent of cases grouped accurately was 72 percent, the proportional reduction in error was .47, and the rank score was .60, which is moderate.

The two variables significantly related to the absence of secession were the presence of external threat and the existence of a general community of outlook. It is suspected that external threat may act to inhibit any internal secession potential in the whole sample; it was, in fact, notably absent in the older, since-failed federations. It is proposed that the absence of external threat contributed to the absence of a sense of unity or common purpose in these states, with the ultimate result being their dissolution. It is not surprising that the presence of a general community of outlook should be related to federal stability, and so this result requires no further discussion. Several of the aforementioned theorists have thus been supported in this section of the analysis.

Long-Term Destabilizing Potential

Independent Variables:

The presence of a territorial or spatial division of power (Terr)

The presence of a written, flexible constitution (Const)

The presence of a bicameral form of government (Bicameral government)

The presence of an external threat or the hope of military expansion (External threat)

The existence of a popular hope for an improved economic position by federating (Hope)

The experience of a previous political association (Prior association)

The existence of similar political and social institutions before and after federation (Polsoc)

Geographical neighborhood among constituent units (Geog)

The presence of flexible elites during the federating process (Flexible elites)

The existence of evidence of administrative efficiency before federation (Admin)

The presence of a general community of outlook (General community of outlook)

The existence of role models (Models)

Dependent Variable: Revolutions

Number = 44

Independent Variable	MLE/Standard Error	Significance
Flexible elites	-1.782	.04

The remaining independent variables for both samples were not significantly associated with revolutions.

The forty-four cases had a Chi^2 significance level of .10, had an r^2 of .27, had 70 percent of the cases grouped accurately, had a proportional reduction in error of .19, and had a rank score of .36, which is low-moderate.

Judging from the statistical results, it seems that the presence of flexible elites during the federating process contributes to the successful inhibition of revolutions in the total sample. One might argue, following the assumptions of Deutsch and Lijphart, that flexible elites are better able to meet the demands of potential revolutionaries than are nonflexible elites.

Dependent Variable: Political assassinations

Number = 44

Independent Variable	MLE/Standard Error	Significance
Bicameral government	-2.075	.02
External threat	-2.943	.002

The remaining independent variables were not significantly associated with political assassinations.

The Chi^2 significance level was .01, the r^2 was .36, the percent grouped accurately was 55 percent, the proportional reduction in error was .17, and the rank score was .55, which is moderate.

Number = 32

Independent Variable	MLE/Standard Error	Significance
Bicameral government	-2.334	.01
External threat	-1.806	.04

The remaining independent variables were not significantly associated with political assassinations.

The Chi^2 significance level was .05, the r^2 was .32, the percent grouped accurately was 66 percent, the proportional reduction in error was .15, and the rank score was .58, which is moderate.

The existence of bicameral levels of government is significantly associated with political assassinations in a negative direction for both samples. This is, of course, as Watts and Lijphart would predict. Democratic federations, which are most likely to have bicameral legislatures, are apparently less prone to political assassinations and other elements of divisiveness during the federating process. The presence of external threat also serves to inhibit widespread dissatisfaction with the federal system, as has been suggested by Riker, Wheare, Maddox, and Dikshit.

Long-Term Legitimacy

Dependent Variable: Small-scale terrorism

Number = 44

Independent Variable	MLE/Standard Error	Significance
Flexible elites	-1.542	.06

The remaining independent variables were not significantly associated with small-scale terrorism.

The forty-four cases had a Chi^2 significance level of .20, had an r^2 of .12, had 44 percent of the cases grouped accurately, had a proportional reduction in error of .10, and had a rank score of .33, which is low-moderate.

Number = 32

Independent Variable	MLE/Standard Error	Significance
Prior association	1.797	.04
Flexible elites	-1.888	.03

The remaining independent variables were not significantly associated with small-scale terrorism.

The thirty-two cases had a Chi^2 significance level of .05, had an r^2 of .18, had 57 percent of the cases grouped accurately, had a proportional reduction in error of .17, and had a rank score of .39, which is moderate.

The presence of flexible elites relates to the inhibition of small-scale terrorism for both samples. It seems that flexible elites are better able to respond to the more dissatisfied elements of society and so can preempt the outbreak of terrorism. It is quite puzzling to find, however, that the prior association of the constituent units is significantly associated to small-scale terrorism in a positive direction. One would expect the opposite result, and it may be that the federating process does not eliminate the problems dating from the colonial era. This does not adequately explain the direction of the association, however, and one is inclined to agree with Riker that prior association is not a necessary condition for stability—nor is there a theoretical reason to believe it should be.

Short-Term Stability

Dependent Variable: Executive tenure

Number = 44

Independent Variable	MLE/Standard Error	Significance
External threat	2.097	.02

The remaining independent variables were not significantly associated with stability.

The forty-four cases had a Chi^2 significance level of .01, had an r^2 of .73, had 47 percent of the cases grouped accurately, had a proportional reduction in error of .18, and had a rank score of .46, which is moderate.

External threat emerges as positively related to executive tenure possibly because a military threat unites citizens around their political leaders for significant periods of time. This finding is consistent with the assumptions of Riker, Wheare, Maddox, and Dikshit.

THE MAINTENANCE OF FEDERATIONS

N-Chotomous Probit Analysis

Independent Variables:

The existence of a continued external threat (External threat)

The existence of a hope for continued economic advantage with federation (Cont. economic advan.)

The presence of two-party or multiparty systems (Multiparty systems)

The presence of political freedom in the federation (Political freedom)

The presence of crosscutting cleavages (Ccleav)

The presence of easy communication across political spheres (Easy communication)

The presence of easy transportation across constituent units (Easy transportation)

The presence of flexible elites (Flexible elites)

The presence of major constitutional change (Constitutional change)

Dependent Variable: Absence of secession potential

Number = 44

Independent Variable	MLE/Standard Error	Significance
Multiparty systems	2.529	.006

The remaining independent variables were not significantly associated with stability.

The Chi^2 significance level for the forty-four cases was .02, the r^2 was .41, the percent grouped accurately was 64 percent, the proportional reduction in error was .06, and the rank score was .30, which is low-moderate.

Number = 32

Independent Variable	MLE/Standard Error	Significance
Multiparty systems	1.975	.02

The remaining independent variables were not significantly associated with stability.

The Chi^2 significance level was .01, the r^2 was .82, the percent grouped accurately was 63 percent, the proportional reduction in error was .18, and the rank score was .41, which is moderate.

The presence of two-party or multiparty systems is positively associated with the absence of secession. It is proposed that when citizens find their demands met within the existing party system, they are less likely to organize secession movements. The Riker and Dikshit positions concerning the importance of parties for the stable federal political system are supported here.

Long-Term Destabilizing Potential

Dependent Variable: Political assassinations

Number = 44

Independent Variable	MLE/Standard Error	Significance
Multiparty systems	-1.469	.07
Constitutional change	2.816	.007

The remaining independent variables were not significant.

The Chi^2 significance level was .01, the r^2 was .56, the percent classified accurately was 66 percent, the proportional reduction in error was 0, and the rank score was .38, which is moderate.

Number = 32

Independent Variable	MLE/Standard Error	Significance
Constitutional change	2.122	.02

The remaining independent variables were not significant.

The Chi^2 significance level was .01, the r^2 was .59, the percent classified accurately was 72 percent, the proportional reduction in error was 0, and the rank score was .48, which is moderate.

Major constitutional changes are positively associated with political assassinations for both samples. A major constitutional change is significant because it either reflects or contributes to disarray within the federal political system. Furthermore, it implies a challenge to the legitimacy of the system by powerful social groups.

Two-party and multiparty systems are associated with the absence of political assassinations for the whole sample. It is suggested, as stated earlier, that when citizens' demands are met by the existing political parties, they are less likely to resort to violence.

Dependent Variable: Civil wars

Number = 44

Independent Variable	MLE/Standard Error	Significance
Cont. economic advan.	-2.892	.002
Political freedom	-2.628	.004
Constitutional change	2.383	.009

The remaining independent variables were not significantly associated with political stability.

The Chi^2 significance level was .001, the r^2 was .68, the percent predicted accurately was 75 percent, the proportional reduction in error was .31, and the rank score was .48, which is moderate.

Number = 32

Independent Variable	MLE/Standard Error	Significance
Cont. economic advan.	-1.985	.02
Political freedom	-1.797	.04
Constitutional change	1.970	.02

The remaining independent variables were not significantly associated with political stability.

The Chi^2 significance level was .01, the r^2 was .88, the percent predicted accurately was 69 percent, the proportional reduction in error was .23, and the rank score was .39, which is moderate.

When a nation experiences continued economic advantage and political freedom, there may be less likelihood for civil war. When economic and political times are good, there is less popular demand for violent change. The results indicate, however, that in the face of major constitutional change and a challenge to the legitimacy of the federal system, dissatisfied groups are more likely to seek violent redress. Several of the theorists of federalism are supported here.

Dependent Variable: Revolutions

Number = 44

Independent Variable	MLE/Standard Error	Significance
Easy communication	-2.39	.008

The remaining independent variables for both samples were not significantly associated with political stability.

The Chi^2 significance level for the forty-four cases was .10, the r^2 was .20, the percent grouped accurately was 45 percent, the proportional reduction in error was .34, and the rank score was .45, which is moderate.

The capabilities for easy communication across political spheres, as first suggested by Deutsch, inhibit the development of revolutions in the total federal sample. When citizens of outlying areas find their demands unmet by the central government, particularly due to failures of communication, revolution becomes a viable alternative. This was often the case in the oldest federations, whose constituent units were often remote and served by inadequate communication outlets.

Long-Term Legitimacy

Dependent Variable: Electoral violence

Number = 44

Independent Variable	MLE/Standard Error	Significance
Political freedom	-2.605	.005
Easy transportation	-2.443	.007
Constitutional change	1.486	.07

The remaining independent variables were not significantly associated with stability.

The Chi^2 significance level was .001, the r^2 was .61, the percent grouped accurately was 68 percent, the proportional reduction in error was .39, and the rank score was .51, which is moderate.

Number = 32

Independent Variable	MLE/Standard Error	Significance
Political freedom	-2.202	.01
Constitutional change	1.57	.06

The remaining independent variables were not significantly associated with stability.

The Chi² significance level was .01, the r² was .60, the percent classified accurately was 69 percent, the proportional reduction in error was .375, and the rank score was .49, which is moderate.

Political freedom is negatively associated with electoral violence in both samples, a finding that is not revealed in chapter 4. Thus it may be that when democratic electoral processes are institutionalized, violent electoral demonstrations are less likely. When authoritarian regimes hold elections that are generally recognized as illegitimate, however, it is possible that violence becomes more likely.

Major constitutional change is also related to electoral violence, and it is proposed again that this reflects a breakdown in a regime's legitimacy, allowing for dissatisfied actors to gain popular support. Finally, the results indicate that the presence of easy transportation across constituent units is negatively associated with electoral violence in the whole sample. Where easy transportation across constituent units existed in the older federations, violence may have been less widespread.

Dependent Variable: Abuse of high office

Number = 44

Independent Variable	MLE/Standard Error	Significance
Constitutional change	1.76	.04

The remaining independent variables were not significantly associated with federal stability.

The Chi² significance level was .10, the r² was .16, the percent classified accurately was 50 percent, the proportional reduction in error was .04, and the rank score was .18, which is low.

Number = 32

Independent Variable	MLE/Standard Error	Significance
Constitutional change	2.091	.02

The remaining independent variables were not significantly associated with federal stability.

The Chi² significance level was .02, the r² was .29, the percent classified accurately was 50 percent, the proportional reduction in error was .2, and the rank score was .51, which is moderate.

The presence of major constitutional change, and the concurrent breakdown in federal legitimacy, are related to the abuse of high office for both samples. It is likely that corrupt leaders are most likely to change constitutions as often as is required to suit their particular needs.

Dependent Variable: Small-scale terrorism

Number = 44

Independent Variable	MLE/Standard Error	Significance
Multiparty systems	-1.796	.04
Easy transportation	-2.509	.006

The remaining independent variables were not significantly associated with federal stability.

The Chi^2 significance level was .01, the r^2 was .44, the percent classified accurately was 73 percent, the proportional reduction in error was .37, and the rank score was .56, which is moderate.

Number = 32

Independent Variable	MLE/Standard Error	Significance
Political freedom	-1.646	.05
Constitutional change	2.24	.01

The remaining independent variables were not significantly associated with federal stability.

The Chi^2 significance level was .01, the r^2 was .49, the percent classified accurately was 72 percent, the proportional reduction in error was .1, and the rank score was .38, which is moderate.

Multiparty systems, effective transportation networks, and political freedom are all related to the restriction of terrorist groups in federations. It is suggested that these conditions are important in easing the frustrations of dissident groups within the established federations. The absence of legitimacy, as represented by major constitutional change, appears to be related to the accelerated growth of small terrorist groups. This is an expected result.

Dependent Variable: Mutiny

Number = 44

Independent Variable	MLE/Standard Error	Significance
Easy transportation	-2.231	.01
Constitutional change	2.099	.02

The remaining independent variables were not significantly associated with federal stability.

The Chi^2 significance level was .01, the r^2 was .32, the percent grouped accurately was 64 percent, the proportional reduction in error was .2, and the rank score was .39, which is moderate.

Number = 32

Independent Variable	MLE/Standard Error	Significance
Constitutional change	1.96	.03

The remaining independent variables were not significantly associated with federal stability.

The Chi^2 significance level was .05, the r^2 was .12, the percent predicted accurately was 57 percent, the proportional reduction in error was .05, and the rank score was .29, which is low.

Ease of transportation across constituent units appears to be strongly associated with the absence of divisiveness, which is represented in this section by the lack of mutinies in the total sample. A federation that has adequate modes of transportation is better able to encourage a sense of common purpose among citizens living in diverse regions of the country. This, in turn, inhibits the development of turmoil or mutiny. When the federation is considered less legitimate by its support groups (police, militia, etc.) due to major constitutional change, however, mutinies are more likely.

Dependent Variable: Plots

Number = 44

Independent Variable	MLE/Standard Error	Significance
Constitutional change	2.137	.02

The remaining independent variables were not significantly associated with political stability.

The Chi^2 significance level was .01, the r^2 was .89, the percent grouped accurately was 70 percent, the proportional reduction in error was .13, and the rank score was .44, which is moderate.

Number = 32

Independent Variable	MLE/Standard Error	Significance
Political freedom	-1.55	.06
Constitutional change	1.89	.03

The remaining independent variables were not significantly associated with political stability.

The Chi^2 significance level was .05, the r^2 was .27, the percent grouped accurately was 63 percent, the proportional reduction in error was .14, and the rank score was .34, which is low-moderate.

A major constitutional change, which is likely related to the absence of federal legitimacy, is positively associated with plots against the regime. It makes perfect sense that dissatisfied social groups would plot against what they regard to be illegitimate regimes. In addition, political freedom is negatively associated with plots for the postwar federal cases. This is not unusual, since social groups in a free society, it can be argued, have less reason to plot against the federal regime.

Short-Term Stability

Dependent Variable: Executive tenure

Number = 44

Independent Variable	MLE/Standard Error	Significance
Constitutional change	-1.65	.05

The remaining independent variables were not significantly associated with stability.

The Chi^2 significance level was .10, the r^2 was .90, the percent predicted accurately was 50 percent, the proportional reduction in error was .05, and the rank score was .26, which is low.

The presence of major constitutional change is negatively associated with executive tenure. If constitutional change implies an absence of federal legitimacy, it is reasonable to believe that illegitimate regimes are less likely to retain power for any length of time.

Dependent Variable: Regular executive transfers of power

Number = 44

Independent Variable	MLE/Standard Error	Significance
External threat	1.837	.03
Cont. economic advan.	2.102	.02
Political freedom	2.131	.02

The remaining independent variables were not significantly associated with federal stability.

The Chi^2 significance level was .01, the r^2 was .60, the percent classified accurately was 84 percent, the proportional reduction in error was .22, and the rank score was .55, which is moderate.

Number = 32

Independent Variable	MLE/Standard Error	Significance
External threat	1.839	.03

The remaining independent variables were not significantly associated with federal stability.

The Chi^2 significance level was .05, the r^2 was .92, the percent classified accurately was 88 percent, the proportional reduction in error was .33, and the rank score was .62, which is moderate.

Again, the presence of an external threat is found to be strongly associated with internal cohesion, in this case represented by regular executive transfers of power.

Dependent Variable: Irregular executive transfers of power

Number = 44

Independent Variable	MLE/Standard Error	Significance
Multiparty systems	-2.13	.02
Easy transportation	-2.871	.002
Constitutional change	2.502	.006

The remaining independent variables were not significantly associated with federal stability.

The Chi^2 significance level was .001, the r^2 was .59, the percent grouped accurately was 75 percent, the proportional reduction in error was .45, and the rank score was .68, which is moderately high.

Number = 32

Independent Variable	MLE/Standard Error	Significance
Political freedom	-1.576	.06
Constitutional change	2.618	.004

The remaining independent variables were not significantly associated with federal stability.

The Chi^2 significance level was .01, the r^2 was .57, the percent grouped accurately was 75 percent, the proportional reduction in error was .2, and the rank score was .53, which is moderate.

Major constitutional change is once more revealed to be a divisive condition with respect to federal stability. The remaining associations demonstrated in this section are of obvious importance to the maintenance of federal tranquillity, which is represented in this case by the absence of irregular executive transfers of power.

Dependent Variable: Major cabinet changes

Number = 44

Independent Variable	MLE/Standard Error	Significance
Multiparty systems	-3.11	.0009

The remaining independent variables were not significantly associated with federal stability.

The Chi^2 significance level was .01, the r^2 was .42, the percent predicted accurately was 66 percent, the proportional reduction in error was .41, and the rank score was .41, which is moderate.

Number = 32

Independent Variable	MLE/Standard Error	Significance
Multiparty systems	-2.977	.001

The remaining independent variables were not significantly associated with federal stability.

The Chi^2 significance level was .01, the r^2 was .48, the percent grouped accurately was 69 percent, the proportional reduction in error was .3, and the rank score was .57, which is moderate.

Democratic multiparty systems are strongly associated with the absence of major cabinet changes for both samples. This further demonstrates, as Riker and Dikshit would suggest, the importance of democratic, competitive party systems to internal federal cohesion.

There are no high rank scores in this chapter, which indicates that the federal theorists' conditions by themselves only partially explain federal instability. The structure, degree of centralization, level of modernization, etc. of the federation are also of great relevance. It seems obvious, however, that flexible, legitimate elites governing within a free, competitive party system in the face of an external threat are most likely to be found in stable federal countries.

CONCLUSION

Comparative federal research is in its infancy. A great many questions concerning the stability of federations will remain unanswered as long as there is a dearth of objective data. However, with the continued scholarly interest in the stability and prosperity of heterogeneous states, both federal and others, that has been expressed in recent years, a concerted effort will likely be made to derive information about a polity's political, economic, and social structure.

A whole series of dependent variables has been tested here. A number have proven to be significantly associated; the majority, as expected, have not. Furthermore, causality cannot, of course, be presumed. However, if one was to establish a federation that would stand the greatest chance of remaining stable, based on the results derived from the history of previous federations, one might seek the attributes listed below.

Such a federation would be composed of many small constituent units owing their first allegiance to a strong central government. It would have an effective two- or multiparty system that would allow for a great deal of political freedom. Furthermore, the federation would be created in the face of a strong military or economic threat, and this threat would not dissipate until a strong sense of national legitimacy developed. This sense of legitimacy would be threatened, however, if there were frequent major constitutional changes.

To further minimize the potential for federal instability, the political elites of such an ideal federation would avoid concentrating national minorities in a small number of constituent units, where the minorities would be in the majority. In addition, the evidence suggests that if one religious group was especially dominant in the federation, there would likely be a struggle between religious and secular interests for the primary allegiance of the population. Historically, this competition has often been associated with federal instability.

Finally, the political elites of such a model federation would govern a modern nation. But, in developed states, leaders would be well advised to discourage rapid economic modernization: the evidence suggests that where rapid economic change exceeds the adaptive capacity of the nation's political institutions, as has often historically been the case, there has been a great deal of internal divisiveness.

The various political elites of such an ideal federation would weigh the costs of federation (less constituent unit independence) against the benefits (increased military protection and economic security) and decide that the benefits outweigh the costs.

One of those federations experiencing the highest level of internal strife at this time is Canada. It might be an instructive exercise to see how many of these "ideal" conditions for federations are present in that country.

Clearly, Canada has a fairly small number of provinces (ten), two of them especially large. Ontario, it can be argued, has historically attempted to dominate the federation, whereas Quebec, finding itself unable to do so, has decided that the costs of political association with the rest of the country might outweigh the benefits. It is most interesting to note that the Quebec nationalists want the province to "have its cake and eat it too"— that is, they want political separation from Canada while retaining economic association. The separatists are not convinced that the costs of doing without Canadian tariff protection, a common currency, and the Canadian market in general outweigh the benefits of their own market economy.

Canada does correspond to the model of an "ideal" federation in that Canadians benefit from a reasonably effective party and judicial system. Indeed, it is probably the case that they are among the freest people in the world. On the other hand, the Canadian federation is no longer subjected to a perceived American military threat, which during the Confederation of 1867 was Canada's primary impetus for unification. In the absence of such a threat, Pierre Trudeau and the Liberal Party attempted to create an external economic threat (the United States) under the guise of a Canadianization of the national economy. This "third option," as it was originally called, did not instill a sense of national purpose in Canadians; and as yet, there has been no great revival of Canadian nationalism. Rather, Canada has embarked on a free-trade agreement with the United States, and Quebec nationalism is at a fever pitch.

The presence of national majorities in a small number of constituent units, where they are in the majority, has proven especially unmanageable in many federations. Canada is an excellent example. The majority (80 percent) of French Canadians are concentrated in one province (Quebec), where they are in the majority. Many political elites in the province are convinced that their particular needs cannot be met within the existing federation and have argued for sovereignty. The ultimate result of this struggle is still in question, but one can argue that if, in the "perfect" world, Canada's ethnic groups had been dispersed across the country—so that their particular interests had been "crosscutting" instead of "asymmetric"—then the country would be far more stable today.

The dominance of the Catholic church, at least within the province of Quebec, has also proven to be a divisive element. Until the Quiet Revolution of the 1960s in Quebec, the church encouraged Québecois to remain closely tied to their communities and culture. The French Canadian was discouraged from going to university or associating with the English-speaking world. Most important, in a political sense, the church commanded the first allegiance of most Québecois and played a greater role in their social and economic lives than did their secular elites.

With the development of hydroelectric power, a higher level of industrialization, the development of a state elite, greater demands for higher education sought by young Québecois, and other factors, the church has played a sharply reduced role in the life of the province. It can be argued, however, that had the church responded to the changing economic climate of the 1950s and 1960s by encouraging the natural evolution of Quebec society, the separatist movement would have had one less reason to grow. This explanation for the declining influence of the church and the growth of separatism in Quebec is by no means universally held and may provoke some controversy.

In contrast to Canada, the United States comprises many of the conditions beneficial to federations. The United States is a federation of many constituent units (fifty), none large enough to attempt to dominate the federation. These constituent units, unlike Canada's, owe their first allegiance to the strong central government in Washington. In addition, the United States, like Canada, benefits from an effective party and judicial system that has proven reasonably adequate to the task of representing and protecting the rights of its citizens.

Furthermore, the United States currently has no potential secessionist minorities concentrated in a few states. The presence of such minorities in the mid-1800s led to a devastating civil war in which a great number of lives were lost to preserve the American federal union. After 1865, however, a strong sense of national legitimacy developed across the country—a legitimacy that remains absent in most of Canada today (with the exception of Ontario).

Finally, the Founding Fathers of the United States expressed remarkable foresight in creating strong, viable political institutions that could adapt to economic and political change as well as to popular demands for greater personal well-being. With the important exception of the Civil War, which was partly a result of southerners' demands for national protection for their economic system and for their "peculiar institution" in the face of rapid industrialization in the North, American institutions and political elites have been able to amend their constitution to meet the changing needs of the times. One is led to conclude that, based on the available evidence, the United States is the federation that best approaches the model of the ideal federation.

In a study ambitious enough to examine the conditions that encourage or undermine the stability of federations, one must proceed with a great deal of caution. It is all too easy to make strong generalizations about how the world is or should be while ignoring the myriad of concepts, ideas, and conditions relevant to the subject. There also remains a dearth of objective data, particularly for the older federations. Above all, it must be remembered that, to some extent, all federations are idiosyncratic. Each has problems particular to itself, and the behaviorist is encouraged to keep this in mind when conducting cross-national research.

Nevertheless, this study has maintained that certain generalizations about the stability and instability of federations can be supported theoretically. Certain significant associations between the independent and the dependent variables have been demonstrated, and as such, they may well make a contribution to the study of federal political stability.

There is one other point worth exploring: the relevant advantages and disadvantages of federations and unitary states in personal minority rights.

Federations, Unitary States, and the Protection of Minority Rights

Historically, many political theorists have argued that the federal structure is one of the most popular vehicles for ensuring that the rights of minorities (be they racial, religious, linguistic, ideological, or class based) within the heterogeneous state are protected, that consensus is encouraged, and that conflict is regulated. Ostensibly, federalism can accomplish these goals because it provides for two or more overlapping jurisdictions, each with substantial autonomy but each subject to an enforceable system of constitutional law.

By contrast, a unitary system is a less popular choice because its structure consists of one jurisdiction in which a majoritarian will can dominate the polity, at times to the detriment of minorities. Power can be decentralized to various forms of local government, but the relationship with the national government is hierarchical. Local governments are associated with distinct, legally bound states and are responsible for discharging functions that the central power considers more appropriate organized locally.

Yet it would be erroneous to suggest that the way in which government is structured lies exclusively within the control of the center. For instance, the central government may find it difficult for political reasons—the existence of relatively powerful local political bases resisting change, for example—to restructure local government according to its own preferences.[7] Some argue that federalism allows more avenues for policy articulation, more institutional remedies for problems, fewer overall demands, and thus less chance for demand overload on the nation's political institutions.[8] On the other hand, it should be acknowledged that the federal system is slower, more complex, and inefficient and that it is subject to higher levels of conflict and regional competition.

The theoretical differences between federations and unitary states are more extensive than is evident in this cursory discussion, of course, but we must not delude ourselves into believing that the differences in practice are entirely clear-cut. Often the distinction between the two structures is quite arbitrary. What are we to make of the quasi-federal structures created to protect minority rights in such unitary states as Cyprus, Belgium, and Israel? Even such classical examples of centralized unitary governments as France or Great Britain make numerous special provisions for distinct minorities and unique regional interests within their respective countries. France has a regional layer of government that, at times, acts as a counterbalance to the central government in Paris. Great Britain allows regional assemblies in Scotland, Wales, and Northern Ireland. Indeed, the central government has allowed the Scots to retain many of the attributes of statehood. The United Kingdom also sustained a quasi-federal parliament in Northern Ireland between 1921 and 1972 and encouraged a loose constitutional relationship with both the Channel Islands and the Isle of Man.

As Sidney Tarrow mentions, in unitary states there are regional and local administrative institutions. "Functional interests . . . range themselves around both the poles of the political system—centre and periphery—and use their territorial leverage to fight out their conflicts of interest."[9] Should the interests of one or more of the different regions in the unitary state conflict with those of the central government, undoubtedly the center would prevail. But most often both levels of government work to avoid inflaming rival passions wherever possible. Furthermore, the histories of federations such as Mexico, Venezuela, and many others are replete with episodes of the central government dominating the constituent units. Clearly, the distinction between federations and unitary governments is very often arbitrary and should be recognized as such.

This should not necessarily be regarded as a problem. Both federal governments and unitary states have similar goals, including the desire to reduce internal conflict. Although theoretically only unitary governments can revoke powers delegated to the regions, in practice most federal constitutions retain the same privilege, at least in times of national emergency. Nor is the use of the federal or the unitary structure the sole means of resolving internal strife. Other conflict-reducing schemes include consociational democracy, (Ian Lustick's discussion of) "control" mechanisms,[10] different forms of sociocultural autonomy, a variety of language accommodations, coercive suppression, confederation, and (Elazar's) compound unitary states, to name just the most prominent.[11]

All of these strategies have strengths and weaknesses depending on the particular country involved, and all of them overlap to varying degrees with one or more of the other conflict-reaction mechanisms. Thus, it is shortsighted to regard the federal or unitary structure as uniquely able to resolve the problems associated with internal strife and political fragmentation.

Perhaps the only clearly discernible difference between the two structures is that it is a bit more difficult in a federation than in a unitary state for the center to encroach on the powers and status of regional governments. Federalism rules out the total elimination of provincial autonomy, a theoretical possibility in a unitary state within the normal procedures of government.[12] Nevertheless, efforts are made in both to construct distinct political and constitutional structures that will accommodate competing interests.

Minority dissatisfaction is a dominant theme in the historical development of the organized modern state and is a central problem of our age. Divisive interests have persisted in particular regions over several generations and have survived despite strong pressures toward mainstream assimilation. In addition, new political leaders seek more political power and varying degrees of autonomy.[13] They reject the tacit historical alliances that co-opted previous generations of ethnic leaders into the central government, and they challenge the legitimacy of the established state system, claiming their moral right to greater autonomy.

Furthermore, minority ethnic groups are often economically disadvantaged. If that is the case, then class conflict and ethnic strife might reinforce each other to provide an impetus to change. Where such divisions correspond with territorial boundaries, that is, when they are asymmetric, the seeds are sown for a nationalist movement. As was demonstrated earlier, asymmetry is, at times, significantly associated with political instability in federal states. If the nation's elites are unable or unwilling to redress the grievances of such groups, there is the potential for a separatist movement.

It should be acknowledged that any federal or unitary state will probably have problems with minorities, for there is discord between the idea of self-determination and the idea of minorities. The idea of self-determination projects a world in which, in the words of John Stuart Mill, "it is in general a necessary condition of free institutions that the boundaries of government should coincide in the main with those of nationalities," in which one's social or political being cannot be realized except among one's own. The idea of minorities, on the other hand, projects a world in which differences are erased by a single standard of citizenship, in which one's social and political being can be realized among anybody. In the past century the idea of minorities has become less

important than the idea of self-determination; groups have chosen, sometimes for reasons of security but often for reasons of self-love or political
and cultural exclusiveness. As a Pakistani nationalist put it in 1947, "Good
government is no substitute for self-government."[14]

Both federal and unitary structures are vulnerable to this regionally
based homogeneity and to separatist threats, and both can violate the civil
rights of minority groups. Unitary states are more obviously culpable in
this regard, but the inability of the American government to reverse the
racist policies of the southern states until the 1964 Voting Rights Act is one
demonstration of the fact that federations are no more able to protect the
rights of minorities than unitary states in the absence of the political will
to do so.[15]

In the same vein, federalism may induce a government to refuse or to
limit adherence to international human rights agreements, or it may
frustrate their implementation. Questions may arise whether the national
government has the authority to adhere to human rights agreements
without the consent of the constituent units and whether it can then
implement these agreements. Federalism is simply not the great panacea
that so many have claimed it to be.

Most nations of the world make explicit provisions for the protection of
minority rights.[16] But a constitution is worth nothing if there is no political
will to ensure that these provisions will be acted on. The Soviet constitution, for example, goes so far as to grant to individual republics the right
to secede from the union, maintain their own armies, and establish their
own constitution. Of course, we have clear evidence in the case of the
Baltic Republics that the Soviet government is not yet prepared to grant
real independence.

For its part, Yugoslavia, at the time of this investigation, also recognized
the principle of constituent unit self-determination. Of course, all the
federal units were, in reality, tightly controlled through the integrated
Communist Party. It is the case now, however, that the federal government
has faced a variety of separatist movements such that the Federation is in
danger of disintegration. Alternatively, the People's Republic of China
contains thirty administrative divisions. Each of these is empowered to
make or impose arrangements peculiar to itself, within limits.

If federalism is associated with the same prejudices and many of the
same problems as the unitary state, and if the constitutional structure or
political institutions cannot, in and of themselves, guarantee minority
rights and political stability, what holds a federation together? The obvious
answer, but one that is too often overlooked, is the degree of political will
present. In this instance, political will means a common self-interest and

identity. The absence of a political commitment to this goal of unity, whether it be within a federal or a unitary state, will make the resolution of internal conflicts that much more difficult. Claude Ake referred to this condition as "the presence of a normative consensus governing political behaviour among members of the political system."[17]

Combined with this condition is the creation of flexible public policies consistent with the will of the population (whatever that might be) and the resulting demonstration of deference and allegiance to the state. In the multiethnic state, the fulfillment of citizens' needs must be accompanied by a sense of fairness to the diverse ethnic groups. If public policy is consistent with the existing political and constitutional structure, then political legitimacy is likely to ensue.

Thus, political will is basic to the resolution of conflict and lasting national unity. Whether the state has a federal or a unitary constitutional structure is not so important. Federalism is not a panacea; indeed, it might provide a preexisting route for demands for autonomy. Instead, what is basic is the will to be flexible to conflicting internal demands and challenges. This condition is not unique to any particular political or constitutional structure.

NOTES

1. Georg Simmel, *Conflict and the Web of Group Affiliations* (Glencoe: Free Press, 1955); Lewis Coser, "Social Conflict and the Theory of Social Change," *British Journal of Sociology* 8 (September 1957): 197–207; James N. Rosenau, ed., *Linkage Politics* (New York: Free Press, 1969).

2. Jean Bodin, *Six Books of the Commonwealth*, abridged and trans. M. S. Tooley (Oxford: Oxford University Press, 1955).

3. Rudolph J. Rummel, "Dimensions of Conflict Behavior within and between Nations," *General Systems Yearbook* 8 (1963): 1–50.

4. K. C. Wheare, *Federal Government*, 4th ed. (London: Oxford University Press, 1963), pp. 40, 50.

5. John Higley, G. Lowell Field, and Knut Groholt, *Elite Structure and Ideology: A Theory with Applications to Norway* (New York: Columbia University Press, 1976), p. 35.

6. William H. Riker, "Federalism," in Fred Greenstein and Nelson W. Polsby, eds., *Handbook of Political Science: Governmental Institutions and Processes* (Reading: Addison-Wesley, 1975), p. 127.

7. For a more complete discussion of this point, see Peter Gourevitch, "Reforming the Napoleonic State: The Creation of Regional Governments in France and Italy," in Sidney Tarrow et al., eds., *Territorial Politics in Industrial Nations* (New York: Praeger, 1978), pp. 28–63.

8. For a more detailed discussion of these points, see, for example, Vincent Ostrom, "Does Federalism Make a Difference?" *Publius* 3, no. 2 (Fall 1973): 197–237; William

Riker, *Federalism: Origin, Operation, Significance* (Boston: Little, Brown and Co., 1964); and William Riker, "Six Books in Search of a Subject, or Does Federalism Exist and Does it Matter?" *Comparative Politics* (October 1969): 135–46.

9. Sidney Tarrow, Introduction to *Federalism and Democratic Theory* by Reginald Whitaker, Institute of Intergovernmental Relations Discussion Paper no. 17 (Kingston: Queen's University, 1983), p. 36.

10. Ian Lustick, "Stability in Deeply Divided Societies: Consociationalism Versus Control," *World Politics* 31, no. 3 (April 1979): 323–44.

11. For a good discussion of these strategies, see, for example, Daniel Elazar, "Urbanism and Federalism: Twin Revolutions of the Modern Era," *Publius* 5, no. 2 (1975): 15–39, and Cynthia Enloe, *Ethnic Conflict and Political Development* (Boston: Little, Brown and Co., 1973), pp. 89–92.

12. This point is made well in Ivo Duchacek, *Comparative Federalism* (New York: Holt, Rinehart and Winston, 1970), p. 194.

13. For a good discussion of this point, see Alvin Rabushka and Kenneth Shepsle, *Politics in Plural Societies: A Theory of Democratic Instability* (Columbus: Charles E. Merrill, 1972).

14. As quoted in the *New Republic*, November 1985, p. 16.

15. William Riker presents the best illustration of this point: see "Federalism," p. 158.

16. For what is perhaps the best quick overview of these constitutional arrangements across many nations, see Daniel Elazar, *Federalism and Political Integration* (Jerusalem: Turtledove Publishing Co., 1979), pp. 215–31.

17. Claude Ake, *A Theory of Political Integration* (Homewood: Dorsey Press, 1969), pp. 1–3.

APPENDIX: THE CODING OF THE INDEPENDENT AND DEPENDENT VARIABLES

In the Appendix, the data are presented as they have been categorized in the study. The raw data are not given because it would be misleading, that is, a reported revolution in a nineteenth-century federation may not be as important as a revolution in a twentieth-century federation. As a result, reported events are classified in terms of degree of importance or intensity across the forty-four federal cases. In this way, the reported incidences of stability or instability can be judged more objectively.

The federations are numbered from 1 to 44; the country numbers appear in the left column of each listing (Ctry).

The dependent variables and the data associated with these variables are presented first. The current federations are coded as of 1983.

Dependent Variable: Absence of secession potential
Value Labels: (2) Stable; (1) Partly stable; (0) Not stable or ended

1.	Argentina (1853–)	2
2.	Australia (1901–)	2
3.	Austria-Hungary (1867–1918)	0
4.	Austria (1919–38)	0
5.	Austria (1945–)	2
6.	United States of Brazil (1891–1934)	0
7.	Brazil (1946–)	2
8.	British West Indies (1958–62)	0
9.	Burma (1948–62)	0
10.	Cameroons (1961–72)	0
11.	Canada (1867–)	1
12.	Central African Federation (1953–63)	0
13.	Central American Federation (1824–39)	0
14.	Chile (1826–27)	0
15.	Grand Colombia (1819–30)	0

16.	Colombia (1853–86)	0
17.	Congo (1960–69)	0
18.	Czechoslovakia (1969–)	2
19.	Ethiopia (1952–62)	0
20.	German Empire (1867–1919)	0
21.	Germany—Weimar Republic (1919–38)	0
22.	German Federal Republic (1949–)	2
23.	India (1953–)	2
24.	Indonesia (1949–50)	0
25.	Federation of Iraq and Jordan (1958)	0
26.	Libya (1951–63)	0
27.	Malaya (1957–63)	0
28.	Malaysia (with Singapore) (1963–65)	0
29.	Malaysia (without Singapore) (1965–)	1
30.	Mali Federation (1959–60)	0
31.	Mexico (1824–36)	0
32.	Mexico (1917–)	2
33.	Nigeria (1960–70)	0
34.	Nigeria (1970–)	1
35.	Pakistan (1947–)	2
36.	Switzerland (1848–)	2
37.	Uganda (1962–67)	0
38.	U.S.S.R. (1922–)	2
39.	United Arab Republic (1958–61)	0
40.	United Netherlands (1579–1798)	0
41.	United States (1787–1861)	0
42.	United States (1865–)	2
43.	Venezuela (1864–)	2
44.	Yugoslavia (1946–)	1

It is interesting to note that seventeen of the twenty-seven failed federations have become or became unitary or military states. One might argue that such a state has therefore not "failed" per se. In response to such an argument, it is worth noting that a majority of these federal-unitary states altered their structures again or dissolved entirely. It should also be mentioned that federations in this study are valued for the very fact that they are federations, for their respective fates can then be more easily contrasted.

LONG-TERM STABILITY WITH DESTABILIZING POTENTIAL: THE ABSENCE OF STRUCTURAL CHANGE AND THE AMOUNT OF POLITICAL VIOLENCE

Dependent Variables: Number of riots; Number of armed attacks; Number of political assassinations; Number of coups d'état; Number of civil wars; Number of revolutions
Value Labels: (0) Few or no reported incidents; (1) Moderate number of incidents; (2) Many incidents

Ctry	Riots	Attacks	Assass.	Coups	Wars	Revol.
1	2	2	2	2	0	2
2	0	1	1	0	0	0
3	2	2	1	0	0	0
4	2	2	2	0	1	0
5	2	2	0	0	0	0
6	2	0	1	1	0	2
7	2	2	1	1	0	2
8	1	2	0	0	0	0
9	2	2	0	1	0	2
10	0	2	0	0	0	0
11	2	2	0	0	0	0
12	2	2	0	0	0	0
13	2	2	2	0	2	2
14	2	2	2	2	2	0
15	0	2	1	1	0	0
16	2	2	2	2	2	2
17	2	2	2	1	2	2
18	0	0	0	0	0	0
19	2	2	0	0	0	2
20	2	2	1	0	0	0
21	2	2	2	2	0	0
22	2	2	0	0	0	0
23	2	2	2	0	0	2
24	2	2	0	0	0	0
25	2	2	0	2	0	2
26	2	2	1	0	0	0
27	2	2	0	0	0	0
28	2	2	0	0	0	0
29	2	2	0	0	0	0
30	2	2	0	0	0	2
31	0	1	1	2	0	0
32	2	2	2	1	0	0
33	2	2	1	1	2	2
34	2	2	1	1	2	2
35	2	2	1	0	2	1
36	1	1	0	0	0	0
37	2	2	0	0	0	0
38	2	2	0	0	0	1
39	0	0	0	2	0	0
40	1	2	2	0	2	0
41	2	2	1	0	1	0
42	2	2	2	0	0	0
43	2	2	1	2	2	2
44	2	2	0	0	0	0

LONG-TERM STABILITY: LEGITIMACY OR THE DEGREE OF LOYALTY

Dependent Variables: (Durfed) Durability of the federation; (Viol) Degree of electoral violence; (Abuse) Level of abuse of high office; (Terror) Level of small-scale terrorism; Number of mutinies; Number of plots; Number of purges; (Gs) Number of general strikes. Value Labels: (0) Few or no reported incidents; (1) Moderate number of incidents; (2) Many incidents

Ctry	Durfed	Viol	Abuse	Terror	Mutinies	Plots	Purges	Gs
1	1	2	2	2	2	2	2	2
2	2	0	0	0	0	0	0	0
3	1	2	2	2	2	2	2	0
4	0	2	2	2	0	2	2	2
5	1	0	0	0	0	0	0	0
6	1	1	1	2	2	2	1	0
7	1	1	1	1	2	2	2	1
8	0	2	0	0	0	0	0	0
9	1	1	0	2	2	2	2	0
10	2	1	0	1	0	0	0	0
11	2	0	0	1	0	0	0	0
12	1	2	0	2	0	2	2	0
13	0	2	2	2	2	2	2	0
14	0	2	0	0	2	0	2	0
15	2	0	2	2	2	2	2	0
16	0	2	2	2	2	2	2	2
17	0	2	2	2	2	2	2	0
18	2	0	0	0	0	0	2	0
19	2	0	2	1	1	2	0	0
20	1	2	2	2	2	2	2	2
21	0	2	0	2	2	2	2	2
22	2	0	0	0	0	1	1	1
23	2	2	2	2	0	2	2	2
24	0	0	0	0	0	0	2	0
25	0	1	1	2	2	2	2	0
26	2	0	2	1	0	2	0	0
27	0	0	2	0	0	0	2	0
28	0	0	2	2	0	0	2	0
29	1	2	2	2	0	2	2	0
30	0	0	0	0	0	0	0	0
31	0	2	1	0	0	2	2	0
32	2	0	1	1	0	1	1	1
33	2	0	2	1	1	1	2	1
34	2	0	2	1	1	1	2	1
35	0	2	2	2	1	2	2	0
36	1	0	0	1	0	0	0	0
37	0	0	2	0	0	0	0	0
38	2	0	0	1	0	0	2	0
39	0	2	2	0	0	2	2	0
40	2	0	2	2	2	2	2	0
41	1	1	0	1	0	1	2	2
42	1	1	1	2	0	0	1	1
43	1	2	2	2	2	2	2	2
44	2	0	0	2	0	2	2	2

LONG-TERM STABILITY: THE LIMITATION OF VIOLENCE—COLLECTIVE PROTESTS

Dependent Variables: Number of protests; Number of riots. Since the latter has already been presented in the first section, only data for protests are given.

Value Labels: (0) Few or no reported incidents; (1) Moderate number of incidents; (2) Many incidents

Ctry	Protests
1	2
2	1
3	2
4	2
5	1
6	2
7	2
8	0
9	1
10	0
11	2
12	2
13	2
14	0
15	2
16	2
17	2
18	0
19	0
20	2
21	2
22	2
23	2
24	0
25	2
26	1
27	1
28	2
29	2
30	0
31	0
32	2
33	2
34	2
35	2
36	0
37	0
38	2
39	1
40	0
41	2
42	2
43	2
44	2

SHORT-TERM STABILITY: STABILITY OF THE CHIEF EXECUTIVE

Dependent Variables: (Exec) Level of executive tenure; (Regtra) Number of regular executive transfers of power; (Irrtra) Number of irregular executive transfers of power; (Unstra) Number of unsuccessful executive transfers of power; (Crises) Number of constitutional crises; (Cabcha) Number of major cabinet changes

Value Labels: All but the executive tenure category are trichotomous. Executive tenure is divided into four categories with: (0) Absence of a legislature; (1) Low level of executive tenure; (2) Moderate level; (3) High level

Ctry	Exec	Regtra	Irrtra	Unstra	Crises	Cabcha
1	0	2	2	2	2	2
2	2	2	0	0	1	2
3	1	2	2	2	1	2
4	1	2	2	2	2	2
5	1	2	0	0	0	1
6	0	2	1	0	1	2
7	0	2	1	2	1	2
8	0	2	0	0	1	0
9	1	2	2	2	2	2
10	3	1	0	0	2	2
11	2	2	0	0	2	2
12	1	2	0	0	2	1
13	1	0	2	2	2	2
14	0	0	2	2	2	0
15	3	0	0	2	0	0
16	0	0	2	2	2	2
17	0	2	2	2	2	2
18	2	2	0	0	0	0
19	0	1	0	1	1	2
20	1	2	2	2	1	2
21	0	2	2	2	2	2
22	0	2	0	0	1	1
23	3	2	0	2	1	1
24	1	2	0	0	2	2
25	0	2	2	0	2	2
26	0	2	0	0	0	2
27	3	2	0	2	1	2
28	3	2	0	0	0	0
29	1	2	0	2	0	0
30	1	2	0	0	0	0
31	0	2	2	2	1	2
32	3	2	0	2	1	2
33	0	1	1	1	1	1
34	0	1	1	1	1	1
35	1	2	1	2	2	2
36	1	2	0	0	1	1
37	0	2	1	0	2	2
38	2	2	0	0	1	2
39	1	2	0	0	2	2
40	0	2	2	2	2	0
41	2	2	0	0	1	2
42	2	2	0	0	0	1
43	2	2	2	2	2	2
44	0	2	0	0	1	1

THE RELATION BETWEEN STRUCTURE AND STABILITY IN FEDERAL GOVERNMENTS

Independent Variables: (Cent) Degree of centralization; (Cunits) Constituent units; (Oversz) Large states; (Lcl) Language cleavage; (Rich) Degree of wealth; (Freedom) Degree of freedom

Value Labels: Cent—(0) No, (1) Yes; Cunits—(0) 1–5, (1) 6–11, (2) 12–50; Oversz—(0) No, (1) Yes; Lcl—(0) No, (1) Yes; Rich—(0) No, (1) Yes; Freedom—(0) No, (1) Partly, (2) Yes

Ctry	Cent	Cunits	Oversz	Lcl	Rich	Freedom
1	1	2	1	0	1	0
2	0	1	0	0	1	2
3	0	0	1	1	1	2
4	0	1	0	0	1	1
5	1	1	0	0	1	2
6	0	2	1	0	0	1
7	1	2	1	0	1	1
8	0	1	1	0	0	2
9	1	1	1	1	0	1
10	0	2	1	1	0	0
11	0	1	1	1	1	2
12	0	0	1	0	0	1
13	0	0	1	1	0	0
14	0	1	1	1	0	1
15	0	0	1	1	0	0
16	0	1	0	1	0	1
17	1	2	0	1	0	0
18	1	2	0	1	0	0
19	0	2	1	1	0	0
20	0	2	1	0	1	1
21	0	2	1	0	1	2
22	1	1	0	0	1	2
23	1	2	1	1	0	2
24	0	2	1	1	0	1
25	0	0	1	0	0	0
26	0	0	1	0	0	1
27	0	1	1	1	1	1
28	0	2	1	1	1	1
29	0	2	1	1	1	1
30	0	0	1	1	0	2
31	0	2	0	1	0	0
32	1	2	1	0	0	1
33	0	0	1	1	0	0
34	1	2	0	1	0	2
35	1	0	1	1	0	0
36	0	2	0	1	1	2
37	0	0	1	1	0	1
38	1	2	1	1	1	0
39	0	0	1	0	0	0
40	0	1	1	0	1	2
41	0	2	0	0	1	2
42	1	2	0	0	1	2
43	1	2	0	0	1	2
44	1	1	1	1	0	0

THE DEGREE OF POLITICAL FREEDOM AND FEDERAL STABILITY

Independent Variables: (Free) Degree of political freedom; (Polrig) Political rights; (Civlib) Civil liberties; (Polter) Political terror

Value Labels: Free—(0) No, (1) Partly, (2) Yes; Polrig—(1) Good, (2) A, (3) B, (4) C, (5) D, (6) E, (7) Bad; Civlib—(1) Good, (2) A, (3) B, (4) C, (5) D, (6) E, (7) Bad; Polter—(1) Good, (2) A, (3) B, (4) C, (5) Bad

The letters A–E represent degrees of freedom from the highest level (A) to the lowest (E).

Ctry	Free	Polrig	Civlib	Polter
1	0	6	5	4
2	2	1	1	1
3	2	5	2	1
4	1	2	4	2
5	2	1	1	1
6	1	5	4	2
7	1	4	3	2
8	2	2	2	1
9	1	4	4	3
10	0	6	6	3
11	2	1	1	1
12	1	4	3	2
13	0	6	5	4
14	1	4	3	2
15	0	5	3	2
16	1	3	3	1
17	0	5	5	3
18	0	7	6	3
19	0	6	5	2
20	1	4	2	1
21	2	1	2	1
22	2	1	2	1
23	2	2	2	2
24	1	4	5	2
25	0	6	6	3
26	1	6	4	2
27	1	3	4	3
28	1	4	4	3
29	1	3	4	3
30	2	3	2	1
31	0	7	6	4
32	1	3	4	2
33	0	5	6	3
34	2	3	2	2
35	2	2	3	2
36	2	1	1	1
37	1	4	4	3
38	0	6	6	3
39	0	6	4	4
40	2	1	2	1
41	2	1	2	1
42	2	1	1	1
43	2	1	2	2
44	0	6	5	3

THE RELATION BETWEEN CENTRALIZATION AND STABILITY IN FEDERAL GOVERNMENTS

Political Centralization and the Federal Constitution

Independent Variables: (Cunits) Constituent units; (Oversz) Large states; (Const) Form of constitution

Value Labels: Cunits—(1) 2–5, (2) 6–11, (3) 12–50; Oversz—(0) No, (1) Yes; Const—(0) Empire, (1) Unitary, (2) Mixed, (3) Peripheral

Ctry	Cunits	Oversz	Const
1	3	1	2
2	2	0	2
3	1	1	0
4	2	0	1
5	2	0	2
6	3	1	2
7	3	1	1
8	2	1	0
9	2	1	1
10	3	1	2
11	2	1	2
12	1	1	2
13	1	1	2
14	2	1	3
15	1	1	3
16	2	0	3
17	3	0	2
18	3	0	1
19	3	1	0
20	3	1	0
21	3	1	1
22	2	0	2
23	3	1	1
24	3	1	2
25	1	1	1
26	1	1	1
27	2	1	1
28	3	1	1
29	3	1	1
30	1	1	2
31	3	0	2
32	3	1	2
33	1	1	1
34	3	0	2
35	1	1	2
36	3	0	2
37	1	1	1
38	3	1	2
39	1	1	1
40	2	1	3
41	3	0	2
42	3	0	2
43	3	0	2
44	2	1	2

The data used in the adaptation of the Canada West study are presented in the text of chapter 5.

Political Centralization and the Federal Party System
Independent Variables: (Ppa) Political party simple; (Ppb) Political party complex; (Ppc) National party success
Value Labels: Ppa—(1) 0, (2) 1 party dominant, (3) 2 party, (4) Multiparty; Ppb—(1) Nonparty nonmilitary, (2) Nonparty military, (3) Nationalist 1 party, (4) 1 party communist, (5) 1 party socialist, (6) Dominant parties, (7) Centralized multiparty, (8) Decentralized multiparty; Ppc—(0) Inappropriate, (1) No, (2) Occasionally, (3) Yes

Ctry	Ppa	Ppb	Ppc
1	1	2	0
2	4	8	2
3	1	6	1
4	1	3	3
5	4	7	2
6	4	8	2
7	4	8	1
8	4	8	1
9	4	7	2
10	1	6	0
11	4	8	2
12	4	7	3
13	1	3	0
14	3	6	2
15	2	3	0
16	3	6	2
17	1	1	0
18	1	4	3
19	0	1	0
20	3	7	2
21	4	8	2
22	4	8	2
23	4	8	3
24	1	1	0
25	1	2	0
26	1	1	0
27	2	6	2
28	2	6	2
29	2	6	2
30	2	3	3
31	1	3	0
32	2	3	3
33	1	2	1
34	4	8	2
35	1	2	3
36	4	8	3
37	2	3	2
38	1	4	3
39	1	3	1
40	4	7	2
41	4	8	3
42	4	8	3
43	4	7	3
44	1	4	3

Political Centralization and Federal Asymmetry

Independent Variables: (Lreg) Language-region correspondence; (Relig) Religion-region correspondence; (Racial) Race-region correspondence; (Cunits) Constituent units; (Oversz) Large states

Value Labels: Lreg—(0) No, (1) Yes; Relig—(0) No, (1) Yes; Racial—(0) No, (1) Yes; Cunits—(0) 2–5, (1) 6–11, (2) 12–50; Oversz—(0) No, (1) Yes

Ctry	Lreg	Relig	Racial	Cunits	Oversz
1	0	0	0	2	1
2	0	0	1	1	0
3	1	0	0	0	1
4	0	0	0	1	0
5	0	0	0	1	0
6	1	0	0	2	1
7	1	0	0	2	1
8	1	1	1	1	1
9	1	1	0	1	1
10	1	1	0	2	1
11	1	1	0	1	1
12	0	1	1	0	1
13	1	1	1	0	1
14	1	0	0	1	1
15	0	0	0	0	1
16	0	0	0	1	0
17	1	1	1	2	0
18	1	0	0	2	0
19	1	1	1	2	1
20	0	0	0	2	1
21	0	0	0	2	1
22	0	0	0	1	0
23	1	1	0	2	1
24	1	1	1	2	1
25	0	0	0	0	1
26	0	0	0	0	1
27	1	1	1	1	1
28	1	1	1	2	1
29	1	1	1	2	1
30	1	1	0	0	1
31	0	0	1	2	0
32	0	0	1	2	1
33	1	1	1	0	0
34	0	1	1	2	0
35	1	0	0	0	1
36	1	0	0	2	0
37	1	1	0	0	1
38	1	1	1	2	1
39	0	0	0	0	1
40	1	0	0	1	1
41	0	0	0	2	0
42	0	0	0	2	0
43	0	0	0	2	0
44	1	0	1	1	1

POLITICAL CLEAVAGE AND FEDERAL STABILITY

Independent Variables: (Religion) Religious homogeneity; (Cath) Percentage of Catholics; (Language) Language homogeneity; (Race) Racial homogeneity; (Balcom) Existence of balanced competition; (Plural) Existence of plural federations

Value Labels: Religion—(0) Heterogeneous, (1) Homogeneous; Cath—(0) Heterogeneous, (1) A, (2) B, (3) C, (4) Most Homogeneous; Language—(0) Strongly heterogeneous, (1) Weakly homogeneous, (2) Strongly homogeneous; Race—(0) Heterogeneous, (1) Homogeneous; Balcom—(1) Fragmentation, (2) Dominant minority, (3) Dominant majority, (4) Balanced competition; Plural—(0) Plural federation, (1) Nonplural federation

The missing cases in the Balcom category refer to the nondemocratic federations.

The letters A–C represent degrees of homogeneity from the lowest level (A) to the highest (C).

Ctry	Religion	Cath	Language	Race	Balcom	Plural
1	1	4	1	1		1
2	1	1	2	1	3	0
3	1	4	0	1	4	1
4	1	4	2	1		1
5	1	3	2	1	4	1
6	1	4	2	0	3	0
7	1	3	2	0	3	0
8	0	2	1	1	1	0
9	1	0	1	1	3	1
10	0	1	0	1		0
11	1	2	0	1	4	0
12	0	0	0	1	2	0
13	1	4	0	0		0
14	1	4	0	0	1	0
15	1	4	0	0		0
16	1	4	0	0	1	0
17	0	2	0	1		0
18	0	2	0	1		0
19	0	0	0	1		0
20	0	2	2	1	2	0
21	0	2	2	1	4	1
22	1	2	2	1	4	1
23	0	1	0	1	1	0
24	1	0	0	0	1	0
25	1	0	2	1		1
26	1	0	2	1	3	1
27	0	0	0	0	4	0
28	0	0	0	0	3	0
29	0	0	0	0	4	0
30	0	0	0	1	1	0
31	1	4	0	0		0
32	1	3	2	0	3	0
33	0	1	0	1	1	0
34	0	1	0	1	1	0
35	1	0	0	1		0
36	1	2	0	1	4	0
37	0	2	0	1	1	0
38	0	0	0	1		0
39	1	1	2	1		1
40	1	2	0	1	3	0
41	1	2	2	0	4	1
42	1	2	2	0	4	1
43	1	3	2	0	3	0
44	1	2	0	1		0

MODERNIZATION, SOCIAL MOBILIZATION, RELATIVE DEPRIVATION, AND FEDERAL STABILITY

Social Mobilization: General

Independent Variables: (Mod) Level of development; (Pop) Population size; (Growth) Population growth rate; (Large) Largest geographic size

Value Labels: Mod—(0) Traditional, (1) Modernizing, (2) Modern; Pop—(0) 5 million or under, (1) 5–15 million, (2) 15 million or more; Growth—(0) Least, (1) A, (2) B, (3) C, (4) D, (5) E, (6) Most; Large—(0) Smallest, (1) A, (2) B, (3) C, (4) D, (5) Largest

The letters A–E represent rates of population growth and geographic size from the lowest levels (A) to the highest (E).

Ctry	Mod	Pop	Growth	Large
1	2	2	2	3
2	2	1	2	4
3	1	2	0	1
4	1	1	1	0
5	2	1	1	0
6	1	2	6	5
7	1	2	4	5
8	1	0	2	0
9	1	2	1	1
10	1	1	3	0
11	2	2	2	5
12	1	1	6	1
13	0	0	0	0
14	0	0	0	0
15	0	0	0	3
16	0	0	0	1
17	1	2	3	2
18	2	2	1	0
19	1	2	3	1
20	1	2	0	1
21	1	2	1	0
22	2	2	1	0
23	1	2	3	3
24	1	2	0	2
25	1	1	4	1
26	0	0	5	2
27	1	1	3	0
28	1	1	2	0
29	1	1	3	0
30	0	0	3	1
31	0	1	0	3
32	1	2	4	2
33	1	2	3	1
34	1	2	1	0
35	1	2	3	1
36	1	2	4	1
37	2	1	1	0
38	1	1	4	0
39	2	2	2	5
40	1	2	5	1
41	0	0	1	0
42	1	2	4	5
43	2	2	1	5
44	1	1	5	1

Social Mobilization: Political Institutionalization

Independent Variables: (Agecon) Age of most recent constitution; (Effect) Legislative effectiveness; (Agepar) Age of the oldest of two parties

Value Labels: Agecon—(0) 0–5 Years, (1) 6–15, (2) 16–35, (3) 36 and up; Effect–(0) None, (1) Ineffective, (2) Partly, (3) Effective; Agepar—(0) 0–9 years, (1) 10–25, (2) 26–50, (3) 51–100, (4) 101 and up

Ctry	Agecon	Effect	Agepar
1	3	0	0
2	3	3	3
3	3	2	3
4	0	0	1
5	3	3	2
6	3	1	2
7	1	1	2
8	0	3	0
9	1	0	1
10	1	1	0
11	3	3	4
12	1	2	1
13	1	1	1
14	0	0	0
15	1	1	0
16	2	1	2
17	1	0	0
18	1	1	0
19	1	1	0
20	3	2	3
21	1	1	1
22	2	3	2
23	2	3	2
24	0	1	0
25	0	0	0
26	1	1	0
27	1	2	0
28	0	2	1
29	2	2	1
30	0	1	0
31	1	0	0
32	3	2	3
33	0	2	0
34	0	0	0
35	1	2	0
36	3	3	4
37	0	1	0
38	3	1	0
39	0	0	0
40	3	2	0
41	3	3	4
42	3	3	4
43	2	3	1
44	1	2	0

Social Mobilization: Inequality

Independent Variables: (Ecineq) Regional inequality; (Class) Class inequality; (Top) % of income held by top 5% of population

Value Labels: Ecineq—(0) No, (1) Partly, (2) Yes; Class—(0) No, (1) Partly, (2) Yes; Top—(0) 0–9, (1) 10–15, (2) 16–20, (3) 21–25, (4) 26–35

Missing values reflect a lack of accurate information.

Ctry	Ecineq	Class	Top
1	1	2	3
2	0	0	1
3		2	
4	2	2	4
5	0	0	
6	2	2	4
7		2	4
8	2	2	5
9	0	0	1
10	2	2	4
11	2	0	1
12	2	2	4
13			
14	2	2	4
15	2	2	4
16	2	2	4
17	1	2	4
18		0	0
19	2	2	4
20	1	0	4
21	0	2	4
22	0	1	4
23	2	2	3
24	0	1	4
25	2	2	4
26	0	0	1
27	0	0	2
28	0	0	4
29	0	1	4
30		2	4
31	2	2	4
32	2	2	4
33	2		
34	2		
35	2	0	2
36	0	0	0
37	0	2	4
38	2	0	
39	2	1	2
40	0	2	4
41	0	2	
42	0	0	1
43	0	1	3
44	0	0	1

Social Mobilization: Particular Aspects of Modernization

Independent Variables: (News) Newspaper readers per 1,000; (Radios) Radios owned per 1,000; (Lit) % literate over age 15; (Univ) University Students; (Cities) % of population in cities over 50 thousand; (Nonag) % in nonagricultural occupations

Value Labels: News—(0) 0–10, (1) 11–50, (2) 51–100, (3) 101–300, (4) 301– ; Radios—(0) 0–10, (1) 11–50, (2) 51–100, (3) 101–300, (4) 301– ; Lit—(0) 0–10, (1) 11–50, (2) 51–100, (3) 101–300, (4) 301– ; Univ—(0) 0, (1) 1–5, (2) 6–20, (3) 21– ; Cities—(0) 0–10, (1) 11–20, (2) 21–30, (3) 31–40, (4) 41– ; Nonag—(0) 0–10, (1) 11–40, (2) 41–50, (3) 51–60, (4) 61–80, (5) 81–100

Missing values reflect a lack of accurate information.

Ctry	News	Radios	Lit	Univ	Cities	Nonag
1	3	4	4	1	4	5
2	4	3	5	2	4	5
3				0	1	3
4		0	2	1	3	4
5	4	3	5	2	3	5
6	0		3	0	0	1
7	1	2	4	2	3	4
8	2	3	4	1	1	4
9	0	0	4	0	0	1
10	0	1	0	0	0	1
11	3	4	5	3	3	5
12	1	1				0
13			0		0	0
14	0		0		0	0
15	0		0	0	0	0
16	0		0	0	0	0
17	0	2	1	0	2	3
18	3	3	5	2	2	5
19	0	0	3	0	0	1
20				1	2	4
21	3	1	2	1	3	5
22	4	4	5	2	3	5
23	1	1	2	1	1	1
24	0	0	1	0	0	0
25	1	1	2	1	3	3
26	0	2	1	0	2	
27	3	2	3	0	0	2
28	2	1	3	1	0	2
29	2	1	3	1	1	2
30	0	0	0	0	0	0
31	0		0	0	0	0
32	3	4	4	1	3	3
33	0	0	1	0	0	1
34	1	2	2	0	1	1
35	0	1	1	1		2
36	4	4	5	2	2	5
37	0	2	2	0	0	0
38	4	4	5	3	4	4
39	1	2	2	1	2	2
40					0	
41	2		4	1	0	
42	3	4	5	3	3	5
43	2	3	4	2	2	4
44	2	3	4	2	1	3

Relative Deprivation and Federal Political Stability

Independent Variables: (Wealth) Prosperous constituent units; (Urban) Degree of urbanization; (Educ) Level of education; (Mail) Level of mail service; (Tele) Level of telephone service; (Gastil) Gastil's political-economic categories; (Top) % of income held by top 5% of population; (Rapid) Rapid economic growth

Value Labels: Wealth—(0) No, (1) Yes; Urban—(0) 0–20, (1) 21–30, (2) 31–60, (3) 61– ; Educ—(0) 0–10, (1) 11–20, (2) 21–40, (3) 41–60, (4) 61–80, (5) 81–90, (6) 91–100; Mail— (0) 0–50, (1) 51–100, (2) 101–250, (3) 251– ; Tele—(0) 0–1, (1) 2–5, (2) 6–20, (3) 21–40, (4) 41– ; Gastil—(0) Socialist, (1) Capitalist-socialist, (2) Capitalist-statist, (3) Capitalist, (4) Other; Top—(0) 0–14, (1) 15–24, (2) 25–30, (3) 31– ; Rapid—(0) 0, (1) 1, (2) 2, (3) 3, (4) 4, (5) 5, (6) 6–

Missing values reflect a lack of accurate information.

Ctry	Wealth	Urban	Educ	Mail	Tele	Gastil	Top	Rapid
1	1	3	5	0	2	2	1	2
2	1	3	6	2	3	3	0	2
3	1			1	0	2		
4	1		2	1	1	3	3	
5	1	3	6	2	3	3		4
6	0	3	0	2	0	2	3	
7	1	2	4	0	1	2	3	6
8	0	1	5			3	2	
9	0	0	4	0	0	0	1	4
10	0	0	0		4	3	3	4
11	1	3	6	2	4	3	0	3
12	1	1			0	2	3	0
13	0	0	0	0		3		
14	0	0	0			2	3	
15	0		0			2	3	
16	0	0	0	0		2	3	
17	0	2	1		0	2	3	6
18	1	3	6	2	2	0	0	3
19	0	0	0	0	0	2	3	6
20	1			3	0	2	3	
21	1	3		1	0	3	3	
22	1	3	6	2	3	3	3	1
23	0	1	2	0	0	2	2	0
24	0	0	1	0	0	3	3	
25	0	2	1	0	0	3	3	
26	0	1	1	0	0	2	0	
27	0	0	3	2	0	3	1	5
28	0	0	3	2	0	3	2	4
29	0	1	3	0	1	3	2	5
30	0	0	0	0	0	3	3	
31	0	0	0	0		2	3	
32	0	3	4	0	1	2	2	2
33	0		1	0	0	2		5
34	0	1	2	0	0	2		5
35	0	1	0	0	0	2	1	0
36	1	2	6	3	4	3	0	0
37	0		2	0	0	2	2	6
38	1	2	6	0	2	0		3
39	0		2	3	0	0	1	
40	1	2				2	3	
41	1			1		3		
42	1	3	6	3	4	3	0	1
43	1	3	4	0	1	2	1	1
44	1	2	4	1	2	0	1	5

THE FEDERAL THEORISTS AND THEIR CONDITIONS FOR
FEDERAL STABILITY

Conditions Associated with the Origin of Federations

Independent Variables: (Terr) Territorial division of power; (Const) Flexible constitution; (Bicam) Bicameral government

Value Labels: Terr—(0) No, (1) Yes; Const—(0) No, (1) Yes; Bicam—(0) No, (1) Yes

Ctry	Terr	Const	Bicam
1	1	1	1
2	1	1	1
3	1	1	0
4	1	1	0
5	1	1	1
6	1	1	1
7	1	1	1
8	1	1	1
9	1	1	1
10	1	1	0
11	1	1	1
12	1	1	0
13	1	1	1
14	1	0	0
15	1	1	1
16	1	1	1
17	1	1	1
18	1	1	1
19	0	1	0
20	0	1	1
21	1	1	1
22	1	1	1
23	1	1	1
24	1	1	1
25	0	1	0
26	1	1	1
27	1	1	1
28	1	1	1
29	1	1	1
30	1	1	0
31	0	1	1
32	1	1	1
33	1	1	1
34	0	1	0
35	1	1	0
36	1	1	1
37	1	1	0
38	1	1	1
39	1	1	0
40	1	1	0
41	1	1	1
42	1	1	1
43	1	1	1
44	1	1	1

Independent Variables: (Extern) Existence of external threat; (Hope) Hope of an improved economic position; (Prior) Some previous political association; (Polsoc) Political and social institutional similarities; (Geog) Geographical neighborhood among states; (Flex) Existence of flexible elites during unification

Value Labels: Extern—(0) No, (1) Yes; Hope—(0) No, (1) Yes; Prior—(0) No, (1) Yes; Polsoc—(0) No, (1) Yes; Geog—(0) No, (1) Yes; Flex—(0) No, (1) Yes

Ctry	Extern	Hope	Prior	Polsoc	Geog	Flex
1	0	1	1	1	1	0
2	0	1	1	1	1	1
3	0	1	1	0	1	1
4	0	1	1	1	1	1
5	1	1	1	1	1	1
6	0	1	1	1	1	0
7	0	1	1	1	1	1
8	0	1	0	0	0	1
9	1	1	1	0	1	1
10	0	1	1	1	1	1
11	1	1	1	1	1	1
12	0	1	1	1	1	0
13	0	1	1	1	1	1
14	0	1	0	0	1	1
15	1	1	0	1	1	0
16	0	1	1	1	1	0
17	0	1	1	1	1	0
18	1	1	1	1	1	0
19	0	1	0	0	1	1
20	1	1	1	1	1	1
21	0	1	1	1	1	1
22	1	1	1	1	1	1
23	1	1	1	0	1	1
24	0	0	1	1	1	1
25	1	1	0	1	1	1
26	0	1	1	1	0	1
27	1	1	0	1	1	1
28	1	1	1	1	1	1
29	1	1	1	1	0	1
30	0	1	0	0	0	1
31	0	1	1	1	1	1
32	0	1	1	1	1	1
33	0	1	1	1	1	0
34	0	1	1	0	1	1
35	1	1	0	0	0	1
36	1	1	1	0	1	1
37	0	1	1	1	1	0
38	1	1	1	1	1	1
39	0	1	0	0	1	0
40	1	1	0	0	1	1
41	1	1	1	1	1	1
42	1	1	1	1	0	1
43	0	1	0	1	1	0
44	1	1	1	1	1	0

Independent Variables: (Admin) Need for administrative efficiency; (Gener) A general community of outlook; (Models) Evidence of role models
Value Labels: Admin—(0) No, (1) Yes; Gener—(0) No, (1) Yes; Models—(0) No, (1) Yes

Ctry	Admin	Gener	Models
1	1	1	1
2	1	1	1
3	1	0	1
4	1	1	1
5	1	1	1
6	1	0	1
7	1	1	1
8	1	0	1
9	1	0	1
10	1	1	1
11	1	0	1
12	1	0	1
13	1	0	1
14	1	0	1
15	1	1	1
16	1	0	1
17	1	0	1
18	1	1	1
19	1	0	0
20	1	0	1
21	1	0	1
22	0	1	1
23	1	0	1
24	1	1	1
25	0	1	0
26	1	0	1
27	1	0	1
28	1	0	1
29	1	1	1
30	1	0	1
31	1	1	1
32	1	1	1
33	1	0	1
34	1	1	1
35	1	0	1
36	1	0	1
37	1	0	1
38	1	0	1
39	1	0	0
40	1	0	0
41	1	1	1
42	1	1	1
43	1	1	1
44	1	0	1

Conditions Associated with the Maintenance of Federations

Independent Variables: (Extern) Continued external threat; (Econ) Continued economic advantage; (Party) Strong two- or multiparty system; (Freedom) Political freedom
Value Labels: Extern—(0) No, (1) Yes; Econ—(0) No, (1) Yes; Party—(0) No, (1) Yes; Freedom—(0) No, (1) Partly, (2) Yes

Ctry	Extern	Econ	Party	Freedom
1	0	1	0	0
2	0	1	1	2
3	1	1	0	2
4	0	1	0	1
5	1	1	1	2
6	0	1	0	1
7	0	1	1	1
8	0	1	1	2
9	1	1	0	1
10	0	1	0	0
11	0	1	1	2
12	0	1	1	1
13	0	0	0	0
14	0	1	0	1
15	0	1	0	0
16	0	1	0	1
17	0	1	0	1
18	1	1	0	0
19	0	1	0	0
20	1	1	0	1
21	0	1	0	2
22	1	1	1	2
23	1	0	1	2
24	0	0	0	1
25	1	1	0	0
26	0	1	0	1
27	1	1	1	1
28	1	1	1	1
29	1	1	1	1
30	0	0	1	2
31	0	1	0	0
32	0	1	0	1
33	0	1	0	0
34	0	1	1	2
35	1	1	0	0
36	0	1	1	1
37	0	1	0	1
38	1	1	0	0
39	0	1	0	0
40	0	1	1	2
41	1	1	1	2
42	0	1	1	1
43	0	1	1	2
44	1	1	0	0

Independent Variables: (Ccleav) Crosscutting cleavages; (Commun) Easy communication across political spheres; (Trans) Easy transportation across cunits; (Flex) Flexible elites
Value Labels: Ccleav—(0) No, (1) Yes; Commun—(0) No, (1) Yes; Trans—(0) No, (1) Yes; Flex—(0) No, (1) Yes

Ctry	Ccleav	Commun	Trans	Flex
1	1	1	1	0
2	1	1	1	1
3	0	0	0	1
4	1	1	1	0
5	1	1	1	1
6	1	1	1	1
7	1	1	1	1
8	0	1	1	1
9	0	1	1	1
10	0	1	1	0
11	0	1	1	1
12	0	1	1	0
13	0	0	0	0
14	0	0	0	1
15	1	0	0	0
16	1	0	0	0
17	0	1	1	0
18	0	1	1	1
19	0	1	1	1
20	1	1	0	1
21	1	1	1	1
22	1	1	1	1
23	0	1	1	1
24	0	1	1	1
25	1	1	1	0
26	1	1	1	1
27	0	1	1	1
28	0	1	1	1
29	0	1	1	1
30	0	0	1	1
31	1	0	0	0
32	1	1	1	0
33	0	1	1	0
34	0	1	1	1
35	1	1	1	1
36	0	1	1	0
37	0	1	1	1
38	0	1	1	0
39	0	1	1	0
40	1	1	1	0
41	0	0	0	1
42	1	1	0	1
43	1	1	1	1
44	1	1	1	1

Independent Variable: (Const) Constitutional change
Value Labels: (0) No, (1) Yes

Ctry	Const
1	1
2	0
3	1
4	1
5	0
6	1
7	1
8	0
9	1
10	0
11	0
12	0
13	0
14	0
15	0
16	1
17	1
18	0
19	0
20	0
21	1
22	0
23	1
24	0
25	0
26	0
27	0
28	1
29	0
30	0
31	1
32	0
33	1
34	1
35	1
36	0
37	1
38	1
39	0
40	1
41	0
42	0
43	1
44	1

BIBLIOGRAPHY

BOOKS

Ake, Claude. *A Theory of Political Integration*. Homewood: Dorsey Press, 1969.

Alexander, William Paul, Jr. "Political Centralization in the Federalism of the United States." Ph.D. dissertation, University of Rochester, 1973.

Almond, Gabriel, and James Coleman, eds. *The Politics of the Developing Areas*. Princeton: Princeton University Press, 1960.

Almond, Gabriel, and G. Bingham Powell, Jr. *Comparative Politics: A Developmental Approach*. Boston: Little, Brown and Co., 1966.

Aron, Raymond. *France: Steadfast and Changing*. Cambridge: Harvard University Press, 1960.

Banks, Arthur S. *Cross-Polity Time-Series Data*. Cambridge: M.I.T. Press, 1971.

Berkowitz, Bruce David. "Stability in Political Systems: The Decision to Be Governed." Ph.D. dissertation, University of Rochester, 1981.

Bluhm, William T. *Building an Austrian Nation*. New Haven: Yale University Press, 1973.

Bodin, Jean. *Six Books of the Commonwealth*. Abridged and translated by M. S. Tooley. Oxford: Oxford University Press, 1955.

Braudel, Fernand. *The Mediterranean World in the Age of Philip II*. New York: Harper Torchbooks, 1975.

Breton, Albert, and Anthony Scott. *The Design of Federations*. Montreal: Institute for Research on Public Policy, 1980.

Brinton, J. Y. *Federations in the Middle East*, Egyptian Society of International Law, Brochure No. 18. 1964.

Buchheit, Lee C. *Secession: The Legitimacy of Self-Determination*. New Haven: Yale University Press, 1978.

Carter, Gwendolen M. *Politics in Africa: Seven Cases*. New York: Harcourt, Brace and World, 1966.

Dahl, Robert A. *Modern Political Analysis*. 3d ed. Englewood Cliffs: Prentice-Hall, 1976.

———. *Polyarchy: Participation and Opposition*. New Haven: Yale University Press, 1971.

Dahl, Robert A., and Edward B. Tufte. *Size and Democracy*. Stanford: Stanford University Press, 1973.

Dahrendorf, Ralf. *Class and Class Conflict in Industrial Society*. Stanford: Stanford University Press, 1959.

Dallin, Alexander, and George W. Breslauer. *Political Terror in Communist Systems*. Stanford: Stanford University Press, 1970.

Davis, Rufus S. *The Federal Principle: A Journey through Time in Quest of Meaning*. Berkeley: University of California Press, 1978.

De Tocqueville, Alexis. *Democracy in America*. New York: Washington Square Press, 1964.

Deutsch, Karl. *Tides among Nations*. New York: Free Press, 1979.

————. *Nationalism and Its Alternatives*. New York: Alfred A. Knopf, 1969.

————. *Nationalism and Social Communication: An Inquiry into the Foundations of Nationality*. 2d ed. Cambridge: M.I.T. Press, 1966.

Deutsch, Karl, et al. *Political Community in the North Atlantic Area*. Princeton: Princeton University Press, 1957.

Dikshit, Ramesh Dutta. *The Political Geography of Federalism*. New Delhi: Macmillan Co., 1975.

Duchacek, Ivo. *Comparative Federalism*. New York: Holt, Rinehart and Winston, 1970.

Durkheim, Émile. *The Division of Labor in Society*. Translated by George Simpson. New York: Free Press, 1964.

Duverger, Maurice. *Political Parties*. Translated by B. North and R. North. New York: Methuen and Co., 1967.

Earle, Valerie, ed. *Federalism: Infinite Variety in Theory and Practice*. Itasca, Ill.: Peacock, 1968.

Eckstein, Harry. *The Evaluation of Political Performance: Problems and Dimensions*. Beverly Hills: Sage, 1971.

Eisenstadt, S. N. *Modernization: Protest and Change*. Englewood Cliffs: Prentice-Hall, 1966.

Elazer, Daniel J., ed. *Federalism and Political Integration*. Jerusalem: Turtledove Publishing Co., 1979.

————. *Self Rule Shared Rule: Federal Solutions to the Middle East Conflict*. Jerusalem: Turtledove Publishing Co., 1979.

Elton, David, F. C. Engelman, and Peter McCormick. *Alternatives: Towards the Development of an Effective Federal System for Canada*. Banff, Alberta: Canada West Foundation, 1978.

Enloe, Cynthia H. *Ethnic Conflict and Political Development*. Boston: Little, Brown and Co., 1973.

Etzioni, Amitai. *Political Unification: A Comparative Study of Leaders and Forces*. New York: Holt, Rinehart and Winston, 1965.

Foltz, William J. *From French West Africa to the Mali Federation*. New Haven: Yale University Press, 1965.

Francis, E. K. *Interethnic Relations*. New York: Elsevier, 1976.

Franck, Thomas M. *Why Federations Fail: An Inquiry into the Provisions for Successful Federation*. New York: New York University Press, 1968.

Friedrich, Carl J. *Trends of Federalism in Theory and Practice*. New York: Frederick A. Praeger, 1968.

Gastil, Raymond. *Freedom in the World: Political Rights and Civil Liberties—1980*. New Brunswick: Transaction Books, 1980.

Gide, A. *Journals*. Vol. 4. New York: Alfred A. Knopf, 1954.

Graham, H. D., and Ted Robert Gurr, eds. *Violence in America*. New York: Signet, 1969.

Gurr, Ted Robert. *World Patterns and Correlates of Conflict*. Beverly Hills: Sage, 1983.

———, ed. *Handbook of Political Conflict: Theory and Research*. New York: Free Press, 1980.

———. *Why Men Rebel*. Princeton: Princeton University Press, 1970.

———. *New Error-Compensated Measures for Comparing Nations*. Princeton: Princeton University Center of International Studies, 1966.

Gurr, Ted Robert, with C. Ruttenberg. *The Conditions of Civil Violence: First Test of a Causal Model*, Research Monograph No. 28. Princeton: Center of International Studies, 1967.

Hamilton, Alexander, James Madison, and John Jay. *The Federalist Papers*. Edited by Benjamin F. Wright. Cambridge: Harvard University Press, 1961.

Hanushek, Eric, and John Jackson. *Statistical Methods for Social Scientists*. New York: Academic Press, 1977.

Hartz, Louis. *The Founding of New Societies*. New York: Harcourt, Brace and World, 1964.

Herman, Valentine. *Parliaments of the World*. London: Macmillan Press, 1976.

Hibbs, Douglas A., Jr. *Mass Political Violence: A Cross-National Causal Analysis*. London: John Wiley and Sons, 1973.

Hicks, Ursula K. *Federalism: Failure and Success*. New York: Oxford University Press, 1978.

Higley, John, G. Lowell Field, and Knut Groholt. *Elite Structure and Ideology: A Theory with Applications to Norway*. New York: Columbia University Press, 1976.

Hudson, Michael. *Conditions of Political Violence and Instability: A Preliminary Test of Three Hypotheses*, Sage Professional Paper in Comparative Politics, no. 01–005. Beverly Hills: Sage Publications, 1970.

Huntington, Samuel P. *Political Order in Changing Societies*. New Haven: Yale University Press, 1968.

Jain, Shail. *Size Distribution of Income: A Compilation of Data*. Washington: World Bank, 1975.

Karnes, Thomas L. *The Failure of Union: Central America, 1824–1860*. Chapel Hill: University of North Carolina Press, 1960.

Kerr, Clark, John T. Dunlop, Frederick H. Harbison, and Charles A. Myers. *Industrialism and Industrial Man*. New York: Oxford University Press, 1964.

Kohr, Leopold. *The Breakdown of Nations*. New York: E. P. Dutton, 1978.

Kurian, George Thomas. *The Book of World Rankings*. New York: Facts on File, 1979.

Lalande, Gilles. *In Defence of Federalism: The View from Quebec*. Toronto: McClelland and Stewart, 1978.

LaPalombara, J., and M. Weiner, eds. *Political Parties and Political Development*. Princeton: Princeton University Press, 1966.

Lenski, Gerhard. *Power and Privilege: A Theory of Social Stratification*. New York: McGraw-Hill Book Co., 1966.

Lerner, Daniel. *The Passing of Traditional Society*. New York: Free Press, 1958.

Lijphart, Arend. *Democracy in Plural Societies: A Comparative Exploration*. New Haven: Yale University Press, 1977.

Linz, Juan, and Alfred Stepan, eds. *The Breakdown of Democratic Regimes*. Baltimore: Johns Hopkins University Press, 1978.

Lipset, Seymour Martin. *Political Man*. Garden City: Doubleday and Co., 1960.

Livingston, W. S. *Federalism and Constitutional Change*. Oxford: Oxford University Press, 1956.

McRae, Kenneth, ed. *Consociational Democracy: Political Accommodation in Segmented Societies*. Toronto: McClelland and Stewart, 1974.

McWhinney, Edward. *Federal Constitution-Making for a Multinational World*. Leyden: A. W. Sythoff, 1966.

May, R. J. *Federalism and Fiscal Adjustment*. Oxford: Clarendon Press, 1969.

Milne, R. S., and Diane K. Mauzy. *Politics and Government in Malaysia*. Vancouver: University of British Columbia Press, 1978.

Mitchell, B. R. *European Historical Statistics*. New York: Facts on File, 1980.

Moore, Barrington. *The Social Origins of Dictatorship and Democracy*. Boston: Beacon Press, 1966.

Nagata, Judith. *Malaysian Mosaic: Perspectives from a Poly-Ethnic Society*. Vancouver: University of British Columbia Press, 1979.

Neumann, Stephanie. *Small States and Segmented Societies*. New York: Praeger, 1976.

Nordinger, Eric A. *Soldiers and Politics: Military Coups and Governments*. Englewood Cliffs: Prentice-Hall, 1977.

Oberle, James Peter. "Consociational Democracy and the Canadian Political System." Ph.D. dissertation, University of Maryland, 1976.

Obler, Jeffrey, Jurg Steiner, and Guido Dierickx. *Decision-Making in Smaller Democracies: The Consociational "Burden."* Beverly Hills: Sage, 1977.

Organski, A.F.K. *The Stages of Political Development*. New York: Alfred A. Knopf, 1965.

Powell, G. Bingham, Jr. *Political Performance in Contemporary Democracies*. Cambridge: Harvard University Press, 1982.

———. *Social Fragmentation and Political Hostility*. Stanford: Stanford University Press, 1970.

Proudhon, Pierre-Joseph. *The Principle of Federation*. Toronto: University of Toronto Press, 1979.

Pye, Lucien. *Aspects of Political Development*. Boston: Little, Brown and Co., 1966.

Rabushka, Alvin, and Kenneth Shepsle. *Politics in Plural Societies: A Theory of Democratic Instability*. Columbus: Charles E. Merrill, 1972.

Rae, Douglas. *The Political Consequences of Electoral Laws*. New Haven: Yale University Press, 1967.

Rae, Douglas, and Michael Taylor. *An Analysis of Political Cleavages*. New Haven: Yale University Press, 1970.

Rastegar, Gholamhossien. "Federalism in Yugoslavia." Ph.D. dissertation, Claremont Graduate School, 1980.

Rhoodie, Nic, ed. *Intergroup Accommodation in Plural Societies*. London: Macmillan Co., 1978.

Riker, William. *Federalism: Origin, Operation, Significance*. Boston: Little, Brown and Co., 1964.

Rippy, James Fred, ed. *Latin America: A Modern History*. Ann Arbor: University of Michigan Press, 1968.

Rosenau, James N., ed. *Linkage Politics*. New York: Free Press, 1969.

Rosenthal, Uriel. *Political Order: Rewards, Punishments, and Political Stability.* The Netherlands: Sijthoff and Noordhoff, 1978.
Russett, Bruce, et al. *World Handbook of Political and Social Indicators.* New Haven: Yale University Press, 1964.
Sartori, Giovanni. *Parties and Party Systems.* Vol. 1. Cambridge: Cambridge University Press, 1976.
Schiller, A. Arthur. *The Formation of Federal Indonesia.* The Hague: Van Hoeve, 1955.
Seton-Watson, Hugh. *Nations and States.* Boulder: Westview Press, 1977.
Shoup, Paul. *The Eastern European and Soviet Data Handbook.* Stanford: Hoover Institution Press, 1981.
Sigmund, Paul E. *Models of Political Change in Latin America.* New York: Praeger, 1970.
Simeon, Richard. *Federal Provincial Diplomacy: The Making of Recent Policy in Canada.* Toronto: University of Toronto Press, 1972.
Simmel, Georg. *Conflict and the Web of Group Affiliations.* Glencoe: Free Press, 1955.
Smelser, Neil J. *The Theory of Collective Behavior.* New York: Free Press, 1963.
Smock, David R., and Kwamena Bentsi-Enchill, eds. *The Search for National Integration in Africa.* New York: Free Press, 1976.
Sofranko, A. J., and R. C. Bealer. *Unbalanced Modernization and Domestic Instability: A Comparative Analysis,* Sage Professional Papers in Comparative Politics, no. 01–036. Beverly Hills: Sage, 1972.
Sorokin, Pitirim. *Social and Cultural Dynamics.* Boston: Horizon Books, 1957.
Steiner, Jurg. *Amicable Agreement Versus Majority Rule: Conflict Resolution in Switzerland.* Chapel Hill: University of North Carolina Press, 1974.
Steiner, Jurg, and Robert Dorff. *A Theory of Political Decision Modes: Intraparty Decision-Making in Switzerland.* Chapel Hill: University of North Carolina Press, 1980.
Taylor, Charles Lewis, and Michael C. Hudson. *World Handbook of Political and Social Indicators.* 2d ed. New Haven: Yale University Press, 1972.
Therborn, Gorcen. *What Does the Ruling Class Do When It Rules?* London: New Left Books, 1978.
Tilly, Charles. *From Mobilization to Revolution.* Reading: Addison-Wesley, 1978.
Tilly, L., and R. Tilly. *The Rebellious Century.* Cambridge: Harvard University Press, 1975.
Tinker, Hugh. *India and Pakistan.* New York: Praeger, 1962.
United Nations Demographic Yearbook (1981).
United Nations Statistical Yearbook and Monthly Bulletin of Statistics (1982).
Von der Mehden, Fred. *Comparative Political Violence.* Englewood Cliffs: Prentice-Hall, 1973.
Watts, Ronald L. *Administration in Federal Systems.* London: Hutchinson, 1970.
———. *Multicultural Societies and Federalism.* Ottawa: Royal Commission on Bilingualism and Biculturalism-Information Canada, 1970.
———. *New Federations: Experiments in the Commonwealth.* Oxford: Oxford University Press, 1966.
Wheare, K. C. *Federal Government.* 4th ed. London: Oxford University Press, 1964.
Young, Crawford. *Politics in the Congo: Decolonization and Independence.* Princeton: Princeton University Press, 1965.

ARTICLES

Ake, Claude. "A Definition of Political Stability." *Comparative Politics* 7, no. 2 (January 1975): 271–83.

———. "Political Integration and Political Stability: A Hypothesis." *World Politics* 19 (April 1967): 488–92.

Aldrich, John, and Charles F. Cnudde. "Probing the Bound of Conventional Wisdom: A Comparison of Regression, Probit, and Discriminant Analysis." *American Journal of Political Science* 19, no. 3 (August 1975): 571–608.

Alker, H. R., and B. M. Russett. "The Analysis of Trends and Patterns." In Bruce Russett et al., eds., *World Handbook of Political and Social Indicators*. New Haven: Yale University Press, 1964.

Armstrong, John A. "Federalism in the U.S.S.R.: Ethnic and Territorial Aspects." *Publius* 7, no. 4 (Fall 1977): 89–105.

Banks, Arthur S. "Patterns of Domestic Conflict 1919–39 and 1946–66." *Journal of Conflict Resolution* 16, no. 1 (March 1972): 41–50.

Barrows, W. L. "Ethnic Diversity and Political Instability in Black Africa." *Comparative Political Studies* 9 (1976): 139–70.

Ben-Dor, G. "Institutionalization and Political Development: A Conceptual and Theoretical Analysis." *Comparative Studies in Society and History* 17 (July 1975): 309–25.

Bertsch, Gary K. "Ethnicity and Politics in Socialist Yugoslavia." *Annals of the American Association of Political Science* 433 (September 1977): 88–99.

Birch, Anthony. "Approaches to the Study of Federalism." *Political Studies* 14, no. 1 (1966): 15–33.

Blondel, J. "Party Systems and Patterns of Government in Western Democracies." *Canadian Journal of Political Science* 1, no. 2 (1968): 180–203.

Brass, Paul R. "Ethnicity and Nationality Formation." *Ethnicity* 3 (1976): 225–41.

Breindel, Eric, and Nick Eberstadt. "Paradoxes of Population." *Commentary* 70, no. 2 (August 1980): 41–49.

Bwy, D. P. "Political Instability in Latin America: The Cross-Cultural Test of a Causal Model." *Latin American Research Review* 3 (1968): 17–66.

Carnell, F. G. "Political Implications of Federalism in New States." In U. K. Hicks, F. G. Carnell, J. R. Hicks, W. T. Newlyn, and A. H. Birch, *Federalism and Economic Growth in Underdeveloped Countries: A Symposium*, pp. 16–42. London: George Allen and Unwin, 1961.

Claeys, P. H. "Political Pluralism and Linguistic Cleavage: The Belgian Case." In Ehrlich St. and G. Wooten, eds., *Three Faces of Pluralism: Political, Ethnic, and Religious*. London: Westmead, 1980.

Cohen, Ronald. "Ethnicity: Problem and Focus in Anthropology." *Annual Review of Anthropology* 7 (1978): 379–403.

Cohen, Youssef, Brian Brown, and A. F. Organski. "The Paradoxical Nature of State-Making: The Violent Creation of Order." *American Political Science Review* 75, no. 4 (December 1981): 901–10.

Connor, Walker. "Nation-Building or Nation-Destroying?" *World Politics* 24 (1972): 339–55.

Coser, Lewis. "Social Conflict and the Theory of Social Change." *British Journal of Sociology* 8 (September 1957): 197–207.

Cutright, Phillips. "National Political Development: Measurement and Analysis." *American Sociological Review* 28, no. 2 (April 1963): 253–67.

Daalder, Hans. "On Building Consociational Nations: The Case of The Netherlands and Switzerland." In Kenneth McRae, ed., *Democracy: Political Accommodation in Segmented Societies*, pp. 107–24. Toronto: McClelland and Stewart, 1974.

Davies, James C. "The J-Curve of Rising and Declining Satisfactions As Cause of Some Great Revolutions and Contained Rebellions." In H. D. Graham and Ted Robert Gurr, eds., *Violence in America*. New York: Signet, 1969.

———. "Toward a Theory of Revolution." *American Sociological Review* 27 (February 1962): 5–19.

Denitch, Bogdan. "The Evolution of Yugoslav Federalism." *Publius* 7, no. 4 (Fall 1977): 107–17.

Deutsch, Karl. "Social Mobilization and Political Development." *American Political Science Review* 55 (September 1961): 493–514.

Duchacek, Ivo. "Antagonistic Cooperation: Territorial and Ethnic Communities." *Publius* 7, no. 4 (Fall 1977): 3–29.

Duvall, R., and M. Welfling. "Determinants of Political Institutionalization and Conflict in Black Africa: A Quasi-Experimental Analysis." *Comparative Political Studies* 5 (January 1973): 387–415.

Eckstein, Harry. "Theoretical Approaches to Collective Political Violence." In Ted Robert Gurr, ed., *Handbook of Political Conflict*, pp. 135–66. New York: Free Press, 1980.

———. "Authority Relations and Governmental Performance." *Comparative Political Studies* 2 (1969): 269–325.

Eisenstadt, S. N. "Breakdowns of Modernization." *Economic Development and Cultural Change* 12 (July 1964): 345–67.

———. "Initial Institutional Patterns of Political Modernization." *Civilization* 12 (1962): 461–72.

Elazar, Daniel. "Urbanism and Federalism: Twin Revolutions of the Modern Era." *Publius* 5, no. 2 (1975): 15–39.

———. "Federalism." In David L. Sills, ed., *The International Encyclopedia of the Social Sciences*. 5: 353–65. New York: Macmillan Co. and Free Press, 1968.

Enloe, Cynthia. "Internal Colonialism, Federalism, and Alternative State Development Strategies." *Publius* 7, no. 4 (Fall 1977): 145–60.

Esman, Milton J. "The Management of Communal Conflict." *Public Policy* 21 (Winter 1973): 49–78.

Fierabend, Ivo, and Rosalind Fierabend. "Aggressive Behaviors within Polities, 1948–1962: A Cross-National Study." *Journal of Conflict Resolution* 10 (September 1966): 249–71.

Fierabend, Ivo, Rosalind Fierabend, and B. A. Nesvold. "Social Change and Political Violence: Cross-National Patterns." In H. D. Graham and Ted Robert Gurr, eds., *Violence in America*, pp. 608–68. New York: Signet, 1969.

Flanigan, William H., and Edwin Fogelman. "Patterns of Political Violence in Comparative Historical Perspective." *Comparative Politics* 3 (July 1970): 1–20.

Geertz, Clifford. "The Integrative Revolution: Primordial Sentiments and Civil Politics in the New States." In Clifford Geertz, ed., *Old Societies and New States: The Quest for Modernity in Asia and Africa*. New York: Free Press, 1963.

Gourevitch, Peter. "Reforming the Napoleonic State: The Creation of Regional Governments in France and Italy." In Sidney Tarrow et al., eds., *Territorial Politics in Industrial Nations*, pp. 28–63. New York: Praeger, 1978.

Grodzins, Morton. "American Political Parties and the American System." *Western Political Quarterly* 13 (1960): 974–88.

Gurr, Ted Robert. "A Comparative Study of Civil Strife." In H. D. Graham and Ted Robert Gurr, eds., *Violence in America: Historical and Comparative Perspectives*, 2d ed., pp. 544–605. Beverly Hills: Sage, 1979.

———. "A Causal Model of Civil Strife: A Comparative Analysis Using New Indices." *American Political Science Review* 62 (December 1968): 1104–24.

Gurr, Ted Robert, and R. Duvall. "Introduction to a Formal Theory of Conflict within Social Systems." In L. A. Coser and O. N. Larsen, eds., *The Uses of Controversy in Sociology*. New York: Free Press, 1976.

Haug, Marie. "Social and Cultural Pluralism As a Concept in Social System Analysis." *American Journal of Sociology* 73, no. 3 (November 1967): 294–304.

Hazlewood, Leo. "Concept and Measurement Stability in the Study of Conflict Behavior within Nations." *Comparative Political Studies* 6, no. 2 (July 1973): 171–95.

Hudson, Michael. "Political Protest and Power Transfers in Crisis Periods." *Comparative Political Studies* 4, no. 3 (October 1971): 259–94.

Huntington, Samuel. "Political Development and Political Decay." *World Politics* 17 (April 1965): 386–430.

Hurwitz, Leon. "Contemporary Approaches to Political Stability." *Comparative Politics* 5, no. 3 (April 1973): 449–63.

———. "Democratic Political Stability: Some Traditional Hypotheses Reexamined." *Comparative Political Studies* 4 (January 1972): 476–90.

———. "An Index of Democratic Political Stability." *Comparative Political Studies* 4, no. 1 (April 1971): 53–56.

Janda, K. "Retrieving Information for a Cooperative Study of Political Parties." In W. Crotty, ed., *Approaches to the Study of Party Organizations*. Boston: Allyn and Bacon, 1968.

Kasfir, Nelson. "Explaining Ethnic Political Participation." *World Politics* 32 (1979): 365–88.

Kesselman, M. "Overinstitutionalization and Political Constraints." *Comparative Politics* 3 (October 1970): 21–44.

Kornhauser, William. "Rebellion and Political Development." In Harry Eckstein, ed., *International War*, p. 24. New York: Free Press, 1964.

Laski, Harold J. "The Obsolescence of Federalism." *New Republic*, May 3, 1939.

Linz, Juan. "Elements of Breakdown." In Juan Linz, ed., *Crisis, Breakdown, and Reequilibration*, 3d ed., pp. 60–61. Baltimore: Johns Hopkins University Press, 1978.

Livingston, W. S. "A Note on the Nature of Federalism." *Political Science Quarterly* 67 (March 1952): 81–95.

Lustick, Ian. "Stability in Deeply Divided Societies: Consociationalism Versus Control." *World Politics* 31, no. 3 (April 1979): 323–44.

McKelvey, Richard, and W. Zavoina. "A Statistical Model for the Analysis of Legislative Voting Behavior." Paper presented at American Political Science Association, New York, 1969.

Maddox, William P. "The Political Basis of Federation." *American Political Science Review* 35 (1941): 1120–27.

Mathews, Russell. "Innovations and Developments in Australian Federalism." *Publius* 7, no. 3 (Summer 1977): 9–19.

May, Ronald. "Decision-Making and Stability in Federal Governments." *Canadian Journal of Political Science* (March 1970): 73–84.

Mayer, Lawrence. "Federalism and Party Behavior in Australia and Canada." *Western Political Quarterly* 23 (1970): 795–807.

Melson, Robert, and Howard Wolpe. "Modernization and the Politics of Communalism: A Theoretical Perspective." *American Political Science Review* 64, no. 4 (December 1970): 1112–30.

Merkl, Peter. "Executive-Legislative Federalism in West Germany." *American Political Science Review* 53 (1959): 732–41.

Morrison, Donald, and H. M. Stevenson. "Measuring Social and Political Requirements for System Stability: Empirical Validation of an Index Using Latin American and African Data." *Comparative Political Studies* 7 (1974): 252–63.

———. "Integration and Instability: Patterns of African Political Development." *American Political Science Review* 66 (1972): 902–27.

———. "Political Instability in Independent Black Africa: More Dimensions of Conflict Behavior within Nations." *Journal of Conflict Resolution* 15, no. 3 (September 1971): 347–68.

Nagel, Jack. "Erratum." *World Politics* 28 (January 1976): 315.

Novak, Michael. "Why Latin America Is Poor." *Atlantic Monthly* 249 (March 1982): 66–75.

Olson, Mancur. "Rapid Growth As a Destabilizing Force." *Journal of Economic History* 23 (December 1963): 529–52.

Ostrom, Vincent. "Does Federalism Make a Difference?" *Publius* 3, no. 2 (Fall 1973): 197–237.

Parker, R. S. "Political and Administrative Trends in Australian Federalism." *Publius* 7, no. 3 (Summer 1977): 35–52.

Parsons, Talcott. "A Sociological Approach to the Theory of Organizations." *Administrative Science Quarterly* 1 (July 1956): 225–39.

Parvin, M. "Economic Determinants of Political Unrest: An Econometric Approach." *Journal of Conflict Resolution* 17 (1973): 271–96.

Purcell, Susan Kaufman, and John F. H. Purcell. "State and Society in Mexico: Must a Stable Polity Be Institutionalized?" *World Politics* 32, no. 2 (January 1980): 194–227.

Rabushka, Alvin, and Kenneth Shepsle. "Political Entrepreneurship and Patterns of Democratic Instability in Plural Societies." *Race* 12, no. 4 (April 1971): 462, 467, 470.

Rae, Douglas. "A Note on the Fractionalization of Some European Party Systems." *Comparative Political Studies* 1, no. 3 (1968): 413–18.

Riggs, Fred. "The Dialectics of Developmental Conflict." *Comparative Political Studies* 1 (July 1969): 197–226.

Riker, William H. "Federalism." In Fred Greenstein and Nelson W. Polsby, eds., *Handbook of Political Science: Governmental Institutions and Processes*, 5: 93–172. Reading:Addison-Wesley, 1975.

―――. "Six Books in Search of a Subject, or Does Federalism Exist and Does It Matter?" *Comparative Politics* (October 1969): 135–46.

Riker, William H., and Jonathan Lemco. "The Relations between Structure and Stability in Federal Governments." In William Riker, ed., *The Development of American Federalism*, pp. 113–29. Norwell, Mass.: Kluwer, 1987.

Rummel, Rudolph J. "Dimensions of Conflict Behavior within and between Nations." *General Systems Yearbook* 8 (1963): 1–50.

―――. "A Field Theory of Social Action with Application to Conflict within Nations." *General Systems* 10 (1965): 183–211.

Russett, Bruce. "Inequality and Instability: The Relation of Land Tenure to Politics." *World Politics* 16 (April 1964): 442–54.

Schneider, Peter, and Anne Schneider. "Social Mobilization, Political Institutions, and Political Violence: A Cross-National Analysis." *Comparative Political Studies* 4 (April 1971): 69–90.

Sigelman, Lee, and Syng Nam Yough. "Left-Right Polarization in National Party Systems: A Cross-National Analysis." *Comparative Political Studies* 11 (October 1978): 355–79.

Snyder, D. "Collective Violence: A Research Agenda and Some Strategic Considerations." *Journal of Conflict Resolution* 22 (1978): 499–534.

Snyder, David, and Charles Tilly. "Hardship and Collective Violence in France, 1830 to 1860." *American Sociological Review* 37, no. 5 (October 1972): 520–32.

Stein, Michael B. "Federal Political Systems and Federal Societies." *World Politics* 20 (1968): 721–47.

Tanter, Raymond. "Dimensions of Conflict Behavior within Nations, 1955–1960: Turmoil and Internal War." *Peace Research Society Papers* 3 (1965): 159–83.

―――. "Dimensions of Conflict Behavior within and between Nations, 1958–60." *Journal of Conflict Resolution* 10, no. 1 (March 1966): 41–64.

Tanter, Raymond, and M. Midlarsky. "A Theory of Revolution." *Journal of Conflict Resolution* 11 (1967): 264–80.

Tarlton, Charles D. "Symmetry and Asymmetry As Elements of Federalism: A Theoretical Speculation." *Journal of Politics* 27 (1965): 861–74.

Tarrow, Sidney. Introduction to Reginald Whitaker, *Federalism and Democratic Theory*, Institute of Intergovernmental Relations Discussion Paper No. 17. Kingston: Queen's University, 1983.

Taylor, Charles L. "Communications Development and Political Instability." *Comparative Political Studies* 1 (1969): 557–63.

Tilly, Charles L. "Does Modernization Breed Revolution?" *Comparative Politics* 5 (1973): 425–47.

Von Vorys, K. "Use and Misuse of Development Theory." In J. Charles, ed., *Contemporary Political Analysis*, pp. 350–66. New York: Free Press, 1967.

Watts, Ronald L. "Survival or Disintegration." In Richard Simeon, ed., *Must Canada Fail?*, pp. 42–60. Montreal and London: McGill-Queen's University Press, 1977.

Weede, Erich. "Income Inequality and Domestic Violence." *Journal of Conflict Resolution* 25, no. 4 (December 1981): 639–54.

Weiner, Myron. "Political Integration and Political Development." *Annals* 358 (March 1965): 52–64.

Welch, S., and A. Booth. "Crowding As a Factor in Political Aggressions: Theoretical Aspects and an Analysis of Some Cross-National Data." *Social Science Information* 13 (1974): 155.

Wood, John R. "Secession: A Comparative Analytic Framework." *Canadian Journal of Political Science* 14, no. 1 (March 1981): 108–34.

Zimmerman, Ekkart. "Macro-Comparative Research on Political Protest." In Ted Robert Gurr, ed., *Handbook of Political Conflict*. New York: Free Press, 1980.

INDEX

ABOUT THE AUTHOR

JONATHAN LEMCO is the author of *State and Development, Canada and the Crisis in Central America, The Energy-Environment Tradeoff*, and *Many Different Tongues*.